Eq
Na

Like the first Reader, this collection examines the grounds that are accepted for inclusion or exclusion of students, and looks at how appropriate support can be guaranteed for people who experience difficulties in learning, who are disabled or who experience social or other kinds of disability. This volume explores national and international contexts for educational practice and research and discusses practical, ethical and political issues which are relevant to undertaking that research.

Part I covers issues facing local government and the consumers of educational services in the UK. Part II compares policy and practice in eleven different countries, and Part III discusses research which explores the issues of equality and diversity in education.

This volume and her sister, *Equality and Diversity in Education 1: Learning, Teaching and Managing in Schools*, are Readers for the Open University course 'Developing Inclusive Curricula: Equality and Diversity in Education' (E829). The two books in the series will appeal to teachers, non-teaching assistants and other school-based staff, parents, disabled people and those who have experienced difficulties in learning, social and health workers, and those working for voluntary organisations.

The other volume in this series is:

Equality and Diversity in Education 1: Learning, Teaching and Managing in Schools
Edited by *Patricia Potts, Felicity Armstrong and Mary Masterton*

This Reader is part of an Open University integrated teaching system. It is designed to evoke the critical understanding of students.

If you would like to study this course, please write to The Central Enquiries Office, The Open University, Walton Hall, Milton Keynes MK7 6AA, for a prospectus and application form. For more specific information write to The Higher Degrees Office at the same address.

Equality and Diversity in Education 2: National and International Contexts

Edited by
Patricia Potts, Felicity Armstrong and
Mary Masterton

London and New York
in association with
The Open University

First published 1995
by Routledge
11 New Fetter Lane, London EC4P 4EE

Simultaneously published in the USA and Canada
by Routledge
29 West 35th Street, New York, NY 10001

Typeset in Garamond by
Florencetype Ltd, Stoodleigh, Devon

Printed and bound in Great Britain by
Biddles Ltd, Guildford and King's Lynn

British Library Cataloguing in Publication Data
A catalogue record for this book is available from the British
Library

Library of Congress Cataloging-in-Publication Data
Equality and diversity in education 2: national and international
   contexts / edited by Patricia Potts, Felicity Armstrong, and Mary
   Masterton.
      p.   cm. – (Open University set book)
   Companion vol. to: Equality and diversity in education, 1. 1994.
   Includes bibliographical references and index.
   1. Special education – Great Britain.   2. Education and state –
Great Britain.   3. Special education.   4. Education and state.
5. Educational equalization.   I. Potts, Patricia.   II. Armstrong,
Felicity.   III. Masterton, Mary.   IV. Equality and diversity in
education, 1.   V. Series.
LC3986.G7E678.   1994   94–26653
371.9'0941 – dc20   CIP

ISBN 0–415–11998–7

Contents

Illustrations

FIGURES

MAPS

TABLES

Preface

This volume and her sister, *Equality and Diversity in Education 1: Learning, Teaching and Managing in Schools*, are the Readers for the Open University course 'Developing Inclusive Curricula: Equality and Diversity in Education' (E829), which is a module within the MA in Education Programme and also the postgraduate component of the Advanced Diploma in Special Needs in Education (D06). The course extends and complements our undergraduate course 'Learning for All' (E242).

The legislation of the late 1980s and early 1990s has transformed the education system in the UK, particularly in England and Wales. Centralisation of control over the curriculum and assessment and decentralisation of funding and management have affected the experience of all learners, from pre-school children to adults. Nurseries, schools, colleges, governing bodies, local education authorities, professional associations, voluntary organisations and parents' groups are all having to rethink their approach in response to the government's measures.

Competition between educational institutions in a commercial marketplace raises questions about the selection and classification of students. What grounds are accepted for their inclusion and exclusion? How can appropriate support be guaranteed for children, young people and adults who experience difficulties in learning, who are disabled or who experience social or other kinds of difficulty?

We expect our students to pursue their own lines of critical enquiry into these policies and practices and we have tried to reflect the diversity of their own interests in the course materials. We are also concerned to develop an awareness of those features of an education system which promote equality of value and opportunity for each student, whatever his or her ability or attainments. These commitments have determined our approach to shaping the contents of these readers, which therefore include:

- discussions of working towards equality in education;
- illustrations of the range of perspectives and interests which exist on educational issues, including parents' and consumers' views;
- encouragement to develop a personal voice and a critical viewpoint, which includes reflecting on educational language and terminology;
- reflections on the process of making enquiries;
- comparative material from around the UK, Europe and beyond;
- discussions of policy and practice in nursery, primary, secondary, tertiary and segregated specialised provision;
- interdisciplinary and interagency material.

Students following the course actively investigate aspects of the education system, on their own or in collaboration. They all undertake three small-scale research projects: one on pupil perspectives, one on curriculum analysis and design and one on policy, decision-making and power. Each Reader contains material to support the stages of each project: to help students work out their research questions, to decide what methods of enquiry are appropriate and to evaluate their findings.

Volume 1 focuses on experiences of learning and teaching and developments which concern individual schools. Volume 2 examines wider national and international contexts and discusses a range of practical, ethical and political issues relevant to the process of doing research.

Forty of the fifty-one contributions have been specially written for these books. The authors are not all white, not all able-bodied, not all men, not all professionals, not all teachers, not all educationally successful. They include both experienced and first-time writers.

Students following 'Developing Inclusive Curricula: Equality and Diversity in Education' will include teachers, non-teaching assistants and other school-based staff, parents, disabled people and those who have experienced difficulties in learning, social workers, health workers and those working for voluntary organisations.

Patricia Potts

Introduction

Patricia Potts

This volume is concerned with national and international contexts for educational practice and research. Part I covers issues facing local government and the consumers of educational services. Part II compares policy and practice in eleven countries outside the UK and Part III discusses research which explores the issues of equality and diversity in education.

The first section of the book presents the perspectives, first, of a group of teachers in a Labour-controlled borough and, second, of senior education officers in a Tory shire county. Julian Wroe argues on behalf of his colleagues in Barnsley's Association of Primary and Special School Headteachers that the government's response to the economic and social consequences of pit closures has been inequitable. Then Nick Henwood describes the ways in which Kent has restructured its education services since 1986. While Nick was preparing his chapter for this book, Roy Pryke, Kent's Director of Education Services, published an attack in the *Times Educational Supplement* on the government's policy for developing a grant-maintained sector, so we have included this alongside. The section concludes with a discussion of the implications for educational equality of the then proposed reorganisation of local government. Kathryn Riley was an elected member of the Inner London Education Authority and she has studied the subsequent effects of its abolition in 1989. She has also studied the work of the Local Government Commission and undertaken independent research for councils uncertain about their future.

In the next section Margaret Peter discusses the sequence of UK education legislation from 1979 to 1994. She reminds us that people saw the Education Reform Act of 1988 as incompatible with the spirit of the 1981 Education Act, but she argues that we should adopt a different view, that it was the 1981 Act that was out of step with the policies of centralisation of the curriculum and assessment and decentralisation of resources that were designed to raise educational standards and create an educational market which would respond to parental choice. John Wright then takes us through the involvement of the Independent Panel of Special Education Advisers (IPSEA) in the passage of the 1992 Education Bill. IPSEA drafted amendments and lobbied an enormous number of relevant groups and individuals. The level of sustained energy and the range of activities required for effective lobbying come across clearly from this chapter. Some of IPSEA's actions were successful, some were not.

Sue Thomas belongs to the Passport Parents Group in Stockport. Her chapter includes both her story and that of her co-member, Gwen. They have experienced a professional approach based on the belief that disability is a disaster and that what families therefore want is a break, a separation. Sue argues that support should aim to avoid separations, building, instead, on the closest relationships that exist for the children and confirming their place in their home communities. She does not see current education legislation as compatible with this view. Colin Barnes ends this section on consumer perspectives with a set of arguments for anti-discrimination legislation that would give disabled people legal rights equal to women and members of ethnic minorities. During the writing of this introduction, the latest in a series of Private Member's Bills has failed to make any progress in the House of Commons due to the tabling of 80 amendments by Tory backbenchers.

In Part II we go abroad. The chapters in this section provide an opportunity to look outwards to a wide range of different settings and to reflect back on the situation we experience in the UK. We include a glimpse of new developments in Eastern Europe and discussions of two of the most rapidly changing societies of the 1990s: China and South Africa.

First, we go through the Tunnel to France, where Felicity Armstrong examined the ways in which children are classified in the education system. She found a medicalised, highly specialised approach to the identification of difficulties in learning. Helen Penn undertook a comparative study of provision for pre-school children in Italy, Spain and the UK and found that services in the UK do not stand up to scrutiny. Harry Daniels has been studying parental involvement in special education across Europe for a number of years and here he compares the different traditions of Denmark, where there is an emphasis on community and parents are included at every stage of decision-making, and Germany, where they are not routinely involved at a community level and where, therefore, parents are increasingly lobbying at national level.

Christine O'Hanlon asks us to look at what is happening in southern Europe, which, she argues, we neglect in comparison to the attention we pay to the richer countries of the north. Spanish educational reforms of the 1980s and onwards have led to a genuinely more inclusive practice for disabled children and young people and those who experience difficulties in learning. In Greece, however, a rhetoric of inclusion has not resulted in progressive practice, for a variety of reasons, including the persistence of rejecting attitudes, the lack of resources and the problem of providing evenly for a scattered rural population. Paul Bennett is an officer of the National

Association of Teachers in Further and Higher Education (NATFHE) and he is involved in the developing European alliance of teacher unions. His chapter contains the story of this alliance and what has been the scope of its activities so far. Nearly 3 million teachers are affiliated across Europe and their voice in policy-making is growing louder.

We travel eastwards for our final contribution from Europe. Marie Cerna discusses recent developments and future aspirations for the education system in the Czech Republic. She hopes that the Soviet climate of depersonalised bureacracy and the denial of educational diversity can be dispelled by a revival of traditional humanist values and the acceptance of equal rights for all students.

With the last three chapters in Part II we go further afield. Early in 1993 Ross Wilson made a study tour from New Zealand to the UK and the United States, to examine policy and practice on the integration into the educational mainstream of disabled children and young people and those who experience difficulties in learning. New Zealand legislation supports a process of integration. The education system, however, like that in the UK, is undergoing reforms to establish an educational 'market-place' and the decentralisation of resource allocation. In my discussion of the reform of special education in China, I have tried to present a picture of the huge scale of the task, which has been given an impetus, both by government aims for universal school attendance and by the rise of a disability rights movement. Zandile Nkabinde's chapter sets special educational provision for black children and young people in South Africa into the context of the inequitable system for all black students. Again, the scale of the task of reform is vast. We shall see what the new government of national unity, under President Mandela, will be able to achieve.

Part III illustrates and critically examines approaches to research which explores issues of equality and diversity in education. Some chapters base their arguments on the close study of individuals or the solving of a particular problem; others draw on a wider range of material to build up arguments about policy.

Susan Brock was employed by a university to study the experiences of its disabled students. She charts the stages by which she developed what she hopes is an equitable relationship with the students. She discusses the idea of 'emancipatory' research, which has been put forward by disabled researchers. Linda Harris works with teenagers who are seen as having 'severe learning difficulties'. Her chapter is an edited version of a project she undertook to try and discover more about two of her students' perspectives on their learning. She found that they preferred activities that took place outside the classroom, that enriching the indoor environment did nothing to increase their participation. She felt that communication with her students would be improved if she worked at their non-verbal skills.

Jenny Morris discusses the kind of relationships that should be developed between researchers and disabled people: she belongs to both groups. She argues that a feminist approach would help to secure an equitable and rewarding experience for participants, but that feminism itself has neglected the area of disability. Feminists therefore need to develop a greater awareness of the diversity of women's experience.

Bill Martin is a blind musician and he had a specific problem: how could he produce compositions in a printed form for his students to work on? Tom Vincent, of the Open University's Institute of Educational Technology, worked collaboratively with Bill on the solution. Their chapter consists of Tom's account of the project, interspersed with Bill's own reflections. In the next chapter, Gloria Pullen, who is deaf, and Lesley Jones, who is hearing, describe their experiences of working together on a long-term project on the views of deaf people. Although they share many characteristics, as white, working-class women and mothers, they are different in an important cultural way, which did have implications for their collaboration.

When Mark Vaughan visited Australia, early in 1993, he collected a wealth of research papers. He was struck by the number of studies that reported on the progress of integration into the educational mainstream of disabled children and young people and those who experience difficulties in learning. These research projects were often commissioned and funded by local or state education authorities, a partnership rare in the UK but which, Mark argues, would be valuable.

Rose Mahony's chapter is an edited version of a research project in which she investigated the relationship between policy and practice in her own area for junior pupils identified as having 'emotional and behavioural difficulties'. The number of young children being excluded is going up fast. A new unit has been set up on the site of a voluntary-run special school, which aims to return the children to the mainstream within two years.

The final chapter in the book is an overview of trends in research since the 1970s. Writing for postgraduate practitioner-researchers, Graham Vulliamy and Rosemary Webb trace how the dominance of a psychological experimental approach has given way, first, to a more qualitative approach and the explicitly political enquiries of sociologists and, second, to the work carried out by disabled people themselves. However, they argue that much of this work still adheres to disciplinary boundaries and does not accommodate questions that arise from, and should be evaluated by, educational practice.

Part I

National contexts for education in the 1990s

A. Educational communities and local government

Chapter 1

'Barnsley bashing'. Communities and schools in the 1990s

Julian Wroe

This chapter sets out in graphic detail the spiral of social, economic and health problems in communities which have seen the destruction of their industrial base. The effect of unemployment and poverty on families and schools in Barnsley is dramatic but the council has been forced to cut local public spending. Barnsley is top of the national league in terms of long-term illness but bottom of the league in terms of the government's Standard Spending Assessment (SSA). Julian Wroe argues that the present system is inequitable.

INTRODUCTION

Barnsley is a Metropolitan District which was formed during local government reorganisation in 1974 from fourteen other local authorities and lies at the heart of what was once affectionately known as the Yorkshire Coalfield. Its industrial base, which once proudly boasted glass, coal and their support industries as major constituent members, now relies almost totally on light industry and the service industry to provide work for the town's 225,000 inhabitants. The following tables will help to set Barnsley in the context of the whole country.

TOP OF THE LEAGUE

Barnsley has a poor health record, with many males, in particular, suffering from long-term occupational diseases such as pneumoconiosis, emphysema and other diseases of the respiratory system. The 1991 Census recorded that 18.5 per cent of all persons in Barnsley suffer from a long-term disabling disease with 34.6 per cent of households containing at least one person with this type of illness. This effectively places Barnsley at the top of the league table of towns and cities with long-term health problems (see Table 1.2).

Table 1.1 Vital statistics

(a) Average income per person:
Barnsley: £8,500
National: £15,800

(b) Unemployment rate:
Barnsley: 15% (up to 24% with the closure of the last of the
town's collieries)
National: 10%

(c) Employment rate between 1981 and 1991:
Barnsley: down by 16%
National: up by 2.7%

(d) Value of housing:
Barnsley: £45,000
National: £65,000

(e) Students entering further education:
Barnsley: 43%
National: 61%

BOTTOM OF THE LEAGUE

Under the system of Standard Spending Assessments on the other hand, through which the government gives 'guidance' as to what local authorities should spend in order to provide a 'standard level of service', Barnsley achieves what in football terms would be deemed an automatic relegation position. With a provisional Standard Spending Assessment for 1993/94 of £597 per head of population, Barnsley appears at the foot of the Metropolitan District League with Manchester lofty champions with an SSA of £951. After having been faced with forced annual cuts in services during recent years, the average Barnsley inhabitant is more than entitled to question the fairness of an SSA system which reduces Barnsley Metropolitan Borough Council to the bottom of five comparative league tables for all service provision in spite of many collections of statistics, including those of the audit commission, confirming that Barnsley is not a high-spending authority.

A DOWNWARD SPIRAL

Expenditure on education suffers accordingly as a result of Barnsley's appallingly low SSA with implied SSA spending needs of a 300-pupil primary school dictating a budget of £537,000 in Barnsley, £661,000 in Manchester and £802,000 in the Tory flagship borough of Wandsworth! An 800-pupil secondary school has an implied spending need of £2,081,000 in Barnsley compared with £2,817,000 in Manchester and £3,113,000 in Wandsworth! Is it plausible that Wandsworth actually needs to spend

Table 1.2 Long-term limiting illness

Town/City	% of all persons
1 Barnsley	18.5
2 Salford	17.4
3 Sunderland	17.4
4 Liverpool	17.3
5 Manchester	17.3
6 Gateshead	17.3
7 South Tyneside	16.9
8 Doncaster	16.4
9 Knowsley	16.3
10 St Helens	16.3
11 Sheffield	16.1
12 Rotherham	16.1
13 Newcastle upon Tyne	16.1
14 Wigan	16.0
15 North Tyneside	15.9
16 Sefton	15.3
17 Wakefield	15.3
18 Wirral	15.1
19 Sandwell	15.1
20 Bolton	15.0
21 Rochdale	14.8
22 Wolverhampton	14.7
23 Tameside	14.5
24 Oldham	14.4
25 Walsall	14.1
26 Birmingham	14.0
27 Bury	13.7
28 Leeds	13.7
29 Calderdale	13.5
30 Bradford	13.4
31 Coventry	13.3
32 Kirklees	12.9
33 Trafford	12.8
34 Dudley	12.7
35 Stockport	12.2
36 Solihull	10.8

Based on the 36 Metropolitan Districts

(*Source*: 1991 Census)

£256,000 (Manchester £124,000) more than Barnsley in providing a standard level of service in a 300-pupil primary school and needs to spend £1,032,000 (Manchester £736,000) more on an 800-pupil secondary school?

This situation has been further exacerbated by the recession which has seen more people out of work and a subsequent larger draw on the national finite figure of resources. The government's low-tax commitment has led to

Table 1.3 Comparison of Standard Spending Assessment (SSA) per adult in all Metropolitan districts, 1992/93

Posi- tion	Metropolitan District	SSA per adult	Other districts as a proportion of Barnsley
1	Manchester	1,488	1.78
2	Liverpool	1,286	1.54
3	Knowsley	1,284	1.53
4	Birmingham	1,282	1.53
5	Bradford	1,230	1.47
6	Wolverhampton	1,184	1.41
7	Salford	1,091	1.30
8	Oldham	1,088	1.30
9	Sandwell	1,080	1.29
10	Rochdale	1,068	1.28
11	Coventry	1,059	1.26
12	South Tyneside	1,028	1.23
13	Bolton	1,022	1.22
14	Newcastle upon Tyne	1,020	1.22
15	Sunderland	1,016	1.21
16	St Helens	1,011	1.21
17	Wirral	1,006	1.20
18	Kirklees	999	1.19
19	Gateshead	989	1.18
20	Walsall	986	1.18
21	Leeds	972	1.16
22	Calderdale	967	1.15
23	Tameside	954	1.14
24	North Tyneside	948	1.13
25	Doncaster	945	1.13
26	Sefton	941	1.12
27	Trafford	932	1.11
28	Sheffield	931	1.11
29	Rotherham	916	1.09
30	Wigan	989	1.07
31	Bury	880	1.05
32	Solihull	872	1.04
33	Wakefield	871	1.04
34	Stockport	867	1.04
35	Dudley	847	1.01
36	Barnsley	838	1.00

greater borrowing and a consequent inability to support industry both large and small, both nationally and locally, thus creating the downward spiral of fewer jobs . . . less spending power . . . fewer jobs . . . even less spending power . . . and so on. The national situation has seen and still sees daily bankruptcy of small businesses, daily repossession of housing and the continual loss of value of property, which leads to mortgages being more

than the value of property, hence the financiers' 'buzz word' of the moment
. . . negative equity.

Barnsley's individual situation is far worse than the national perspective.
With the lack of support for the coal industry the government has compounded Barnsley's already sorry situation. Pit closures have increased the
town's already high rate of unemployment and this has itself led to an
increase in the draw on the local budget, particularly that of the education
budget which supports families through the scheme of aid, an entitlement
which rightly allows children of families in receipt of Income Support access
to free school meals and clothing allowances. Communities which grew up
around the closed collieries are being decimated in a way unheard of since
the wholesale closures in the steel and shipbuilding industries in the early
1980s. Lack of community income to support the community has led to the
withdrawal and closure of community services. Erosion of the community
focus has led to a lack of communal heart . . . a total lack of purpose.

'FAMILY' LIFE

The quality of home life for families affected by the closures both in the coal
and related industries has suffered due to lack of income with no resources
for 'extras'. David is aged 27, is married with two children and was a face
worker at the pit for seven years. His colliery closed three years ago and he
was made redundant. With his redundancy payment he bought a new car,
paid for a family holiday and now, three years later, finds that his wife has
left him and the children for a new life. David is also penniless, having now
used up his redundancy money. There is little prospect of him finding work.
This scenario will undoubtedly be repeated as the stress which surrounds
wholesale unemployment facilitates the decimation of families. The experience of communities which have already suffered the ravages of pit closures
suggests that the different perception of the 'role model', and the consequen-
tial 'low image', will lead to an increase in vandalism and crime and the loss
of community pride (Barnsley is already hailed as the crime capital of South
Yorkshire!). The self-perpetuating cycle of deprivation leads to the total
erosion of community spirit and ultimately to the death of the community
itself.

COMMUNITY, CULTURE AND EDUCATION

The children of Barnsley are hard hit. Due to the multitude of interconnected factors to which we have already referred, Barnsley finds it hard
to meet the needs of its children. Its schools, as already discussed, are
considerably underfunded and continually find it difficult to meet the social
and educational needs of the children in their care. Families struggle to
provide the solid emotional base upon which young lives are built whilst

communities which once boasted choirs such as the Dodworth Male Voice Choir and brass bands such as the Grimethorpe Colliery Band now find it impossible to meet the cultural needs of their citizens. At a time when more children are in need, Barnsley's schools are deserted by a central government which bases its Standard Spending Assessments on data which lack economic and unemployment indicators and fail totally to recognise the problems of coalfield communities. Education budgets are continually eroded as Barnsley Council wages its annual fight to keep spending below the level unfairly dictated by SSAs and policed by capping strategies, with the consequence that schools find their buying power severely restricted. Schools find it impossible to afford the comfortable pupil–teacher ratio, adequate resourcing, teacher expertise and high-standard accommodation which would allow them to compete successfully in central government's education market-place.

Large classes are being held together by a professional commitment which papers over the cracks purely for the sake of Barnsley's children and Barnsley's future.

Under the average salary-into-school-budget/actual-salary-out-of-school-budget scenario, schools are penalised for employing experienced teachers. School development during enforced educational change is impossible within the limited finance available. Mandatory exceptions within the LEA Budget continue to be eroded as less money can be targeted at areas such as welfare, scheme of aid and educational psychology. School buildings continue to be neglected as planned maintenance spending suffers annual shrinkage.

SUPPORT FOR PRIMARY EDUCATION

A primary school in a once-mining suburb of Barnsley, which now sees inhabitants drifting to pastures new, is faced with horrendous budgetary problems in carrying a £30,000 deficit on a budget of £180,000. It effectively has £150,000 to meet expected expenditure of £180,000 during the financial year 1993/94. It has cut staffing by two during the last twelve months in an effort to reduce overheads and currently has four classes of thirty and one mixed infant class boasts thirty-four members with no extra support. All classes have representatives from at least two age groups whilst one class has members from three different age groups, again with no extra support. Teachers, who struggled with the teaching and administrative demands of an ideal class size of twenty-five children, find it almost impossible to deliver the broad, balanced and enriched curriculum to which they know their pupils are entitled. Morale is low. The situation is due not to mismanagement by the school but to a drastic fall in roll caused by the rapid shrinkage of a once-proud industrial community. Barnsley LEA acknowledges, understands and sympathises with the school's calamitous situation, but is unable to offer financial support in the current financial climate. Services such as Barnsley's Scout Dike Outdoor Education Centre and its Performing Arts Development Service, upon which schools and their teachers have heavily depended for curriculum support, enrichment and In-Service Training, suffer repeated closure threats as the council endures its annual battle to set the required SSA dictated budget.

AN UNEVEN PLAYING FIELD

How can Barnsley be expected to achieve even moderate success in the education market-place when the playing-field is so obviously uneven? Every child in Britain has an entitlement to the same quality of teacher expertise, resources, pupil–teacher ratios and accommodation, irrespective of geographical or political location. This cannot be achieved without a common national funding policy based on all local authorities receiving the same Standard Spending Assessment for Education for each pupil. There would need to be a Positive Action Element of extra funding to bring all schools up to a nationally-accepted standard of staffing, resourcing and accommodation. Funding based on nationally equitable pupil-share of national educational finance from central government would at least remove one of the inconsistencies which discredit the educational league tables upon which the government's education market-place depends.

Barnsley and its communities are victims of government policy which is either ill-thought-out, vindictive or both! Standard Spending Assessments are supposed to provide a simple and stable formula for guidance as to what local authorities should spend in order to provide a standard level of service. This cannot be justified in Barnsley's case, particularly when the relationship between SSAs and capping criteria dictate expenditure levels which do not allow for the adequate resourcing of its services, when SSAs totally fail to recognise high unemployment, low levels of educational attainment, the need for economic regeneration of its decimated communities, low incomes and the high mortality rate, which is associated with the incidence of chronic illness associated with the mining industry.

CONCLUSION

It is evident that outdated formulae are used to determine Standard Spending Assessments which, instead, need to be made annually on the basis of developing requirements. How can central government close the last of Barnsley's collieries, decimate their dependent communities and fail to amend the criteria upon which the funding of the local services is based? Until there is a complete review of the methods of the determination of local authority spending by central government the people of Barnsley cannot be adjudged to receive a standard level of service equal to that of the Wandsworths and Manchesters of this world. A complete case of Barnsley bashing, I presume?

Chapter 2

Local authorities in the 1990s.
A county perspective: Kent

Nick Henwood

*Kent is a large shire county and conservative by tradition. Since 1986 its
education department has undergone a series of restructurings in response
both to calls for efficiency and accountability and its changing role in the
context of the growing number of grant-maintained schools. Nick
Henwood charts these transformations for us and discusses the impact that
they have had on the provision of educational services to all children and
young people.*

HISTORICAL BACKGROUND

Local authorities are all different. There is no 'typical' authority. Because
their historical roots are in local accountability they quite properly reflect
local priorities – and the local electorate. Thus an Inner London authority
will have very different characteristics from a shire county. A shire county in
the south of England is likely to be quite different from a County Council in
the north. The views in this paper are based on experience in Kent, the
'Garden of England'.

Kent is a large local authority which, apart from some trimming of its
London borders, has remained substantially the same since the County
Council was formed in 1891. It has over 700 schools and a school population
exceeding 230,000. In addition to geographical stability, Kent remained
under Conservative control continuously until the local government elections of 1993, after which there was no overall control. Its stability and
innate conservatism have been reflected in resistance to change in its education service during the 1960s and 1970s – a time when most authorities
were committed more or less willingly to comprehensive reorganisation of
secondary education. Although some parts of Kent were reorganised, much
was not, and the county continues to have a higher proportion of selective
schools than any other local education authority (LEA). Kent's unique
character is also reflected in a wide variety of types of school organisation in
the many relatively small centres of population, which themselves vary –

from London fringe to highly rural. Kent's natural tendency towards being inward-looking has been further encouraged by geographical factors. It is virtually a peninsula, bounded by London and its very different culture to the west. Its proximity to Europe and the prospect of the Channel Tunnel are also of increasing importance.

Not surprisingly, Kent's view of local government has valued stability and a perception of traditional values. With a history of tight budgeting, its administration was centralised, formal, friendly and, perhaps, perceived by some to be paternalistic. The Education Service was managed along conventional lines. Until 1986 a central headquarters office in Maidstone managed both operational and policy issues. There was a network of thirteen divisional education offices, ensuring close contact with schools and their governing bodies. They administered local services such as transport, admissions and welfare. To some extent the divisional office staff identified more closely with schools than with the central Education Office, and were valued by schools for that very reason.

WINDS OF CHANGE

By the mid-1980s many local authorities were working closely at the organisation of their education departments. This was the period of the '3 Es' – economy, efficiency and effectiveness. There was also a marked shift away from traditional bureaucratic approaches to administration.

In 1986 a major restructuring of the divisional organisation was undertaken, following a review by external consultants, Price Waterhouse. They recommended the creation of six new areas with greater management responsibilities and reduced overheads. Central services were restructured but there was limited commitment to the devolution of responsibility.

The year 1986 also saw the appointment of a new chief executive, Paul Sabin, and coincidentally the publication of the 1986 Education Act, which began in a tentative way to increase the power of governing bodies and to put power closer to schools.

Paul Sabin came to Kent, something of a 'sleeping giant', with a determination to change the way in which the County Council, Kent's largest employer, did its business. He rapidly pressed for change linked to three themes: proximity to the customer; management not administration; and financial accountability. The Education Service was large, inevitably bureaucratic, relatively remote and struggling with its budget! The new approach struck a chord with some education managers who were far from unaware of the need for changed approaches. The restructuring of the department became a movement towards devolution – not just within the department but also to schools. Kent started planning its local management scheme for schools in 1987.

Figure 2.1 shows the pre-1989 structure. Immediate contact with schools,

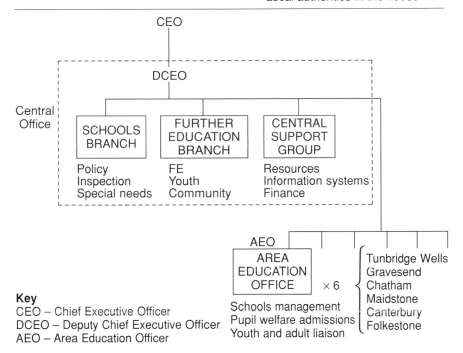

Figure 2.1 Pre-1989 structure of Kent's Education Service

the Youth Service, Adult Education and support for individuals is through six substantial area offices. Policy, co-ordination of county-wide issues and the inspection/advisory service were located centrally.

Kent was beginning to change. Like other authorities it could see that decision-making should be devolved where that could result in service improvement. The LEA's role was becoming more strategic and enabling – supporting the providers of education rather than directing the process. That change of approach was not without difficulties. Schools had long been dependent on the LEA for quite detailed decision-making and LEA offices were accustomed to that relationship. 'Letting go' was not easy. For some of the elected members of the County Council the emphasis on management by schools and by officers led to a questioning of the respective roles of officers and members. The fundamental role of members in dealing with constituency business and taking an active role in resolving problems is relatively simple with a centralised administrative structure, whereas a devolved system of management accountability can be seen to move powers away from members.

By 1988 it was apparent that further devolution was necessary to achieve the new objectives and Price Waterhouse as external consultants were used to advise on major restructuring. Meanwhile, on the national scene, the government was moving towards the Education Reform Act. In Kent, preparation for restructuring continued with a close eye on the progress of the bill through Parliament and an awareness that the role of local authorities was about to undergo major change. The greater emphasis on decision-making at school level was generally welcomed. There appeared to be scope for successful development of the partnership between schools and the LEA. Decisions about the quality of provision and management would be made at school level. The LEA's reduced role was as planner, resource allocator, enabler and service leader.

The organisational response to the Education Act was to structure three interconnected functions: operations, strategy and quality assurance. Operations was about enabling service delivery – its aim was to support school management and ensure effective direct services provided by the department (e.g., support for pupils with special educational needs). It was also concerned with grants and more tactical issues such as school reorgani-sations. Strategy was concerned with forward planning, developing policies and ensuring coherence of the service. Quality assurance was about moni-toring and reporting on the quality of all aspects of the service – in schools, the Education Department and other services (see Figure 2.2).

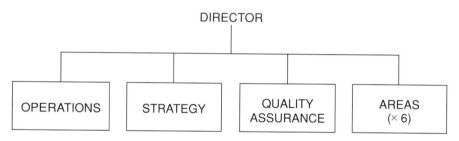

Figure 2.2 Post-1989 structure of Kent's Education Service

The conceptual structure was designed to support schools and individual students, but with an acceptance that schools would become increasingly autonomous through the development of local management – which the 1988 Act had made statutory. It was recognised that the early 1990s would be a period of change as schools took on their new responsibilities. There was a commitment to a further review in 1992 when local management of schools (LMS) and the National Curriculum would be well on the way to full implementation.

The earlier creation of six areas was proving popular with schools, which appreciated the proximity of support and the increased responsiveness resulting from their becoming 'one-stop shops'. The new operational man-agement of the service was through the six areas – each with an area director – having budgetary responsibility and management of most aspects of the service (schools, support for pupils with special needs, curriculum support, adult education, youth, careers). The rapid development of local management was facilitated by six area-based local management 'champions'. National Curriculum developments were managed by substantial area curriculum support staff.

A new chief education officer, Roy Pryke, was appointed in December 1988 to the post of Director of Education Services. The changed job title reflected the new role of the authority – in supporting and enabling the provision of education rather than directly managing it.

During the next two years the local management scheme was extended to all schools and the National Curriculum was introduced successfully, despite some national wavering. The new structure was well received and Kent was bold enough to carry out a Market and Opinion Research International (MORI) survey in 1990. It revealed increasingly confident management but mixed public reaction to education services. Meanwhile, the new approach to quality assurance included inspecting area offices and other parts of the administration as well as schools, in an uncomfortably objective fashion!

Two areas of business were particularly problematic – budgetary control and support for children with special education needs. Although care was taken with setting up new budgetary systems, reorganisation at the same time as the wholesale delegation of school budgets created major pressures. In addition, the LEA's non-delegated budget comprised those areas of needs-driven expenditure which had always proved difficult to control (for example, special needs support and home-to-school transport). It became evident that management of both in a devolved structure requires particular skill, persistence and good guidelines. The budgetary pressures being felt by Kent during this period were replicated in other LEAs.

IMPACT OF GRANT-MAINTAINED STATUS

The opportunity for a school to opt out of LEA control to become grant-maintained (GM) was originally seen as a route for a minority of schools. That is still the case in 1993 but the government's arguments have gradually increased support for the GM sector – now perceived as government policy for all secondary schools and some primary schools.

By September 1993 there were sixty-eight grant-maintained schools in Kent (fifty-four secondary and twelve primary schools). Although that is less than 10 per cent of the total of maintained schools in Kent, it is a significant number. Why did that come about and what did it mean for Kent as a local education authority? The change of direction did not come about through legislation. In a sense, it would have been easier to manage had that been the case. Ministerial statements and an increasing financial bias in favour of GM schools gradually mapped out policy. Even the 1993 Act, although facilitating GM status, did not make it mandatory.

The earliest schools in Kent to apply for grant-maintained status did so largely because they were dissatisfied with the LEA. Some felt threatened by reorganisation proposals. Others felt constrained by an authority which was choosing not to adopt comprehensive education while they wanted to admit pupils of all abilities to their non-selective high schools. A second tranche of schools felt less antagonism to the LEA but were attracted by the financial inducements being offered. The relatively low levels of education expenditure in Kent, coupled with some major school building problems made the financial aspects of GM attractive. In addition to an initial grant, early GM schools received an enhanced level of funding for services no longer being provided by the local authority and also a high chance of success in bids for building improvements. In some schools GM status was a natural next step towards greater autonomy following several years of enjoying the benefits of local management.

Faced with interest in GM status, the Education Committee adopted a neutral standpoint. It wished well those schools leaving the LEA but remained relatively agnostic about the GM movement. With financial advantages and the prospect of continued goodwill and services available from the LEA, more schools in Kent chose GM than was the case in many other authorities.

The immediate impact of GM on the LEA was not great as GM schools represented a small minority. However, by 1991 the financial impact was beginning to be felt. In that year the Department of Education and Science assumed a 16 per cent budget addition for former LEA services – a sum far greater than the LEA had actually spent on the GM schools. Although that addition was eventually reduced to the actual average expenditure, the financial impact was significant – particularly since school budgets were based on pupil numbers whereas LEA services equate more closely to the number of schools. The Education Committee decided to offset the cost of GM by increasing the annual budget – requiring £10 million by 1993/4. The administrative budget was reduced and a gradual realignment of services began.

The authority was finding it increasingly difficult to exert leadership at a strategic level. For example, it made attempts to rationalise provision to take surplus places out of use and standardise the age of secondary transfer at 11 plus in line with Key Stage 2 of the National Curriculum. Where proposals were perceived as a threat or ran counter to the ambitions of an individual school, there was a tendency to apply to become grant-maintained. Some early GM approvals appeared to ignore sound planning in favour of increasing the number of GM schools, although there were notable exceptions, such as refusal to agree GM proposals by middle schools where an overall change in transfer age was proposed. However, gradually, the county felt a significant change in its ability to manage a system to the benefit of the whole community.

Secondary school admissions was one area of activity where a loss of coherence was felt. GM schools are not constrained by LEA schemes for secondary school transfer and the partnership between schools and the LEA began to become more difficult. Many GM schools showed a willingness to co-operate but changes to their age range and status resulted in strain. The situation in Canterbury was particularly interesting. All but one of its eight secondary schools became grant maintained. School admissions in a selective system were delicately balanced and there was great pressure on selective places. However, the LEA was no longer in a position to determine the outcome. It had rapidly become apparent that even a relatively small percentage of GM schools will have organisational implications for the whole authority.

THE STRATEGIC LEA

The changes brought about directly by the Education Reform Act and less directly by GM schools are not the only factors affecting the role of the local authority. The establishment of the Office for Standards in Education – with its four-yearly inspection programme for all schools – was brought about by a transfer of funding away from LEAs and resulted in immediate changes for LEA inspectorates. It is important to put that change in the broader context of government legislation requiring compulsory competitive tendering for both 'blue collar' staff (manual) services and 'white collar' staff (professional and administrative) services. In addition, the impending Review of Local Government with its preference for single-tier unitary authorities is likely to bring further significant change.

After the 1992 General Election it was anticipated by some that local education authorities might well be abolished. The 1992 White Paper 'Choice and Diversity' did not deliver the death blow – but also failed to identify a clear way ahead.

The 1993 Act has left many unanswered questions – especially in respect of the future role of LEAs. It lays important and increased responsibilities on LEAs for the delivery of services to individuals but continues to leave the development of the schools sector to market forces. Whereas schools are encouraged to become self governing (i.e., grant maintained) there is no legislation to make them do so. Thus LEAs are left wondering what role they have to fulfil – at least in the interim.

However, there are key responsibilities which many LEAs would continue to identify as important. They relate to quality improvement; the planning of school places and the securing of education for every child; support services to schools, and information to schools and the community at large. The 1993 Education Act does not remove these responsibilities although it places them in a context which will be increasingly difficult to sustain.

Kent is not alone in feeling itself unsure about the overall direction of national policy at the present time (1993). It has already decided to move into the market-place in respect of services to schools. In 1993 it established Kent Education Support Services – a grouping of support services for schools which is ready for further delegation of schools budgets and to sell to GM schools 'at the margin'. Increasingly, the provision of services is seen to be not necessarily the sole preserve of the local authority, which becomes the purchaser or commissioner of services on behalf of others – whether schools or individuals. There is a concentration on those services which a local authority does well and a wish to delegate those where other providers might be more appropriate. For example, most LEAs are good providers of curriculum support and specialist personnel advice. In contrast, good-quality information systems support and financial services are also available elsewhere. At present only mainframe computer services in Kent have been fully privatised ('outsourced' – the selling of the entire function including staff to an external commercial organisation) but there is the prospect of further development as has occurred in other authorities.

The extent to which this new approach to the role of a local authority is to be adopted will be determined in part by the wish of the authority to control services where it feels there is a strategic advantage in having influence – in other words, where the authority believes it can add quality to the process of learning in its community. Decisions will also be influenced by legislative and financial pressure applied by central government – and they may well be the determining factors.

A GENERIC ROLE

Kent's response to further change has resulted in realignment of its functions. The continued and increased role of the LEA is reflected in a generic branch called 'Customer and Community Services'. It encompasses all services to individuals, from Special Educational Needs to Youth and Adult Education (see Figure 2.3).

Its creation reflects an LEA's substantial and main residual responsibilities as schools become more and more autonomous. The 1993 Education Act reinforces the responsibility of the LEA for services to individuals and there is increasing concern to ensure multi-agency co-operation in devising support plans. That is particularly true for children and young people with special education needs where Education, Health and Social Services need to work together – and provide links beyond the years of statutory education. There are other powerful examples, such as work with disaffected youngsters, truants and juvenile offenders.

Although there is an increasing wish to bring together the work of the Education and Social Services departments in Kent, their professional differences (as well as similarities) are recognised. They remain major organisa-

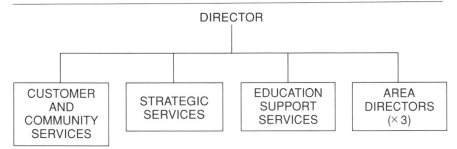

Figure 2.3 Post-1993 structure of Kent's Education Service

tions where there are less obvious benefits of closer amalgamation, such as contemplated in some small authorities, where the span of management responsibility is less.

A second branch, Strategic Services, brings together the functions of purchaser of services, policy development and review – the core functions of the LEA as the provider of education resources to the community. Area offices remain a key local focus for service delivery. Area directors are now principally concerned in the assurance of quality and local policy issues relating to the provision of places and school organisation.

FUTURE PERSPECTIVES

There is no doubt that local government – of education at least – is at a crossroads. Its role has been successively reduced since 1986 and has reached a point where, should the grant-maintained initiative really take hold (and it has not yet done so) the way ahead can lead to the handing over of responsibility for strategic planning and the budget to the Funding Agency for Schools (FAS) in York, quality assurance to the Office for Standards in Education (OFSTED) and welfare and admissions matters increasingly to litigation. That would imply a managed process of transferring responsibility, but no such process exists. It was the lack of coherence and a perceived need to re-establish an education partnership which led Kent's Director, Roy Pryke, to speak up vociferously in the *Times Educational Supplement* (Pryke, 1993).

Currently, LEAs share responsibilities with the FAS for planning when an LEA has 10–75 per cent of its schools grant maintained, unless the LEA chooses to hand over all responsibility to the FAS. It is hard to see how a policy which lacks clear edges can survive without further review. Already policy applies unevenly to different LEAs and the post-1944 Act view of the education service as a national system, locally administered, is fading. Choice and diversity were never intended to provide a basis for easy planning and LEAs continue to manage the service and support schools and individual pupils during a period of major instability. The current review of local government is unlikely to reduce that instability in the foreseeable future. After 100 years, local democracy has increasingly less influence in the English counties although the case for a partnership with education – central government, schools, churches, community and local authority – may never have been stronger.

NOTE

The views expressed are personal and not those of Kent County Council.

Chapter 3

Opting into irrelevance

Roy Pryke

First published in the *Times Educational Supplement*, 1 October 1993, pp. 12–13. ©
Times Supplements Ltd 1993.

*In Chapter 1 you have read the criticisms levelled at the government by
Julian Wroe on behalf of his colleagues in Barnsley schools. This is what
you might expect from mining (now ex-mining) communities, solidly
Labour. Here is another attack on recent policy, this time from a south-
east Tory heartland, Kent. During the time that Nick Henwood was
writing his chapter for this book, his Director of Educational Services,
Roy Pryke, published the following broadside in the* Times Educational
Supplement. *The response to the article, from inside and outside Kent,
was noisy.*

The partnership is over, or so they say. Returning from summer hills and
beaches, hapless civil servants and education officers look at the future
envisaged in the new Education Act.

This year's Act is not just a continuation of Kenneth Baker's 1988 Act. It
signals radical change in the management of education and seems designed to
impair the partnership between local authorities and central government in
providing a varied and comprehensive education service in every area – a
national system locally administered which has produced genuine progress.

We survey the future and many of us, in schools, offices and policy
chambers, believe it will not work unless there is an early *rapprochement*
between central and local government.

Reflect on the results of the 1988 Education Act. For the past five years
local education authorities have worked with schools to bring about the
revolution of local management.

Most headteachers I know are handling local management brilliantly.
LMS started in LEAs, was adopted as national policy and implemented
between schools and LEAs within a Department for Education framework:
the proven partnership leading to success.

We have also had a major supporting role in implementing the National Curriculum – but spot the difference. The National Curriculum was taken over by national bodies and lost connection with the realities of the classroom. In the end the monster had to be tamed by Sir Ron Dearning.

Now, despite its faltering, we have a serious problem with the policy of schools opting out. The effects are not immediately obvious, but they are insidious and in the end they will be extremely damaging. My concern is that what was originally a minor and perceivably beneficial element of Kenneth Baker's Act is threatening to undermine the quality of the education service wherever more than a sprinkling of schools become grant-maintained.

The opting-in to a grant-maintained sector is a misfit policy which is damaging the success of local management and the potential of the National Curriculum. I write from first-hand experience of Kent as a 'leading-edge' authority, with almost half of its 126 secondary schools grant maintained. The impact on the primary sector has been minimal – only twelve out of 570 have changed status.

The grant-maintained policy is in reality irrelevant. It is hitting the wrong targets and is counter to local management and the National Curriculum. But it is causing substantial damage to the finances of local authorities, reducing the money available for local authority 'self-governing' schools and diminishing our capacity to support schools in their management of curriculum, finance, contracts, personnel and property.

LMS has placed decision-making where the action is and increased the involvement of the local community and the local autonomy which GM policy claims to seek. The mould was broken five years ago through LMS, not GM.

The push from the Department for Education (DFE) for schools to opt out seems to us directly involved with schools, to have little or nothing to do with improving education and everything to do with the emasculation of locally-accountable influence in favour of centralisation of power.

The current and future cost in terms of wasted energy and misdirected funding is substantial. When we are desperately seeking to raise educational standards for the sake of all our futures, such waste is unacceptable.

As a simple example, each large primary school which opts out takes with it the amount of finance which is needed to establish a nursery class. Is the development of the GM sector going to contribute more to raising standards than the extension of nursery education?

There is a way to avoid the morass which continuation of the current incoherent and seemingly unplanned management of the public education service is heading towards. But let me first demonstrate from real experience why someone expected to develop effective schools and make best use of available resources is so concerned.

While opting into the GM sector has scarcely affected many LEAs, I imagine that every chief education officer with GM schools has a file of issues which have occurred in the last couple of years. Here are some of mine.

INEQUITABLE FUNDING OF SCHOOLS

- Public acknowledgement of preferential treatment of the first few hundred GM schools' building programmes;
- double-funding of GM schools whereby they receive both services and the money to buy those services;
- protection of the first batch of GM schools so that they have better funding than other GM schools;
- the exclusion of LEA secondary schools from DFE funds to develop technology, which is supposed to be a priority for the education service nationally;
- the loophole which allows a school that has overspent the previous year to opt out, leaving all the other LEA schools to pay that school's debt.

UNSATISFACTORY BUDGET ARRANGEMENTS

- One-fifth of GM schools suffering mid-year budget cuts and another fifth still without their budgets four months into the financial year (we had given all Kent GM schools last March a close calculation of what they could expect: so what is the DFE's problem?) and mysterious arrangements for auditing GM school accounts with no information made public;
- under the Common Funding Formula for GM schools, potentially damaging arrangements which may eventually be extended to impose on all schools a crude national formula with marginal local variations but ignoring the arrangements of local authorities, have been made to respond to schools' circumstances. This is producing the constitutional absurdity of Council Tax payers' money being handed to the Funding Agency for Schools (FAS) quango in York for distribution to government schools in a way which has not been decided by a body accountable for how the money is raised or spent.

ADMISSION AND EXCLUSION OF PUPILS TO GM SCHOOLS

These are not being properly monitored by the DFE, allowing the schools to pick and choose pupils, widen ability intakes to selective schools, end arrangements such as those in Waltham Forest for the education of blind and partially-sighted children, 'cool out' disaffected pupils without going through the proper procedures and refuse to take pupils excluded from other schools. This is leading to a real fear among excellent non-GM schools that they will become 'sink schools'. We now have schools choosing pupils, instead of parents having more choice.

POOR INFORMATION ON QUALITY

Just one report so far on GM schools of a general kind from the Office for Standards in Education (OFSTED) inspectors based on visits to eighty-one schools and concluding that 'there is no significant difference in the quality of teaching between GM and other maintained schools'. Kent parents have had access to LEA inspection reports on individual county schools for the past four years. There have been GM schools in Kent now for four years and not a single government inspector's report on them has been made public.

INCONSISTENT POLICY-MAKING

Two Maidstone 11–16 schools went GM and were then allowed to develop sixth forms. Shortly after, three more Maidstone GM schools in similar circumstances wanted to do the same and the DFE refused permission. The result was frustration and bewilderment for the disadvantaged schools, dismay for anybody who wants strong, broad and efficient 11–19 education.

IGNORING LOCAL CONCERNS

A grammar school in Canterbury in inadequate premises has not opted out, confounding our attempt to make provision closer to children's homes and to stem the flow of children from outlying areas into a city which has terrible traffic congestion. The school is now being encouraged to seek a funding programme for expansion.

WASTED MONEY ON SURPLUS PLACES

There are over 8,000 surplus places in GM schools in Kent which nobody is doing anything about even though removal of surplus places is rightly a central link of DFE policy.

Where do we go from here? Contrary to the tone of much of the debate, LEAs and their chief education officers have a common agenda with the DFE.

Since the 1988 Education Act we have worked assiduously to secure maximum practicable parental choice, well-managed and self-governing schools, implementation of the National Curriculum, professional and cost-effective support for schools and clear accountability both to parents and to schools.

Whatever new management superstructure is established, be it direct control from the DFE, regional bureaucracy and government or the FAS collaborating with the Further Education Funding Council and Training and Enterprise Councils, there are five functions vital to the quality of education which need to be carried out locally.

These are: quality improvement, planning of school provision, securing education for every pupil, support and information to schools and the community, and support services to schools.

Heads of LEA self-governing and state GM schools have no doubt about the need for this. To quote from a recent letter from the head of a Kent GM school: 'I believe that debate should include all parties.'

When I discussed with GM heads clause 293 about trading, they made it clear they want access to the LEA services which we shall eventually be unable to provide because we shall be trading 'beyond the margins'.

Schools appreciate the good quality and responsive service, with no hidden extras, which LEAs have long provided without fuss. LMS has broken the mould. Few LEAs were the bureaucratic oppressors of schools which some national politicians like to depict.

The DFE initiative on local management has now separated the analysis and response to a school's immediate needs, which is properly placed with the headteacher and governing body, from strategic planning.

All that remains is to decide who should have the planning function and everything that flows from it and to establish equitable funding for all schools.

The only fact we have been told so far by the DFE about its approach to planning is that the new FAS quango, which looks as though it will carry out this function, is to be based in York. From next April it will have an influence on about 40 LEAs where more than 10 per cent of pupils in the primary and secondary sector are in GM schools. More than three-quarters of these pupils are in the south-east.

It is really intended that there will be no regional bureaucracy to bring York closer to the action in Bromley, Essex and Kent. In these three LEAs it is possible that the threshold will be crossed and responsibility will pass to the FAS. A distant, non-accountable and costly bureaucracy will be established.

With just a few months to go, we still do not know how the planning for the opening, extending or closing of schools will operate. The duties and powers are to be split between the FAS and the LEAs.

Split authority is no authority. We cannot conduct business on the basis of arrangements whereby planning powers are both parallel and shared (whatever that means) and which assume that everybody will try to make it work, with the escape route that if things go wrong the Secretary of State will intervene. How many extra ministers and civil servants will that require?

There is no indication yet how the interests of parents are to be addressed. My department handles two million enquiries a year from the public. Nobody is suggesting that even a small proportion of these are frivolous. So who will handle them if we do not? Would the local MPs be ready to handle hundreds of extra enquiries from their constituents each week?

Already parents are confused. They write to me to sort out admissions problems or complaints relating to GM schools. All I can do is to tell them to approach the governing body (who may well have been party to the decision causing parental concern) or to write to the Secretary of State.

That is a long way from the clear accountability we have for LEA schools where, if they need to go beyond the school, parents can seek help from the area education director or from me and, if not satisfied, can enlist the support of a member of the LEA.

Democracy may not always work smoothly but at least the parents know they can have a say at the ballot box if they are not satisfied with how the local member has handled their concerns. Where does the responsibility really rest in the new scheme? Without diminishing the new status and self-sufficiency of schools, it seems essential for all LEA and GM schools to operate within a framework. My preference would be for that framework to have a local democratic base. That could also help to preserve the vital connection with other agencies such as police, social services and housing departments.

Perhaps existing GM schools could be given a new kind of voluntary-aided status in recognition that they wish to remain at arm's length from the local body. What is evident is that the current arrangements are confusing, incoherent, wasteful and corrosive. They lack clear accountability to parents and the wider public. New thinking is urgently required.

I know from talking to 400 Kent heads just how much most of them dislike the prospect of moving from the LEA to the DFE. They know, as I do, of the extra stress and workload GM heads are suffering and they believe that the interests of their pupils and communities are best served if they remain as self-governing schools within the LEA.

Research shows that the GM policy has done nothing and can be expected to do nothing to benefit children. I am forced to conclude that the proposals for GM schools will damage rather than improve state education.

Now that the clamour surrounding the Education Act has passed, can we have the rational argument and dialogue? Unless there is a secret plan to nationalise education very soon, which would at least give us a clear way ahead, we need to reach agreement quickly before the educational system is undermined.

My concern, and that of my politically hung County Council, is to secure sound and coherent management of the public education service for all children and communities. That does not necessarily mean through LEAs, although nobody has come up with anything better. Is it possible for the children's sake that we could have the same open review of policy which has brought sense to the National Curriculum?

Chapter 4

Local government reorganisation and its implications for educational equality

Kathryn Riley

This chapter examines the impact of changes to the structure, funding and management of local government on children and young people identified as having 'special educational needs'. Kathryn Riley was an elected member of the Inner London Education Authority (ILEA) in the 1980s and she draws on her experience and research to discuss the consequences of the abolition of the ILEA for educational equality. She concludes with a discussion of the Local Government Review and how far proposed changes will confirm or erode children's educational rights.

INTRODUCTION

Over the last decade, central government and local government have been playing a long and complicated game of poker. Central government has been the dealer and has dealt itself all the aces and trumps. The rules of the game have been determined by the unwritten British Constitution in which local government is the creation of central government – a creature of statute. But what the government makes it can also unmake.

The results of the game to date have been that central government has reasserted its power over local government. It has set a new framework for the public sector which challenges professional and producer control; introduces a market philosophy; creates competition; and introduces new forms of consumerism (articulated in the Citizen's Charter) which emphasise individual rights. A range of non-elected bodies has also been created to take responsibility for many aspects of local services from local authorities. A further dimension to these changes is proposals currently being considered by the Local Government Commission, to reorganise county and district local authorities.

This chapter explores the impact of these changes for children identified as having special educational needs.[1] What have been the effects of the new emphasis on individual rights? When the stakes have finally been counted – will he or she be a loser or a winner?

NEW RIGHTS AND FREEDOMS?

The period from the 1981 Education Act up to the mid-1980s saw a steady increase both in the number of children and young people taught in mainstream provision and in expenditure on special educational provision.[2] Over the last decade, however, special needs provision has operated in an uncertain and contracting financial climate: a climate made more complex by new assertions about rights and choices and by increased competition between schools.

The 1988 Education Reform Act asserted the rights of parents to choose a school. But the right to choose a school is in reality the right to state a school preference, the right to appeal if that preference is not satisfied, but not the right of access to a school, or the right to certain levels of performance. The Parent's Charter guarantees the right of parents to know what is taught, but not the right to influence it. The rights for parents articulated in the 1988 Act and the Parent's Charter are therefore essentially guarantees of process, rather than guarantees of outcomes.

Some aspects of parental rights – particularly in relation to the statementing process – have been strengthened by recent legislation.[3] However, the climate of competition created by the 1988 Education Reform Act; the introduction of market-economy principles; and the introduction of severe financial controls on local government spending have combined to create new obstacles for children with special education needs and an overall reduction in the levels of service available.[4]

Competition between schools has created winners and losers. The losers certainly include children with behavioural difficulties who increasingly risk exclusion from school. Processes of selection of pupils for secondary schools are also reducing the opportunities for the child seen to have educational needs.[5] Complaints to the local government Ombudsman from the families of children with special needs have escalated, as a result of reduced resources and greater public awareness of the ombudsman's role.[6]

The 1993 Education Act: an articulation of rights

The issue of rights is central to the implementation of the 1993 Education Act. The Act reaffirms the rights of children and young people with special needs to be educated in mainstream schools but is likely to create new tensions and difficulties. In the words of Sir Malcolm Thornton (Conservative Chair of the Select Committee on Education):

> If we really believe that special educational needs are going to get a better deal under the new legislation than under the old system, then this is the biggest triumph of hope over experience that I have ever encountered.[7]

The central problem of the 1993 Act is that it promises more than it can deliver in that:

- it encourages GM schools to consult local authorities about special needs, *but* denies LEAs the power to ensure that GM schools accept pupils with special needs;
- it increases parents' rights of appeal against LEA special needs decisions, *but* withholds from LEAs an overall lead on special needs in their locality, thereby limiting the extent of parental redress.

The Act is premised on a notion of individual rights which assumes that all individuals will be in a position to exercise their rights effectively. It symbolises a final move away from the egalitarian goals of the 1960s and 1970s, towards a newly-emerging meritocratic framework.[8] It is the dawning of the new era in which *'equality is now the key anti-conservative concept'* (David Willetts MP, past director of the Conservative 'think-tank', the Centre for Policy Studies).[9] It also continues the process of fragmentation begun by the 1988 Education Reform Act, increasing the climate of competition between schools and the marginalisation of the educational role of the local authority begun by the 1988 Act.

THE ROLE OF THE LOCAL AUTHORITY IN SUPPORTING CHILDREN IDENTIFIED AS HAVING SPECIAL EDUCATIONAL NEEDS

But how valid are government criticisms about the failure of the LEAs? Have LEAs successfully provided for the children seen to have spent educational needs? Three reports, all published in 1992, suggest that not all local authorities have adequately discharged their responsibilities for special needs in the past. But the reports also point to the lack of lucidity and direction from central government and the lack of resources to implement the 1981 Act.

Report I, a joint HMI/Audit Commission report identified a number of problems which included a lack of clarity about what constitutes special needs; a lack of systems to ensure that schools and LEAs were accountable for their work; and a lack of incentives for LEAs to implement the 1981 Act.[10] Report II (which was sponsored by the National Union of Teachers and the Spastics Society), focused on the costs of ensuring access for pupils with disabilities to mainstream schools. It also found a lack of clarity (from both central and local government) about what constitutes special needs.[11]

Report III, a management action report (also produced by the Audit Commission and HMI), found substantial evidence of good practice in LEAs.[12] The report praised Clwyd, for example, for the clarity of its policies; Lincolnshire for its performance measurement system; and Leeds for the purposeful way in which it tackled surplus places in special schools and successfully reallocated resources to mainstream schools.

The three reports together provide a clear action framework for both central and local government. But as the context for change remains uncertain, two critical questions as yet remain unanswered:

- Given the reduced capacity of the local authority to plan for special needs provision, can the improvements recommended in the three 1992 reports be achieved?
- If local government reorganisation goes ahead, will it improve, or damage the opportunities to provide effective special needs services?

LOCAL GOVERNMENT REORGANISATION: THE ILEA EXPERIENCE

The new education framework which has developed as a consequence of the 1988 Act and subsequent legislation is one which leaves the special needs child vulnerable both to market forces and to the consequences of organisational change. The abolition of the ILEA (which came about as a result of back-bench intervention – led by Michael Heseltine – during the Committee stage of the 1988 Act) provides an example of how provision for the special needs child can be squeezed by major organisational upheaval.

In 1991 I undertook a review of the administrative and service consequences of the abolition of the Inner London Education Authority and the transfer of services to the twelve inner London boroughs. The findings from that study (which is reported more fully elsewhere),[13] were that there had been both gains and losses from the reorganisation and from the creation of unitary authorities in the London Boroughs.

The actual gains were in a range of small discrete tasks, or in the delivery of services which required responses to individual needs, such as statementing. The potential gains depended on the willingness and ability of the new authority to refocus and co-ordinate their services, such as those for the early years.

In terms of losses, there was general agreement by participants in the study that the ILEA had provided visionary leadership and that the abolition of the ILEA had denuded London of a strategic authority which could provide an overview of the educational needs of London. There was unanimity in the view that the most significant strategic loss had been in the planning and overseeing of provision for special educational needs. (Table 4.1 summarises the gains and losses as a consequence of abolition.)

Although the initial intention of many of the London boroughs had been to work collaboratively across borough boundaries, to enhance the quality of planning (in special educational services as in other areas), and to maximise limited resources, this aspiration has not been realised. The pressures

Table 4.1 Gains and losses as a consequence of the abolition of the ILEA

Actual gains from having a smaller LEA

Discrete services
e.g., bus passes, school transport

Services which require responses to individual needs
e.g., statementing, allocation of school places

Services which need a local focus
e.g., non-statutory services, e.g., youth provision

Services which require a quick but differentiated response
e.g., small repairs and property maintenances

Potential gains from the creation of unitary authority

Opportunity to co-ordinate services more effectively
e.g., services for young children

Opportunity to develop particular emphasis
which meets local community needs

Services best provided by a larger strategic authority (such as the ILEA)

Specialist services
e.g., such as legal advice and financial services to schools

Special Educational Needs

Strategic overview and educational leadership

Overall research, monitoring and evaluation

---

on the new authorities to deliver the local service and manage the competition inherent in the Education Reform Act (for pupils, tender of contracts, etc.) reduced the opportunities for co-operation and joint planning.

Since abolition, gaps and duplication have emerged in special needs provision. Boarding school provision has been a particularly contentious area. Expertise has been lost, for example, about particular types of placements, or the provision of specialist equipment.

As a consequence of abolition of the ILEA and government determination to reduce levels of spending, London has witnessed a steady haemorrhage of services. Support for children with behavioural difficulties – a group which lacks a significant public lobby – has diminished beyond recognition. Services such as withdrawal groups and support for educational psychologists have been reduced in most boroughs.

The ILEA experience suggests that special needs provision is vulnerable during a process of major organisational change, and the creation of smaller local authorities. The vulnerability of those services increases when the major imperative to change is financial.

THE REVIEW OF LOCAL GOVERNMENT

Apart from continued uncertainties about the role of the LEA, the other wild-card for local government is the outcome of the work of the Local Government Commission.

In December 1990 the Secretary of State for the Environment announced his intention to undertake a wide-ranging review of local government, including its territorial structure. The Commission's brief was to review the two-tier council system in the English shires and to examine *'whether a unitary structure (i.e. one tier of local government) would better reflect the identified interests of local communities and secure effective and convenient local government'* (Policy Guidelines, para. 3). Sir John Banham was appointed in March 1992 as Chair of the Local Government Commission with the brief of reviewing county and district authorities in five tranches, over a sixteen-month period.

The commission began its work in August 1992 and reported on the authorities in the first tranche (Avon, Derbyshire, Durham, Cleveland, Gloucestershire, Humberside, Isle of Wight, Lincolnshire and North Yorkshire) by the early summer of 1993. It recommended the replacement of all the local authorities in the first tranche review by a range of unitary authorities. Its recommendations provoked intense criticism from supporters both of county councils and of district councils.

Central to this criticism was the charge that the commission lacked a clear view about the role and purposes of local government and assumed that changing structures would change outcomes. The commission was also criticised for its lack of consistency; for its failure to acknowledge critical issues about local government such as the reduction in local choice (symbolised by virtually universal capping of local authority spending); the centralisation of control by ministers; the replacement of elected councillors by ministerial appointees; and the fragmentation of local governance.[14]

Publication of the recommendations was soon followed, however, by indications from ministers that the future direction of the work of the commission was uncertain, although recommendations in the first tranche would go ahead.[15] Autumn 1993 murmurings suggest, however, that the commission will continue.

Although the situation in England remains confused, proposals for Wales have now been finalised – again against a backdrop of bitter opposition – and will come into effect in April 1995. The present thirty-seven Welsh districts and eight County Councils will merge into twenty-one single-tier authorities whose responsibilities will include education. If current proposals for

Scotland are implemented the existing system of fifty-three district councils, nine regional councils and three islands councils will be replaced by twenty-five new all-purpose single-tier authorities by 1996.

Whether the changes in the English authorities such as Avon, whose fate appears to be sealed – eight new unitary authorities – and the Welsh and Scottish authorities will improve, or diminish, opportunities for children with special needs remains to be seen. But the omens are not good.

Although the abolition of the ILEA does not provide a direct parallel with proposed local government reorganisation, it remains the nearest comparable restructuring. As was suggested earlier in the chapter, the experience of the ILEA has been that children identified as having 'special educational needs' have been losers, as a consequence both of local government reorganisation and of diminishing educational resources.

At this stage one can only speculate about the implications of local government reorganisation for special needs. In the short term, the work of the commission has drained time and energy from local government, as both officers and elected members prepare, consult and amend proposals and contemplate their fate. The long-term prospects are not good. On the basis of the ILEA experience, special needs provision is particularly vulnerable on reorganisation and may well deteriorate in those areas where a County Council has offered a strategically-planned and locally-delivered service in the past. Quality services are at risk.

WINNERS OR LOSERS?

It is difficult to tot up the gains and losses overall for disabled children and those who experience difficulties in learning over the last few years, in the increasingly uncertain world of local government. The gains are those of greater clarity about special needs and a clearer articulation of the rights of parents, which gives them some protection from the excesses of professionalism. But the gains are dependent on parents themselves having the energy and 'know-how' to promote the individual rights of their child and on their capacity to operate within the new meritocratic framework.

The losses are those created by the excesses of the market and by the introduction of a new meritocratic philosophy in which there will always be winners and losers. Competition, markets and selection are integral to the creation of this new meritocracy. But meritocratic notions of excellence based on selecting the most able, sit uneasily with special educational needs and the recognition of individual worth. The new consumerism fails to recognise that the special needs consumer is not the same as the supermarket shopper and cannot exercise the right not to buy commodities in the same way.

Central government has mainly gained in the local government poker game and is likely to continue as a winner. The emphasis of the Local

Government Commission on structures and reducing the costs of local government is unlikely to improve the access and opportunities for the child with special needs. In general, local authorities empowered by central government to plan strategically and deliver comprehensive resources locally are not part of the government's game-plan.

The hope for the future is that the government may yet make concessions (as it has on curriculum and testing) and recognise that in the new meritocracy not all children are equal competitors.

REFERENCES AND NOTES

1 The special needs child is defined as a pupil with a short-term learning difficulty, as well as one who has profound handicaps. According to the Audit Commission and Her Majesty's Inspectorate (HMI), this figure constitutes some 20 per cent of all pupils (see also reference 10).

2 A study carried out in 1991, for example, by the National Foundation for Educational Research (NFER) found that 15 per cent of a sample of eighty-one LEAs reported that schools had made cuts in special needs posts and support (Fletcher-Campbell, F. with Hall, C. (1993), *LEA Support for Special Needs*, NFER–Nelson).

3 According to *Hansard* (7 June 1993), the number of pupils statemented has risen from 137,000 (approx.) in 1986, to 162,000 (approx.) in 1992.

4 A review of special needs education, carried out by Klaus Wedell in 1993 for the National Commission, detailed evidence of the increasing problems which schools faced in meeting special needs requirements. It indicated a general deterioration in provision as a result of overall fiscal constraints on local authorities (and therefore also schools); the funding formulae to schools of local financial management which was largely weighted on student numbers; and the move towards the publication of league tables of school performance (Wedell, K. (1993), *Special Needs Education: The Next 25 Years*, National Commission on Education, Briefing Paper no. 14, May).

5 There is evidence to suggest, for example, that grant-maintained schools are increasingly choosing pupils. A study carried out by Leicester University of forty-seven grant-maintained schools found that just under one-third selected pupils by either academic, social or economic criteria (*Times Educational Supplement*, 1 May 1992).
   A study conducted for the Association of Metropolitan Authorities has also raised questions about whether grant- maintained schools are using subjective criteria to select pupils (Morris, R. (1993), *Choice of School: A Survey 1992–3*, Association of Metropolitan Authorities).
   A particularly stark example of the consequences of choices exercised by GM schools emerged in July 1993, with evidence that a grant- maintained school in Waltham Forest had ended a twenty-year agreement with a special school to teach blind and partially-sighted children: a decision which denies the rights and choices of those parents and children (*Guardian*, 24 July 1993).

6 *Times Educational Supplement*, 17 September 1993.

7 Sir Malcolm Thornton, quoted in the *Times Educational Supplement*, 11 December 1992.

8 This issue is developed more fully in Riley, K. A. (1994), *Quality and Equality: Promoting Opportunities in Schools*, Cassell, London.

9 Willetts, D. (1992), *Modern Conservatism*, Penguin, London.
10 *Getting in on the Act: Provision for Pupils with Special Educational Needs, the National Picture* (1992), The Audit Commission and Her Majesty's Inspectorate, HMSO, London.
11 *Within Reach: Access for Disabled Children to Mainstream Education* (1992), The National Union of Teachers, in Association with the Spastics Society, London.
12 *Getting the Act Together: Provision for Pupils with Special Educational Needs*, (1992). *A Management Handbook for Schools and Local Authorities*, The Audit Commission and Her Majesty's Inspectorate, HMSO, London.
13 Riley, K. A. (1993), 'The abolition of the ILEA: some implications for the restructuring of local government', *Public Money and Management*, 13 (2), April–June, pp. 57–60.
14 Stewart, J. (1993), 'The Local Government Review itself reviewed', *European Policy Forum*, July.
15 *Local Government Chronicle*, 16 July 1993.

National contexts for education in the 1990s

B. Educational consumers and legislation

Chapter 5

Trends in law: fifteen years of education policy-making, 1979–94

Margaret Peter

From the Conservative Party Manifesto of 1979 to the passing of the 1993 Education Act, the rhetoric of raising educational standards has led the way to an increasingly centralised system, with a declining role for both local education authorities and institutions of teacher education. Where does policy for disabled students and those who experience difficulties in learning fit in? Does it? People complained that the 1988 Education Reform Bill was out of step with the spirit of the 1981 Act and its support for a more integrated system. Margaret Peter takes a different view and argues that it is the 1981 Act that is out of step with the sequence of legislation passed since 1979.

Ten days before GERBIL – the Great Education Reform Bill – was published in 1987 I interviewed the then Secretary of State for Education, Kenneth Baker, for the *British Journal of Special Education*. The interview lasted seventeen minutes. He arrived late and left on time. During pauses between questions (submitted beforehand by request), he paid studious regard to the retying of the shoe-laces on his left foot and displayed a keen interest in a sudden hooting which came from Waterloo Station below the Department of Education and Science (DES) Offices at Elizabeth House. Answers came smoothly from a prepared sheet and only once was he caught unawares. It happened when he was told that not all children with statements of special educational needs and comparable levels of learning difficulties were in special schools, that policy and practices varied from one local authority to another and that many of these pupils were being taught in the mainstream. Only the flicker of an eyelid and a fleetingly intent look indicated that he had learned something new. When the Education Reform Bill appeared in November, the suspicion about the marginalising of pupils with special needs that I had felt during the interview was confirmed. There was only one reference to pupils with special educational needs and one to special schools.

The Secretary of State was not alone in his surprise. During the passage of the 1988 Bill through Parliament and when, with many amendments on special educational provision, it finally became law, critics of government policy on special educational needs complained that it was out of step with the 1981 Education Act. They argued that it went against the 'spirit' of the 1981 legislation, which had cautiously encouraged integration. It promoted a market forces approach which ran counter to coherent provision for children with disabilities and learning difficulties and it created league tables of achievements in which children with learning difficulties would be seen to fail.

I believe that a more realistic response is to look at the situation the other way round. Surely it was the 1981 Act which was out of key? Out of step with the orchestrated suite of legislation which started up in 1979, when the Conservatives returned to power and which continues to be played into the 1990s? In what ways was the 1981 Act at variance with the Conservatives' master plan for educational revolution? To attempt to answer these questions we need to look at the 1981 Act in the wider context of Conservative policy and legislation over the past fifteen years.

The Conservative Party manifesto for 1979 gave some clues to its agenda for education over the years ahead. One of its 'five tasks' was 'to support family life', an aim partly to be achieved by raising standards of education. It committed the party to doing so through promoting 'higher standards of achievement in basic skills', 'national standards in reading, writing and arithmetic monitored by tests worked out with teachers and others', strengthening the Inspectorate and placing more emphasis on practical skills and discipline-keeping in teacher training. The manifesto also introduced parents' 'right to choice' and implied that, armed with the examination results in the prospectuses which schools would have to publish, they would be able to choose their child's school and exercise greater influence over education – an essential condition for the unleashing of market forces in the legislation which lay ahead.

At the same time, inflation was to be controlled and waste, bureaucracy and over-government would be reduced. While there was no explicit reference to plans to erode the powers of local education authorities (LEAs) and to create the conditions for more centralised control – part of the hidden agenda – there was a telling allusion to Southwark's plans to spend £50 million on building another town hall.

These related themes of raising standards of achievement and of parental 'choice' as ways to improve overall standards of education were carried into the first Act in the Conservative law-by-law strategy to change the education system. The 1980 Education Act stressed parental choice or, more accurately, qualified rights for parents to express a preference for the school they wanted their child to attend and it gave them the right of appeal if they disagreed with the LEA's decision. Choice was extended further for 'less well off' parents whose children were academically capable of gaining government-assisted places at independent schools. Parents' influence was extended through the right to be represented on governing bodies. All these changes impinged, though only slightly as yet, on the activities of LEAs. At the same time schools were having to expose pupils' achievements, and were being prepared for the later introduction of market forces, through the duty to make public their admission arrangements and examination results.

The Education Act on special educational provision came a year later. It was wrung from a reluctant government after the Warnock Report had been published in 1978, on the understanding that there would be no extra money to kick-start it into action. Neil Kinnock, then leader of the Labour Party, compared it with Brighton Pier: 'good as far as it goes but not much of a way to get to France'.

With hindsight it can be seen as a diversion from the main thrust of Conservative education strategy for the 1980s. It did not offer 'choice' of school to parents whose children were attending special schools or in need of 'special educational treatment'. It did not refer to the monitoring of standards through tests or to the publication of pupils' examination results. It went against the Conservatives' hidden agenda by increasing rather than diminishing local authorities' duties in relation to pupils with special educational needs, which consisted of responsibility for the complex processes of statutory assessment and statementing, although it did increase LEAs' accountability for the resources it expended on pupils with statements. It focused too much attention on too few children, Warnock's '2 per cent', who had very different requirements for support from the high fliers whom the government and its middle-class supporters most wanted to help. It laid the foundation for a growing clamour on behalf of the neglected '18 per cent' for whom provision was frequently inadequate. Its attempts, through Section 2(5), to raise standards by improving schools' awareness, identification and provision in relation to pupils whose educational needs were not seen as acute enough to warrant a statement were half-hearted. Governors' duties to secure these improvements were nebulous.

Two years later the 1983 Conservative manifesto appeared. It returned to the key themes, including parental choice and improving standards. 'Giving parents more power is one of the most effective ways of raising educational standards', stated the section on schools. It announced the publishing and following-up of HMI reports on individual schools – previously kept secret, renewed emphasis on school attendance in order to reduce truancy, and encouraged schools to keep 'proper records of their pupils' achievements' and to carry out externally graded tests. Although the manifesto was published just a month after the 1981 Education Act had come into force, there was no mention of the party's policy for students seen to have special educational needs, who therefore remained in their cul-de-sac, off the highway of mainstream education.

Three years on, the 1986 (No. 2) Education Act further pursued the same themes and, in most respects, applied them to both mainstream and special schools. This Act was intent on raising standards and enlarging the responsibilities of governing bodies at the expense of LEAs. It strengthened governors' and schools' responsibilities for the curriculum, conduct, the appointment of staff and the presentation of an annual report to parents. Significantly, it advanced another of the government's aims, to transfer budgetary control from LEAs to schools by giving governors the responsibility for spending capitation grants. The Act also gave central government some control over local authorities' in-service training, with its provision for specific grants for training in areas determined by the Department of Education and Science. These are now known as grants for education, support and training (GEST).

When it was passed in November 1986, this Act prepared the ground for the publication of the Great Education Reform Bill a year later, as did the Conservative Party manifesto published in May 1987. *The Next Move Forward* foreshadowed not so much a move as an upheaval. The section headed 'Raising Standards in Education' heralded four major reforms. These included a 'national core curriculum' for all pupils aged 5–16, budgetary control devolved to all secondary schools and most primary schools within five years, and increased parental choice, notably through expansion of popular schools and an increasing array of selective, specialised and independent schools as alternatives to the comprehensives maligned by Tory voters. As in the previous manifesto there was no mention of special educational provision.

When GERBIL was published six months later, in November 1987, it provoked massive condemnation and fear of the damage it was likely to inflict upon pupils with special educational needs. It united disability charities, teachers' unions, parents, religious groups and many other organisations in demands for an unprecedented number of amendments. Members of both Houses were lobbied, at both public and private meetings, by letters, telephone calls and drinks in the bar. Like hundreds of others I went to meeting after meeting to voice objections, draft amendments and, with other editors and writers on education, to express opposition in specialist journals and the national press. Many more amendments on special educational needs appeared on the face of the bill and some concessions were extracted from the government, but none went to the hard core of the Act. Its central pillars, an enforced National Curriculum and testing, local management of schools, open roles and schools' ability to opt out of LEA control all remained erect.

Attempts to remove the strait-jacket of the heavily prescriptive National Curriculum and the assessment arrangements were doomed from the start. The National Curriculum was the cornerstone of the Conservatives' strategy for raising standards in schools. Through the common testing and assessment system it created a single measure for parents to compare pupil achievements in different schools. In theory at least, they (and the schools) could exercise choice, especially at Key Stage 2 when pupils were in their last year at primary school and when these results could encourage a return to backdoor or open selection at 11 plus.

This was the Act that the 1980 and 1986 (No. 2) Acts had been waiting for. It was the one that most radically set out to raise standards and promote parent choice and which also built on the foundation of the earlier legislation to introduce local management of schools. It whittled down the responsibilities of LEAs still further and at the same time the Secretary of State acquired many new powers.

The Act was widely criticised for the threat it posed to the tender plant of integration which had been mildly encouraged by Section 2(3) of the 1981 Education Act. There were fears that pupils with learning difficulties, who would be labelled as 'failures' on the 10-level scale, would be unwelcome in ambitious mainstream schools and that, with locally-managed and diminishing budgets, links between special and mainstream schools would be difficult to fund. Fears like these have now turned into reality in some areas.

It was predictable, however, that appeals from lobbyists would not succeed in persuading the government to modify the statutory basis of the National Curriculum, with its age-related key stages for teaching and testing. The government seemed almost pathologically anxious, at the time, about any concession that could undermine its carefully devised system to use the National Curriculum to foster improvements in teaching and learning, parental choice and competition among schools. When official statements on the National Curriculum were liberally interpreted in early drafts of the National Curriculum Council's Curriculum Guidance 2, *A Curriculum for All* (1989), they elicited a reaction approaching consternation from official sources and 'subversive' sentences were amended or removed with only the smallest concession on the wording to do with the age-related key stage requirements. It would be another four years before the government accepted recommendations, from Sir Ron Dearing, in December 1993, that the range of levels which could be taught at key stages should be broadened so that children still at level 1 could be included in work at Key Stages 2 and 3 along with their peers (see also Peter 1992).

The 1988 Act did, however, lay the foundations for raising standards for some pupils with special educational needs, particularly those in special schools. The 1981 Act had left them out on a curricular limb. By giving all pupils the implicit right to a broad and balanced curriculum, including the National Curriculum, the 1993 Act was to open up opportunities to include subjects like science, history and modern foreign languages, where few or none of these had been taught in most special schools before. It also offered a framework for continuity, progression and curriculum-based assessment, and it stimulated higher expectations of what pupils with disabilities and learning difficulties could achieve.

The next Act, the Education (Schools) Act 1992, harked back to the promise in the 1979 manifesto about strengthening the inspectorate. It launched an entirely new system of four-yearly cycles of school inspections administered by the Office for Standards in Education (OFSTED). OFSTED was the latest government department to be enlisted in the efforts to raise standards, and special schools were brought fully into the new system. Some of the special units for pupils with special educational needs, however, could still slip through the inspection net. It was only in 1994, after OFSTED inspections had begun, that *all* designated special units were brought within the inspection system. Changes in the status of designated units under the 1993 Education Act and the closing of a loophole in inspection arrangements, after the publication of articles in the *British Journal of Special Education* (for example, Chorley 1993) and the *Times Educational Supplement* (for example, Pyke 1993) contributed to the full inclusion of units in the inspection system.

The 1992 Conservative manifesto, issued in March, looked towards the 1993 Education Act and the 1994 Education Bill on teacher training (at the time of writing still wending its way through Parliament). It repeated the government's commitment to 'high standards' and to its belief in 'partnership with parents, choice in schools and a good grounding in the basic skills all children need to make a success of their lives'. Its tasks included completing the Nationa Curriculum's introduction, tests for 7-, 11- and 14-year-olds by 1994, annual publication of schools' performance and several initiatives to widen choice of schools, including the scope for grant-maintained schools to change their character if consistent with parents' wishes and the wide needs of the local area. Again there was no mention of special educational needs despite the fact that the bill, when it appeared some months later, incorporated most of the 1981 Education Act and devoted one of its six parts to special educational provisions.

In integrating many of the provisions of the 1981 Act into the wider framework of the 1993 Education Act, as well as enabling parents of pupils with statements to express a 'choice', or rather a preference, about the school their children should attend, the government has moved further in bringing legislation on special educational needs into line with the provisions of the other education acts it has introduced since 1980. However, two inconsistencies remain. These are, first, the increased rather than diminished importance of local education authorities in relation to special educational provision and second, the likelihood that resources will continue to be allocated disproportionately on pupils with statements at the expense of raising standards of achievement for the notional 18 per cent.

Will the Code of Practice succeed in removing these inconsistencies? As long as the government retains the statutory procedures for making assessments and statements the gap between the main thrust of Conservative policy and its provisions for special educational needs will continue to exist in law. It is conceivable, however, that practice could close the gap. In LEAs where schools closely follow the three tightly defined and school-based stages of assessment and are determined to find ways of tackling pupils' difficulties without resorting to statements, dwindling resources may be spread more evenly to raise standards of achievement instead of being concentrated on a small, statemented minority. If this happens it will also reduce the extent of LEAs' activities under the assessment and statementing procedures of the Act. Conversely, LEAs' powers and influence may stream amoeba-like into other directions offered by the Code. The 1993 Education Act has been described as a 'law to last the century'. Time will tell. Five years are a long time in policies as well as politics.

REFERENCES

Chorley, D. (1993), 'OFSTED prepares for special inspections', *British Journal of Special Education*, 20(4), pp. 127–8.

Dearing, R. (1993), *The National Curriculum and its Assessment Final Report*, School Curriculum and Assessment Authority, London.

Department for Education (DFE) (1993), *Code of Practice on Provision for Children with Special Needs*, Department of Education, London.

Department of Education and Science (DES) (1978), *Children with Special Needs*, HMSO, London.

National Curriculum Council (1989), *A Curriculum for All*, NCC, York.

Peter, M. (1992), 'Writing clearly: contributing to the ideal comprehensibility situation', in Booth, T., Swann, W., Masterton, M. and Potts, P. (eds) *Learning for All 1: Curricula for Diversity in Education*, Routledge, London.

Pyke, N. (1993) 'Inspections pledge broken', *Times Educational Supplement*, 24 December 1993.

Chapter 6

From Bill to Act: the passing of the 1993 Education Act

John Wright

This chapter illustrates the possibilities for, and limitations on, transforming draft legislation as it passes through the Houses of Parliament. John Wright is a full-time worker for the Independent Panel for Special Education Advice (IPSEA), one of the groups which sustained an active campaign to secure amendments to the 1992 Education Bill. He begins by describing the work of IPSEA, which includes a concern to influence education law. Some of IPSEA's proposed amendments to the Education Bill were successful and others were not. The chapter concludes by acknowledging those who have supported IPSEA and by outlining IPSEA's priorities for the rest of the 1990s.

INTRODUCTION

This chapter documents the response of one voluntary organisation – the Independent Panel for Special Education Advice – to the changes in special education law brought about by the enactment of the 1993 Education Act. It falls into five sections. The first section introduces IPSEA and explains why we welcomed government proposals for legislative change. The second section sets out how, as a small underfunded charity, we attempted to influence government thinking on the changes needed. The third section lists our successes. The fourth lists our failures, including the failure to influence government thinking in one key area – parental access to information – and sets out the case we are still arguing (i.e., as of March 1994), in the hope of persuading the Department for Education to amend the Draft Code of Practice in a way which would give parents a right of access to all information held by a local education authority (LEA) on their child. Finally, in the fifth section we acknowledge the people who helped IPSEA with this work and record our preliminary thoughts on how some of the issues raised will be carried forward to the future.

IPSEA'S CONCERN WITH THE LAW

IPSEA was established in 1983 with the aim of providing free second professional opinions for parents who were unhappy with LEA accounts of their children's special educational needs. We are a limited company and a registered charity and rely entirely on donations for the work we do.

From the start, it was clear that independent professional opinions, on their own, would rarely be sufficient to persuade a recalcitrant LEA to fulfil its legal duties towards children and young people with special educational needs. For the law provided too many loopholes: LEAs could not be challenged if they refused to assess children; could not be kept to a reasonable deadline for completing assessments and issuing statements; could not be forced to be specific in the way they worded statements; could amend statements on a whim without having to produce professional evidence or opinion that amendment was needed, etc.

So, in addition to providing parents with independent professional opinions on their children's needs, IPSEA's volunteers (and administrator) were quickly drawn into providing advice on LEA's legal duties and advocacy for children with special educational needs and their parents.

From 1990 on, IPSEA lobbied for changes in the 1981 Education Act. We publicised individual cases, wrote articles in the press and offered ourselves for radio and TV interview on the issues as often as we were able. Together with MP Jack Ashley we drafted an Early Day Motion, tabled by Ashley, which attracted the support of over 250 MPs from all political parties.

EARLY DAY MOTION No. 718

This House notes that, by refusing to assess children with special educational needs and issue Statements describing their specific requirements, a growing number of Local Education Authorities are dodging their legal obligation to make appropriate provision; deplores this disregard of legal obligations, and calls upon the Government to ensure that all Local Education Authorities fulfil their legal duties under the 1981 Act.

Tabled by Jack Ashley on 17 April 1991

Naturally, IPSEA was pleased when, in early 1992, the government announced their intention to make changes to the law on special education with a view to tightening up the procedures and protecting children's rights to appropriate provision.

HOW IPSEA LOBBIED

The government's White Paper was issued (in a blue cover) late in July 1992. It set out four proposed changes to the law on special education, to be included in Part III of the 1993 Education Act. These were: to impose time limits on LEA assessments; to allow parents of statemented children to state a preference for a school; to produce a Code of Practice which would impose strict guidelines on LEAs in fulfilling their duties under the new law; to establish a tribunal to hear parents' appeals.

We posted photocopies of these proposals to around 130 parents (selected from those who had contacted IPSEA for advice over the previous year) and to our volunteers. We asked for comments on the changes proposed and for thoughts on what else needed to be changed. We received responses from twenty-eight individual parents (in two cases, the paper had been passed on to local parents' groups and comments included those of group members) and from five IPSEA volunteers. On the basis of these responses and our own casework we prepared a formal response to the White Paper (against a September deadline), broadly welcoming the changes proposed by the government, but identifying eighteen additional areas where we believed change was needed to the law.

Between October 1992 and January 1993, while the Department for Education were considering comments received on the White Paper, we published and circulated an expanded version of our response to the White Paper, titled 'Putting right the 1981 Education Act'. This set out detailed arguments for the (now twenty-two) further changes which we believed were necessary, drawing on our casework for examples of abuses under the 1981 Education Act. 'Putting right . . .' was sent to all the parents we had consulted, our volunteers and directors, 109 voluntary and statutory organisations in the parents'/children's rights/disability fields, all MPs and sixty members of the House of Lords.

IPSEA urged all parents and concerned professionals to see or to write to their own MP, seeking assurances of support for a wider change than that which the government were proposing. We published a leaflet titled 'How to lobby your MP' to help people who would be doing this for the first time.

The first draft of the 1993 Education Act was published at the end of October 1992. Some of the issues identified in 'Putting right . . .' had been taken on board by the DFE at the White Paper stage and were reflected in clauses in the draft legislation. These were: responsibilities of 'new' LEAs to meet children's needs when families move area; a parental right to request formal assessment; a fixed procedure for reviewing statements.

The next stage involved drafting specific amendments to the Bill. By December 1992 we had produced twenty detailed amendments, together with briefings for MPs. Again, these were circulated to parents, to our own volunteers and to organisations in the voluntary sector. Responses were positive: e.g., the Association for Spina Bifida and Hydrocephalus, the Association for All Speech Impaired Children and the Child Growth Foundation wrote to the Secretary of State endorsing all of the IPSEA amendments. The British Psychological Society reprinted and circulated the amendments and briefings under their own imprimatur (acknowledging IPSEA as their source).

In January the government announced a guillotine on the committee stage of the Bill which would limit the time for discussion of amendments to Part III (dealing with special education) to one and a half days. Although pointless to argue against, IPSEA issued a press release condemning the guillotine and wrote (again) to parents, volunteers and voluntary organisations urging them to protest to the Secretary of State and to their own MPs, and to restate the case for IPSEA's twenty amendments.

As the Bill progressed through the Commons Committee, the Lords Committee and Lords Report stages, a number of our amendments were tabled by members. Of those actually voted on, only one was passed. This was an amendment proposed in the House of Lords by Lady Warnock which was promptly thrown out by the government when the Bill returned to the Commons. In most cases, our amendments were withdrawn by the members who had tabled them in response to assurances from government ministers that the issues they raised would be taken care of either in subsequent regulations or in the proposed Code of Practice.

When the draft Code of Practice was released (at the time of writing it has still to be finalised), IPSEA again circulated parents, volunteers, voluntary and statutory organisations, MPs and members of the House of Lords with comments. These focused on twelve areas where we believed the Department for Education had got it wrong. Some of the arguments we were making were ones which ministers had already conceded in the House of Commons and the House of Lords and given assurances on but then, we assume, forgot about when it came to actually writing the Code.

SUCCESSES

By the spring of 1994, it was possible to begin to gauge IPSEA's successes and failures. From the list of changes argued for in 'Putting right the 1981 Education Act' we were able to spot eleven (including the three referred to above) which had been incorporated by the government into the Act or the draft Regulations (giving them the force of law) or in the draft Code of Practice (creating a qualified legal duty on LEAs). In summary, these changes are:

1 Parents will be given the right to request a full formal assessment of their child (Act).
2 When families move, new LEAs will have a duty to maintain the old LEA's statement (Act).

3 Parents will have a right to appeal if a statement fails to name a school (Act).

4 Reviews of statements will have to follow standard procedures (Act and Regulations).

5 When LEAs refuse to statement children following assessment, parents will have a right to seek professional advice (Code).

6 Parents will have a right to receive copies of professional advice when statements are reviewed (Regulations).

7 Parents will have a right to receive copies of professional evidence when LEAs propose to amend statements (Code).

8 Parents will have a right to receive copies of professional evidence when LEAs propose to drop statements (Code).

9 Parents will have the right to know professionals' opinions on the type of school that would best suit their child, e.g., mainstream or special school (Regulations and Code).

10 Schools will have specific duties towards children with special needs who do not have statements, including the duty to review arrangements made for them and to involve parents in those reviews (Code).

11 A child's non-educational needs will be specified in a statement (Regulations).

12 Views of the child/young person will be ascertained as part of formal assessment (Code).

13 Statements will normally have to quantify in terms of hours the special teaching or ancillary provision to be made (Code).

14 There will be an inhibition on placement of children without statements in special schools. These are to be termed 'emergency placements' (Code).

15 Statements which change a child's placement will normally have to be issued or amended in time to allow parents to appeal, i.e., before the beginning of the term preceding the proposed change (Code).

Of course, some of the other organisations in the special needs field were also arguing for many of these changes, and at the end of the day it is not realistic for any one group to claim credit for influencing government thinking.

In fact IPSEA worked closely with some of these other groups on particular issues. For example, we debated with the Centre for Studies on Inclusive Education (CSIE) the desirability of a principled amendment which would create a straightforward duty on LEAs to integrate children with special needs. Ultimately, we backed an amendment drafted by CSIE which, if adopted, would have given LEAs six years' breathing space before having to implement the duty to arrange total integration for children with special needs. IPSEA also sent a representative to address meetings of the Education Law Advice Service (ELAS) and the Special

Education Consortium, an umbrella group steered by the Council for Disabled Children. We helped make up a delegation from the Consortium to meet Eric Forth, Under-Secretary of State for Education, and we had a further meeting with DoE officials in our own right to discuss problems over the emergent new legislation.

In addition to pushing for the changes we believed were necessary, we responded as vigorously as we were able when we came to suspect that unforeseen and unheralded changes were being pushed through. For example, when the Bill was published it appeared that parents were to be given a veto over their child's integration. IPSEA challenged the government on this, recruiting the support of a leading education solicitor (Peter Liell) and a leading education barrister (John Friel). Although the government stubbornly refused to alter the manifestly ambiguous wording of the law with regard to integration, unequivocal assurances were given by ministers (and recorded in *Hansard*) that no veto has intended; and the Code of Practice was equally emphatic on this point.

FAILURES

To some of our amendments there was no echo of government sympathy. Those amendments which would have strengthened children's rights to be integrated in mainstream schools and increased the rights of access for physically disabled pupils were rejected by the government at Commons Committee stage. As was an amendment which would have committed professionals in law to act in the child's best interests and another which would have given LEAs a duty to make provision for special needs children on the basis of maximising their potential.

ACKNOWLEDGEMENTS AND PLANS FOR THE FUTURE

Our lobbying cost IPSEA around £5,000. It had not been foreseen and therefore involved spending money which we had not raised in advance. Thankfully, the Yapp Educational Trust responded positively to an application for grant aid in retrospect, giving us £4,975.

One-time Conservative Party agent Allan Bradley gave valuable advice on planning our lobbying, urging us in particular to concentrate on getting as many parents of special needs children as possible to meet with MPs and explain the problems they had had (rather than joining the professional lobbyists in the bars and smoke-filled rooms of Westminster). Bradley also drafted our leaflet 'How to lobby your MP'.

Rachel Hodgkin, then of the Children's Legal Centre but now working at the National Children's Bureau, read and commented on all of our proposed amendments. We followed her advice on how to word our amendment to the letter, as we did the advice of solicitor Richard Poynter, who has worked without remuneration for IPSEA on many occasions over the last six years.

Wyn Griffiths, Labour Member of Parliament for Bridgend, tabled and argued for IPSEA's amendments in the House of Commons. Lady Davina Darcy de Knayth, a cross-bencher, was tireless and skilled in presenting our concerns in the House of Lords. Lady Darcy has been a Director of IPSEA for a number of years and is herself disabled.

Last but not least we acknowledge the input of the parents we consulted again and again. In essence, the arguments we made were their arguments, arising from their experiences as parents of children with special educational needs. Further, if IPSEA had a hand in influencing the shape of the new law, it was as a result of individual parents responding to our call for lobbying of individual MPs.

The Code of Practice can be amended and improved, once government is convinced of the need for change. IPSEA plans to keep parents informed of developments under the new Act (coming into force in September 1994) and, in turn, to ensure that we are ourselves constantly informed by parental experience of the new procedures. Our recently launched newsletter, *Special Edition*, will help us in this task, as will our ever-expanding network of volunteers who advise and support young people with special educational needs and their parents.

Chapter 7

Parents' perspectives: towards positive support for disabled children and those who experience difficulties in learning

Sue Thomas

Sue Thomas is a founder member of the Passport Parents' Group, Stockport. In this chapter she uses the detail of her own experiences with her daughter, Elizabeth, to illustrate her view that services are based on the assumption that disability is a disaster and that, therefore, professional support frequently consists of taking children away from their parents, to give them a break. Sue argues that these separations undermine parents' confidence and weaken the most valuable foundation for the children's development, namely, their relationship with the most committed adults. She urges parents to reassert their personal responsibility for their children and demonstrate to professionals and politicians the diverse range of positively normal lives.

INTRODUCTION

For sixteen years I was a nurse. I became a senior sister, then a clinical teacher. I left to look after my foster daughter Elizabeth. Her parents felt they couldn't cope with Elizabeth's disability. They were advised to go home and to leave the baby in hospital while they thought about the rest of the family and how they would all cope. They came back only for a short visit, to say goodbye. By the time Elizabeth and I met she was three-and-a-half years old, had lived in a children's home for three years and had suffered a failed foster placement. She was described to me as a profoundly disabled child that functioned at a two-month level. She couldn't sit up, she had no control over her body, she was unresponsive, didn't sleep, didn't eat, couldn't cope with adults or children going outside, or loud noises. Elizabeth was very underweight, she moaned all day except when she screamed.

Elizabeth and I had to really struggle to get to know each other, to trust each other, but now, six years on, she attends her local mainstream school full time; she has many friends who come and stay with her and she goes and stays with them.

I managed to do this with the help of a support/campaign group I helped to set up, by reading as much information as I could get my hands on, by going to conferences, workshops, council meetings, by meeting parents from different areas, by talking to disabled people and making alliances with workers who wanted to change the way services are provided, by facing a host of fears, by being very stubborn. Now I've realised how lucky I was fighting my battle just at the right time. Many parents who came after me and who worked equally hard have failed to 'win' a place for their child. I say lucky to win since it has hardly anything to do with 'rights' or meeting the child's real needs.

In this chapter I would like to contradict some of the traditional thoughts, feelings and ideas surrounding the world of disability. I want to show people that there is another more positive, active and hopeful world in which they can live. It's hard work though, since you have to retrieve the sense of personal responsibility which we (all community members) unthinkingly have let slip to our politicians and government officials, both local and central.

I begin with a brief overview of society's attitudes. Then I tell my own story and Gwen, another member of the Passport Parents' Group, tells hers. I go on to discuss the approach of the parents' group as a whole and what we see as the likely effect on our children of the 1993 Education Act. I conclude with my hopes and fears for the future.

THE OPPRESSIVE SOCIETY

I propose that our society oppresses disabled people and their families. Unless the systems and professionals who work in them take this oppression into account then any new policies or procedures will be interpreted according to the old ways or attitudes and so lose their effectiveness, which ultimately will lead to families being disempowered. The term disempowerment means that power is taken away, causing a negative type of dependence, the loss of confidence, personal power and skills.

The disempowering of a family with a child who has special needs starts even before the child is diagnosed. It begins when the parents were young and had no contact with disabled children and adults.

All children, wherever they live, have the right to be provided with correct and full information about the world around them. This means positively and accurately reflecting the reality of our multiability, multicultural, multiracial society in every aspect in all nurseries, playgroups, crèches, schools and leisure activities.

A childhood bereft of disabled adults and children will leave a developmental black hole for non-disabled adults, which will attract fear, prejudice and traditional thoughts, feelings and ideas.

A childhood filled with diversity gives the adult experiences to draw upon. If disabled people were given full access to education, housing, transport, leisure activities and jobs then parents would have sufficient role models to reflect on.

When No One Answers

A child sees me
Naturally curious,
He looks to his mother,
'Why?'
'Shh!' is her answer.
Time passes;
We meet again,
The child and I,
I smile recalling his curiosity
This time he isn't curious though
He picks up a stone,
Throwing it in my direction he yells,
'Get ya mental'
Where did he learn that?
Surely not his mother,
Her only answer was
'Shhh'

(Robert Williams; written at the age of twelve)

The silence surrounding disability speaks strongly and affirms the negative beliefs and fears. The messages from the media are sharp and clear. Disabled people and their families are either brave, heroic, angels, saints or charity cases, dependent, helpless, burdens, useless.

Society believes that if the disability cannot be cured or if the disabled person cannot compete on non-disabled persons' terms (e.g., the child having to be continent or able to walk, etc., before being allowed to attend a mainstream school) then the person and his/her family have a bleak and unhappy future.

MY STORY

Although I had been a nurse I had very little experience in looking after a child and no understanding of disability issues. When I decided that I would try to look after Elizabeth, the experts, with all good intentions, decided that I would need a lot of help and support. The way this was translated was to give me one weekend in four off. They arranged for a family to care for Elizabeth, in their own home. To maintain this they thought it would be good for Elizabeth to spend at least one short visit per week with them.

I agreed with this; it sounded logical and because I felt at a loss I gave my trust and responsibility to the experts.

Elizabeth and I really struggled. I was a single mother, I had no mother to help me, I was totally on my own except for her going to school and the session a week when Elizabeth went to the other carers. I was exhausted by the time the first weekend off came. I was so looking forward to it. Elizabeth went off and I kept wondering if I was a good enough Mum since I was so tired I needed a break from my child within the first month.

I set off on the bus to see my friends just like I used to five weeks ago when I was not a mother. A feeling came over me that this life was easier, no sleepless nights, no crying child, no guilt or wondering if I was doing it right, etc., etc. But this was the life I had decided to end, why had I got it back so soon? The old life was comparatively easy. I wouldn't have to change, I wouldn't have to go through the uncertainty and guilt, but this wasn't the life I wanted though it was so attractive to me. Within the first month, I got my first inkling what my new life was going to be like. It was going to be hard, I had to learn to become a Mum, putting Elizabeth first before all others.

I knew there was something wrong with the arrangements; my friend who had two children under two didn't have weekend breaks, especially a month after having a child.

Elizabeth came home. I was so pleased to see her. I'd missed her. I was frightened that she would have forgotten me, even though I didn't know whether she remembered me in the first place. Elizabeth screamed the place down, she couldn't eat or drink or sleep. The other carers had said she had a good time so that was proof to me that she didn't like being with me. I knew I was no good.

The social worker called, she tried to reassure us. I was devastated, what should I do? Elizabeth's ex-foster mother rang me up and asked how we were managing. She told me that that was what happened to her, so she had to have more and more respite care. It got to the stage when she was having every weekend away.

I thought a great deal, and I had to take my courage in my hands. I decided to tell the social worker that I didn't want any more weekends off. She was very disturbed with my decisions and she tried to persuade me to continue with this kind of support.

Elizabeth settled slightly, but every time she went to the other family she came back agitated, highly strung, so eventually I decided to stop the visits. That took a lot of determination and courage. I thought I was letting everyone down. I wasn't sure I was doing the right thing, I was finding it very difficult to cope with Elizabeth and all the changes in my life, I needed help, but I didn't know what sort of help I needed, I just had a feeling that the help I was getting was actually putting our relationship in jeopardy.

When my friends had babies their mothers came to help them. They offered them advice, support and practical help not just with the baby but with the housework. Of course I couldn't expect this sort of help, could I?

For eighteen months I received no practical help from the social services (this was because I had refused the only help they could give me). I began to believe, and in some ways it was true, that I was the only person in the world that could look after Elizabeth. This way of thinking had an effect on my whole attitude. It became a downward spiral: the more I believed in the partial myth the more real it became. I was then lucky to come across a voluntary organisation that was very experienced in looking after people in their own homes. Crossroads sent a lady to look after Elizabeth for two hours a month, the lady had a great effect on me, it wasn't just the practical help that was important, it was what she said.

She would talk to me like I imagine a mother would talk to her daughter. She didn't assess Elizabeth, she just got to know her. We talked about the whole of her not just her problems. By doing so her problems seemed to lose their great significance. That doesn't mean to say that I found any great solutions but my life started to become more normal, still full of struggle just like everyone's life.

The fact that she could learn how to look after Elizabeth gave me confidence. I started to ask friends to help me. I had to learn how to show them how to look after her, which took a bit of time. As they did favours for me I did favours for them. Since Elizabeth has attended mainstream school the opportunities for support have really increased. I've come to the conclusion that the type of support I need I can only get by understanding what I need and then being in charge.

GWEN'S STORY

Paul, my eldest son, is 12 years old, nearly 13. I'm slowly realising that what the special schools do is not only to lull you into a false sense of security, but also to put your focus on the wrong things. I mean I would listen to the teacher assessments of Paul. Every year every part of his behaviour, his development, his progress would be analysed and then once his faults were established they would tell my husband and me the action they would take as if it would somehow make him complete. He always made progress. I wanted to believe it; in actual fact I was desperate to hear it, but when I look back he hasn't made much progress. Don't get me wrong. I'm really proud of Paul just like any mother. I basically want what any other Mum wants for her child. I want Paul to do his best, to get as good an education as possible, to have friends, to have a good future.

I'm realising that Paul will always be dependent on people, to help him get about, to have a good life.

I've had to attend umpteen reviews where the teachers would talk about Paul's pencil grip or his lack of concentration, etc. I fell into the trap of believing that was all he needed from his time spent at special school. But then one of my friends asked me what I wanted for Paul in the future. I didn't really know, I'd not really thought about it, I just thought the school would somehow prepare him, they always kept on telling me that they had his best interests at heart, I latched on to that and just carried on with the day-to-day activities.

Then at the review I asked the headteacher what Paul's future was going to be like. He told me that he would always be dependent on someone; he would never be able to live on his own or to go out on his own. He would probably spend most of his time at home or in a day-care setting. He said people like Paul, who have moderate learning difficulties, become completely lost in the community. There are few services for them so they idle their time away living with their parents until they become too much of a burden. There are a few colleges that accept people with learning difficulties, and a few places that have vocational job schemes, but these are limited and are a temporary solution.

I was shocked and it took me quite a time to understand the full implications. I asked the headmaster about Paul having non-disabled friends and the headmaster told me that he thought that Paul may get some one-sided friends. That he would make non-disabled friends but they would not make friends with him. I was shattered by his outlook. It struck me that if he thought the outlook for people like Paul was really so bleak then why did he continue doing the same thing with them? Maybe it was because he couldn't think of another way.

I've now decided to take matters in my own hands – what have I got to lose? Even though that meeting stunned me, at last I know where we stand. Paul has got some friends from attending local Cubs and Scouts, I've always allowed him to play in the street, so the children know him and accept him. So I know it is possible for him to have double-sided friends.

I decided to think about the future and what I wanted for Paul. For instance, it would be great for him to go to the local pub for a drink, for the people there to know him, not necessarily to make a fuss but to accept him, to understand if he got a bit excited and to point him in the right direction if necessary. If he couldn't manage on his own then to go with a friend; it would be wonderful if he had the choice. I would like him to have a little job, maybe just around the corner at our local garage. He likes cars, he could sweep up or make cups of tea.

To do all this he has to be in his local community, meeting, playing, growing, laughing with all sorts of people of all different age ranges. He will have to gain confidence and get used to meeting people.

Then I thought, how can he do this when every day since he was 5 he has been sent off to school away from his neighbourhood to meet other children who are also miles away from their communities.

I've decided I'm going to try really hard to work out what Paul really needs, just to see if I can change his prospects. I know it's going to be frightening. I'll do it step by step. I've got to do it, there is no other way.

THE PASSPORT PARENT'S GROUP

As members of Passport, at first we thought that we needed to fight for better services, since they kept on telling us that the reason that they could not meet our needs was because of the shortage of resources. As we began to understand their fundamental limitations, we started to look for other ways, such as how we can become as independent as possible, without cutting off our noses to spite our faces.

Mainstream school for our children is the most important issue we campaign for, and we try and empower ourselves as much as we can. We have found that most people will help us if approached properly but we've had to learn skills and find courage to do so.

We also bring people together, not just parents but professionals from all the services and we're making links with disabled people's groups.

The traditional view of bringing up a child with disabilities is that it is very tiring, burdensome, that there is not much joy to it. This is constantly reaffirmed by service workers, who will have this view unless they have seen a different approach. Therefore it becomes a self-fulfilling prophecy. To help the exhausted parent they set up schemes with all good intentions but with the idea that the disabled child is a problem. Since the services have limited resources, if the parent needs more than a few hours of support the child is usually removed from the home.

The fact that the child and the parent are slowly but relentlessly being separated from the community is seen as the result of the disability rather than the measures that have been taken to support the family. From birth, the professionals have been giving the parents a one-sided view of what they and their child require. Because both professionals and parents know of no other way, it is not surprising that, when the parents are asked what they require, they just echo what they have been told over the years.

A NEW FRAMEWORK FOR THE 1990s

The 1993 Education Act comes into effect on 1 September 1994. Section III will replace the 1981 Act and proposes to extend the rights of parents whose children have 'special educational needs'. The Act will establish an Independent Regional Tribunal to hear parents' appeals against the terms of the statements of special educational needs written about their children. There will also be a time limit that the LEAs have to keep to when drawing up a statement.

Under Sections 157 and 158 of the Act, the Secretary of State must issue and send out a draft copy of a Code of Practice. This Code gives practical guidance to local education authorities and governing bodies of all main-tained schools on the discharge of their functions under Part III of the Act towards all children with special educational needs. LEAs and governing bodies must have regard to the provisions of the Code. So do most other bodies, including, for example, district health authorities and local authority social services.

The Code will cover:

- early action to meet special educational needs;
- partnership between parents, schools, LEAs and other agencies;
- the support for which schools will be expected to take responsibility;
- the criteria for maintaining statements, and the procedures involved;
- the role of voluntary agencies;
- the rights of parents and children and young people concerned.

The Code recognises a continuum of special educational needs and it advocates the general adoption of a staged model of assessment. It contains criteria for the making of statutory assessments and statements, guidance for provisions and on the conduct of annual reviews.

Phillippa Russell, Director of the Council for Disabled Children, writes: 'Although there has been some disappointment that the Act (and hence the Code which informs it) continues to lay a qualified duty to integrate, there are new opportunities.' She goes on to discuss the benefits of the school-based stage of assessment hopefully preventing the escalation of problems which often led to exclusion or referral out of mainstream school. This of course doesn't take into account the children that have never been to mainstream school but went straight to segregated schools. For parents that are committed to mainstream education, there is virtually no change, as the LEA has a duty to consider mainstream school placement for all children, and parents have the right to name their chosen school in the proposed statement, but there are still three let-out clauses:

1 the child receiving the special provision which she/he requires;
2 the provision of efficient education for children with whom the child will be educated;
3 the efficient use of resources.

Time will only tell if this new piece of legislation has any real effect, once it has been interpreted by the officers of the LEAs, governors and teachers. With all good intentions, if legislation is not followed by staff training in disability issues and more exposure to disabled people then, as with all legislation, it is open to interpretation and a traditional course can be taken.

How can a local education officer who never went to school or made friends with a disabled person, who doesn't live near or work with somebody who is disabled, ever manage to imagine that a child who is multiply disabled can be fully included into mainstream education?

How can that ever be a real option to him? How can he ever discuss this option with a parent? How can he advise local councillors on new policies for including disabled children in local mainstream schools? Until he can do this he will be disempowering parents, as parents believe that he is the expert and knows all the options.

Disabled people's organisations and many parents' groups talk about their rights whereas the professionals talk about the parents' and disabled person's needs. The rights of parents to expect their disabled child to be fully included into mainstream school, leisure activities and employment is fundamental. If the professionals continue to consider these rights merely as needs then society will continue to find excuses to segregate, exclude, devalue and disempower.

Many parents put their complete faith in professionals thinking that professionals understand and know best, but I propose that professionals do not understand how disabled people and their families are oppressed by our society and the systems that serve it. Until the professionals understand and take steps to diminish this oppression, parents will continue to be disempowered.

REFERENCES AND FURTHER READINGS

Ahmed, S. (1991), 'Routing out racism', *Community Care*.

Audit Commission (1992), Available from the Department of Education and Science.

Eckersley, L. (1992), 'Breaking the news', *Nursing Times*, 88(51).

Femail Testimony (1990), in Barrister Blunt (ed.), 'Why we had to give our baby away', *Daily Mail*.

Fido, R. and Potts, M. (1991), 'The way they were', *Community Living*, 4(3).

Flynn, G. (no date), *A School System in Transition*, Waterloo Region Roman Catholic Separate School Board, Ontario.

Humphries, S. and Gordon, P. (1992), *Out of Sight: The Experience of Disability 1900–1950*, Northcote House Publications Ltd, Plymouth.

Hyde, S. (1989), 'The forgotten holocaust', *Community Living*, 3(2).

Jupp, S. (1992), *Making the Right Start*, Opened Eye Publication, Hyde.

Lane, J. (1991), 'Race equality and child care', *Child Right*, 75.

Leonard, A. (1992), *A Hard Act to Follow*, The Spastics Society, London.

Lonsdale, S. (1991), 'Out of sight, out of mind', *Community Care*, 862.

McKnight, J. (1987), 'Regenerating community', *Social Policy*, Winter.

North Western Regional Health Authority (no date), *Breaking the News*, Regional Advisory Group on Learning Disability Services.

Oswin, M. (1978), *Children Living in Longstay Hospitals*, Spastics International Medical Publications, London.

Rieser, R. and Mason, M. (1990), *Disability Equality in the Classroom: A Human Rights Issue*.

Stainton, T. (1992), 'Big talk small steps', *Community Living*, 6(1).

Stainton, T. (1992), 'The seed of change', *Community Living*, 5(4).

Stockport Metropolitan Borough (1991), *Services to People with Learning Disability*, Policy Document, Part 3, Section 2.

Wolfensburg, W. (1975), *The Origin and Nature of our Institutional Models*, Human Policy Press, Syracuse.

Chapter 8

The case for anti-discrimination legislation

Colin Barnes

First published in Barnes, C. (1991) *Disabled People in Britain: The Case for Anti-Discrimination Legislation*, Hurst and Co., London, in association with the British Council of Organisations of Disabled People (BCODP).

A range of arguments has been put forward in the UK to justify opposition to measures that would make discrimination against disabled people illegal. They include: that an adequate definition of 'disability' is impossible, that legislation would therefore be too complex to draft and that it would drive a wedge between disabled and non-disabled people. Colin Barnes refutes each of these arguments in turn and then specifies the terms of an anti-discrimination law. He argues that such a law has to be based on the notion of social 'rights', not individual 'needs'.

Clearly, the traditional ideological justifications for discrimination are well entrenched within the core institutions of our society. After more than a century of largely state-sponsored education, disabled children and young people are still not legally entitled to the same type of schooling as their non-disabled peers. The overwhelming majority of British schools, colleges and universities remain unprepared to accommodate disabled students within a mainstream setting. Thus, many young people with impairments have little choice but to accept segregated 'special' education which is both educationally and socially divisive, and which fails to provide them with the necessary skills for adult living. Moreover, by producing educationally and socially disabled adults in this way the 'special' education system perpetuates the false assumption that disabled people are somehow inadequate, and thus legitimises discrimination in all other areas of social life, particularly employment.

Discriminatory attitudes and institutionalised practices which work to the disadvantage of disabled people in employment are well established within the British labour market. They are conspicuous in the policies and practices of employers and employment agencies, public and private. As a result, disabled people are more likely to be out of work than non-disabled people, they are out of work longer than other unemployed workers, and when they do find work it is more often than not low-paid, low-status work with poor working conditions, thus accelerating the discriminatory spiral in which many disabled people find themselves.

The overwhelming majority of disabled people and their families are forced to depend on welfare benefits in order to survive. Further, the present disability benefit system does not even cover the cost of impairment and effectively discourages those who struggle for individual autonomy and financial independence. The inevitable outcome is a life of extreme economic deprivation and excessive bureaucratic regulation and control; in other words, poverty and dependence.

This dependence is compounded by the present system of health and social support services, most of which are dominated by the interests and concerns of the professionals who run them and the traditional assumption that disabled people are unable to take charge of their own lives. While disabled people may no longer be forced to live in residential institutions, their opportunities for economic and social integration are severely restricted due to a lack of information, appropriate technical aids and a comprehensive personal assistant service. Hence, many are compelled to rely on informal unpaid helpers – usually family or friends. Current provision, therefore, denies disabled people not only opportunities to live independently within the community, but also the dignity of independence within the context of personal relationships and the family home.

This cycle of dependence is intensified by a largely hostile physical environment in housing, public transport and the built environment generally. Although the need for personal mobility has become increasingly apparent in recent years for all sections of society, particularly for work, disabled people continue to be confronted with inaccessible homes, transport systems and public buildings.

Moreover, along with unemployment, a lack of money and a heightened and unnecessary dependence on others, environmental factors are crucial in excluding disabled people from the kind of leisure and social activities which the non-disabled community takes for granted; indeed, some sections of the leisure industry are evidently unwilling to cater for disabled people. Discrimination is compounded for disabled people who are women, and members of ethnic minorities and the gay community.

Until quite recently disabled people did not have a credible collective voice to articulate their views and so successive governments have been able to avoid and even deny the extent of institutional discrimination against disabled people. But a large part of the responsibility for this lies with a succession of British governments. Although there is a growing consensus in democratic countries that disabled people have the same basic human rights as non-disabled people, and that governments should ensure that disabled people are able to achieve a standard of living equal to that of their fellow citizens (UN 1988), this has not yet come about in the British Isles. Yet Britain was one of the first western nations to establish the notion of basic human rights for disabled people in law with the setting up of the welfare state in the early 1940s; everything that has been happened since has been a gradual retreat from this position. Although the British government endorsed the United Nations Programme of Action Concerning Disabled Persons in 1982, it has consistently refused to implement policies which would enable disabled people to attain a lifestyle comparable to that of their non-disabled neighbours.

As we have seen, the Education Act 1944 specified that disabled children should be educated alongside their peers, and the Disabled Persons (Employment) Act 1944 attempted to secure employment rights for disabled people. But non-enforcement of these tentative rights, coupled with the gradual but intensifying drift from rights-based to needs-based policies, has served to underline the traditional individualistic approach to disability, the very opposite of what is needed. This is evident in each area discussed in this study.

In education, while reiterating the principle of integration, the Warnock Report and the 1981 Education Act both explicitly emphasised the importance of the concept of special educational needs within the education system as a whole. This is a policy which has justified not only the continued segregation of a substantial part of the student population, but also the exclusion of minority languages and cultures from the mainstream sector, in particular the language and culture of the non-hearing community. In the crucial area of employment, the data show that the government's lack of commitment to the employment quota scheme and its obvious preference for voluntary policies of persuasion have not only resulted in a failure to provide disabled people with meaningful employment, but also emphasised the traditional divisions between disabled and non-disabled workers.

Although it has been officially acknowledged that disabled people and their families received significantly lower incomes than the rest of the population (owing to institutional discrimination in the labour market and the additional costs which impairment incurs), recent changes to the disability benefits system will not change this situation. Indeed, the shift away from statutory entitlement in favour of discretionary awards distributed by semi-independent organisations with limited budgets, following the introduction of the 1988 social security reforms, signals a significant erosion of disabled people's rights as well as an intensification of unnecessary bureaucratic regulation and control.

A similar situation exists regarding health and social support services for disabled people. Although the transition from rights-based to needs-based provision can be traced back to the 1948 National Assistance Act, it has intensified in recent years. Although the 1948 Act placed a duty on local authorities to provide residential accommodation and some services for disabled people, it also acknowledged the historical involvement of charities in these areas and so permitted the local authorities to designate responsibility for provision to voluntary agencies if they so wished. An inevitable outcome of this was a proliferation of residential institutions of one form or another run by charitable trusts and private agencies, and the failure of local authorities to develop appropriate community-based services. Moreover, contrary to the views of some non-disabled observers (Topliss and Gould 1981), the 1970 Chronically Sick and Disabled Persons Act did little to change this situation.

The 1980s saw a further retreat from the notion of rights as a result of the inclination towards voluntary rather than statutory-based services of a succession of policy-makers in both local and central government. While the introduction of the 1986 Disabled Persons (Services, Consulation and Representation) Act paid lip-service to the idea of meaningful collaboration between service users and providers, there is evidence of widespread disregard for the law within local authorities which has hitherto been ignored by central government. Moreover, it has recently been announced in the House of Commons that key sections of the 1986 Act which would have secured the right of disabled people to have an advocate had they needed one, and given them the right to ask local authorities for services and to have a written statement on their needs assessment, are not to be implemented (*Hansard* 1991). Clearly, despite the talk of choice and consultation emanating from a growing number of politicians of both left and right, current provision is still controlled by mainly non-disabled professionals who decide what services disabled people should have, when they should have them, and how they should be delivered.

Although there is an increasing shortage of accessible homes, there are no policy initiatives to remedy this in either the public or the private sector, and segregated special-needs housing remains central to the government's community care programme. The prevalence of special-needs transport systems is also likely to remain the norm rather than the exception because, even though the Department of Transport supports the desirability of accessible public transport systems in principle, it is clear that it will be well into the twenty first century before they become anything like a reality. Moreover, although policy-makers have endorsed disabled people's rights of access to public buildings with the recent amendments to the Building Regulations, it is clear that these measures will not eradicate discrimination within the context of the built environment, particularly in the leisure industry, where inaccessible buildings exclude disabled people to a large extent from mainstream recreational pursuits.

Indeed, the rhetoric of individual needs is central to the arguments of those who have successfully opposed measures to reinforce the rights of disabled people. First, it has been suggested that defining disability would present major problems in disagreements over equal rights. In 1983, for example, one government supporter noted that to establish that discrimination had taken place the 'extent of the disablement would have to be proved, which can be very distressing' for a disabled person (*Hansard* 1983, p. 1250). Such a position seems somewhat hollow since until recently policy-makers appeared content to allow disabled people to have their impairments measured in this way in order to receive the benefits and services to which they are entitled. None the less, given the strength of feeling against discrimination among disabled people and their desire to remove it this is likely to be one test that many would welcome.

Second, on discrimination in perhaps the most important area of all, employment, the Department of Employment's consultative document *Employment and Training for Disabled People* reiterated an argument which has been repeated constantly by opponents of anti-discrimination legislation throughout the 1980s. It states: 'A major difficulty is that disability, unlike race or sex, can be relevant to job performance and what to some might seem like discrimination may in reality be recruitment based on legitimate preferences and likely performances' (DE 1990, p. 30). This implies that discrimination is indeed acceptable on the grounds that disabled workers are not as productive as non-disabled workers.

Such arguments are difficult to understand particularly when, since the early 1970s, successive governments have spent a large amount of public money telling employers the opposite, namely that given the appropriate equipment (which the government is willing to provide) disabled workers are as productive as non-disabled workers. Further, the same publication reports: 'There is clear evidence that most people with disabilities can be as productive as the general population. . . . Even severe handicap, whilst clearly giving rise to difficulties, has frequently been overcome' (DE 1990, p. 14).

Third, it has been suggested that an anti-discrimination law would be complex to draft and therefore uncertain in its application (DE 1990). This point is difficult to understand in the light of developments abroad and the fact that there is support for the drafting of such legislation within the legal profession. If this type of legislation would present major problems for those charged with interpreting it, this would surely not be the attitude of lawyers.

There is a fourth argument that anti-discrimination legislation would exacerbate traditional divisions between disabled and non-disabled people; this point is often used in relation to employment, for example 'the relationship between people with disabilities and employers might be damaged and the task of persuasion made much harder' (DE 1990, p. 39). However, it is difficult to see the logic in this, considering that all the evidence hitherto has shown widespread support for anti-discrimination legislation among the general public. Also, since most employers have proved particularly unresponsive to policies of persuasion, it is probable that anti-discrimination legislation could only have a positive effect on the employment of disabled people.

This continual denial of equal rights to disabled people by successive British governments is all the more astonishing when other disadvantaged groups have some protection under the law, and when legislation to combat institutionalised disablism is becoming increasingly common throughout the western world. The overtly unequal treatment accorded to disabled people in Britain has prompted an almost universal demand from disabled people and their organisations for similar legislation in Britain, and it is a demand which is likely to increase in strength.

What these organisations are demanding is comprehensive anti-discrimination legislation which (a) establishes a suitable framework to enforce policies ensuring the integration of disabled people into the mainstream economic and social life of the community, such as the employment quota scheme, and (b) provides public confirmation that discrimination against disabled people for whatever reason is no longer tolerable. This would be legislation emphasising social rights rather than individual needs, and focusing on a disabling society and not individual disabled people.

For such legislation to be truly effective, disabled people would inevitably need access to the kind of medical and other information which historically has been used to justify their economic and social subordination. Thus an essential addition to anti-discrimination legislation would be laws facilitating freedom of information going beyond providing access to information held on computers and in local authority files. Locked medical cabinets would need to be opened and the unofficial documents which are kept as ways of avoiding information disclosure, as with current practices which require information to be provided to parents under the statementing regulations of the Education Act 1981, would need to be made available.

There will also be a need for some kind of mechanism offering disabled people individual and collective redress. This can only be accomplished by the adequate funding of the nationwide network of organisations controlled and run by disabled people themselves. As we have seen, it is these organisations which have put the issue of institutional discrimination on to the political agenda, and which are best fitted to ensure its eventual eradication.

The abolition of institutional discrimination against disabled people is not a marginal activity; it strikes at the heart of social organisations within both the public and the private sectors. It would not be possible to confront this problem without becoming involved in political debate and taking up positions on a wide range of issues. It is imperative, therefore, that any mechanism for enforcement should remain independent of government influence and control. Indeed, as Gregory (1987) has shown, one of the chief reasons for the relative failure of the Sex Discrimination Act 1975 and the Race Relations Act 1976 to remove sexism and racism in Britain has been the semi-autonomous status of the Equal Opportunities Commission and the

Commission for Racial Equality. Their semi-autonomy has become a double-edged weapon in the hands of unsympathetic governments: because they are independent, they can be ignored, and because they are not independent, they can be subdued through government control of funds and appointments. Hence, both organisations have been forced to concentrate on policies of education rather than enforcement – the opposite of what is needed.

However, none of these policies by itself is likely to prove successful. First, anti-discrimination legislation without freedom of information and a supportive network of disabled people will simply benefit the legal profession. Second, access to information by itself will almost certainly expose disabled individuals to further professional mystification and exploitation. Third, support for organisations of disabled people without an appropriate framework guaranteeing basic human rights would effectively neutralise the only collective voice that disabled people have in this country. But an integrated policy similar to that suggested above would provide a means of addressing institutional discrimination effectively and thus eliminating it.

It could be argued that institutional discrimination against disabled people is so entrenched within British society that it is unrealistic to think that its eradication is possible. Those who take this view need to be reminded that no one in contemporary Britain lives in the 'real world'. They need to be made aware that all human beings live in a socially created world and that institutional discrimination is nothing more than a social creation and as such could be got rid of. While the policies outlined above might not remove institutional discrimination overnight, they would certainly contribute significantly to its demise.

REFERENCES

Department of Employment (DE) (1990), *Employment and Training for Disabled People*, consultative document, Department of Employment, London.
Gregory, J. (1987), *Sex, Race and the Law*, Sage, London.
Hansard (1983), 11 February.
Hansard (1991), 25 March.
Topliss, E. and Gould, B. (1981), *A Charter for the Disabled*, Basil Blackwell, Oxford.
United Nations (UN) (1988), *A Compendium of Declarations on the Rights of Disabled Persons*, United Nations, New York.

Part II

Europe and beyond

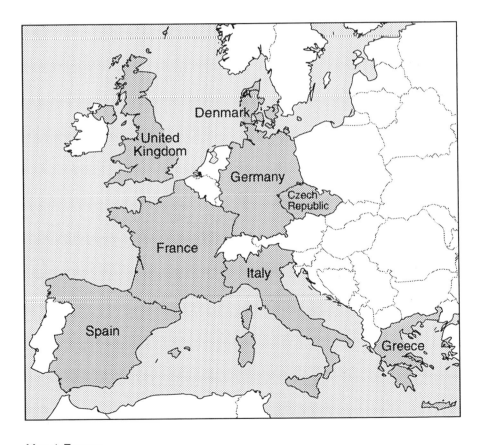

Map 1 Europe

Chapter 9

'Appellation contrôlée': mixing and sorting in the French education system

Felicity Armstrong

Structures and practices in the French education system for assessing, categorising and segregating students ignore the characteristics, interests and needs which they all have in common. The 1989 Education Law – the 'Loi Jospin' – asserted the right of all children and young people to an 'inclusive education'. This chapter looks at two settings, a large primary school and a special school in the Paris region, to find out how far they have been affected by this legislation.

INTRODUCTION

This chapter is about the French education system and some of the structures and practices which lead to the inclusion or exclusion of different groups of children and young people from ordinary schools and colleges. The 'Loi Jospin' passed in 1989 declared the right of all children and young people to an 'inclusive education' (Law no. 89-486 of 10 July 1989). However, many are in settings which are not part of the service provided by the Ministry of Education, but which come under the Ministry for Health or the Ministry for Social Services (Magnier 1990). It is not yet clear how many of these young people will be included within the ordinary education system in the future.

I have called this chapter *Appellation contrôlée: mixing and sorting in the French education system* because it is about the way in which young people in France are labelled and channelled along different routes within – and beyond – the education system. *Appellation contrôlée* refers to the official categorisation and labelling of French wines.

My interest in the French education system goes back some years to the late 1960s when I was a part-time student in Paris, then a teacher and – years later – the parent of a child in a French primary school.

At first, the French system looks relatively democratic. Children can all have a place at a nursery, they follow a common curriculum and there is an explicit commitment by the government not to introduce setting and streaming according to perceived attainment.

STRUCTURE OF THE SYSTEM

The French school system is arranged in the following way:

3–6 years *Ecole Maternelle*
6–11 years *Ecole Elémentaire*
11–15 years *Collège*
15–18 years *Lycée professionnel* or *Lycée d'enseignement général*

The early years and primary education

Although school is not obligatory until the age of 6 years, nearly all 3-year-olds attend nursery school (Thelot and Esquieu 1993). Children spend five years at the *école élémentaire*. During that time they all follow a common curriculum and there is no explicit setting according to perceived attainment.

Secondary schooling, classification and selection processes

Students aged 11–15 spend four years at their local *collège*. Although these schools are supposed to be non-selective, a process of overt sorting takes place after the second year at the *collège* at the age of 13. Those students who are not considered suitable for an 'academic' route through the remainder of their education are put into classes where they will follow a path leading in the direction of the *lycée professionnel*. This kind of *lycée* prepares students for the world of manual and skilled labour and they normally take an exam called the *Certificat d'Aptitude Professionnelle* (the CAP) The CAP is not a diploma representing a standard of general education; it is a diploma for a technical skill. There is a CAP in carpentry and a CAP in butchery, for example.

In theory the *lycée professionnel* can start at 14, but usually students stay at the *collège* until they are 16. Many parents are reluctant to see their son or daughter forced to choose a trade at the age of 14 and hope that they will make the kind of academic progress that will give them broader opportunities. Parents cannot be forced to allow their child to be moved to the technical stream but pressure can be exerted. Frequently they are told that if their child is to stay in the academic stream he or she will need to repeat a year so that they can *rattraper* (catch up), although since the 1989 law this cannot be enforced.

The *lycée d'enseignement général* is for students who are going to take the French *baccalauréat*, the examination taken at the age of 18 which leads on to university entrance.

There is clearly a division of the general school population taking place at the age of 13 on the basis of perceived abilities and expected socio-economic orientation. A psychologist I spoke to explained:

> It's a division which takes place basically on class lines. The middle class takes the route to higher education and the working class head for the factory or service industries. There are plenty of exceptions, of course, but basically that's what happens.

Teacher training

Recent legislation has introduced radical changes in the training of teachers, setting up the new *Instituts Universitaires de Formation des Maîtres* (University Institutes for Teacher Training). These changes, introduced by a socialist government, could well be reversed by the right-wing government which came to power in the elections of March 1993 (Holyoake 1993). All intending teachers now have to have a degree before undertaking further initial teacher training. (The notable exception to this rule is mothers of three or more children. They are not required to have a degree. This exception is a hangover from earlier legislation.)

Those wishing to teach children with disabilities or difficulties in learning must be fully qualified teachers with three years' experience in ordinary schools. Each category of disability has its own training course, usually lasting one year full-time in a national training centre. This is followed by a further year of teaching practice. Teachers in special education are on full pay during this period of their training but once qualified they earn about £40 a month more than their colleagues in ordinary schools and classes. There are many reasons why teachers want to qualify in a branch of special education, but one frequently given is the desire for a permanent teaching contract which, while being assured to a fully qualified teacher in a special school or institution, is often not available to teachers in ordinary schools.

A NEW LEGISLATIVE FRAMEWORK

In June 1975 The Law of Orientation In Support of Handicapped People was passed which laid the foundations for greater participation in all aspects of ordinary community life. Although this law confirmed the right of all children and young people to an education which should meet their individual needs, it did not take any steps towards dismantling the complex system of different schools and institutions for children and young people with disabilities and difficulties in learning.

The Jospin Law of 1989

The main tenet of this law was to make the education system and progress within it more accessible to a greater number of children and young people. Unlike the 1981 Act in Britain, the 'Loi Jospin' did not focus on children and young people with disabilities and learning difficulties but on all pupils. The proposals which were designed to help those experiencing difficulties were part and parcel of those designed to change the way in which all children were taught.

The Loi Jospin set a target for the year 2000: 80 per cent of school-leavers would have the *baccalauréat* and the remaining 20 per cent the *Certificat d'Aptitude Professionel* (CAP). To achieve this, reforms are being implemented which are designed to 'raise standards' in schools.

Since September 1991 a number of changes have been introduced, especially in primary schools. The degree to which they have been fully implemented and the speed at which it has been done has varied according to the commitment and determination of headteachers and governing bodies.

'Learning cycles'

One major change is the emphasis on responding to the needs of the individual child, recognising that children learn at different speeds and in different ways. Primary and nursery education has been divided into cycles of three years and there is no longer a system of 'repeating' a year when certain levels have not been reached.

The first 'cycle of learning' spreads across the *école maternelle* and into the first year of primary school, the second cycle covers the middle three years of the primary school and the third cycle the last three years before pupils move on to the *collège*. Although the three cycles are planned to spread across three years each, in fact a cycle can last anything from two years to four years, depending on the individual rhythm of each child, although the shortening or lengthening of a cycle can only take place once during the primary stage of a child's education (Kerviel 1991, pp. 22–3).

'Needs' and 'competences'

Teachers in primary schools are being urged to adopt collaborative approaches to teaching. Each school is free to organise children into teaching groups which they consider are best suited to their pupils and to the physical organisation of the school. Pupils may be grouped according to the cycle they are in rather than by age, and the same teacher can stay with one class for the whole of one cycle. It will also be possible to teach pupils grouped according to 'competences' or 'needs'. The meaning behind these terms is not yet clear. Government circulars, however, do not recommend the grouping of pupils according to level of attainment on the grounds that this would lead to the development of different streams in the education system of 'good' and 'less good' pupils, although in fact the system of channelling students along different routes is well established when they reach *collège*. It will be interesting to see how the grouping of students at primary level works out in practice and the extent to which teachers are willing and able to draw a distinction between grouping according to 'needs' and 'competences' and grouping according to levels of attainment.

'Integration classes' – the introduction of the 'CLIS'

The law also introduced plans for major changes in the provision for some disabled children and some who experience difficulties in learning. *Classes d'integration scolaire*, known as 'CLIS' (Classes for educational integration), are being established for pupils who are deaf, blind or who have a physical disability, and there will also be some of these classes for young people with autism (Circulaire no. 91–304 dy 18 November 1991, Education nationale: Ecoles). These CLIS are regarded as 'integration classes' although they are really special classes added on to ordinary schools. The aim of the CLIS is to make it possible for some young people to move out of special segregated provision and have some experience of ordinary schools. In fact, they often spend much of their time in the special classes with their own teacher, joining the rest of the school at lunchtimes and making visits in the afternoons when possible. Theoretically the system is designed to be flexible so that some pupils can spend an increasing amount of time in ordinary classes until they become fully integrated.

SELECTION PROCEDURES IN SPECIAL EDUCATION

There are two district commissions in each district, one for pre-school children and those in elementary education and the other for those of secondary age, which meet to make decisions about the appropriate educational setting for each pupil seen as experiencing difficulties. Their responsibilities have been delegated to them by the Departmental Commission for Special Education which has the power to delegate decisions concerning integration which do not require any additional finance. Proposed changes in provision for individuals and groups of pupils which entail expenditure can only be dealt with at the departmental level.

When a child is in difficulty in school the parents are informed and their file is sent to the district commission. This body, in consultation with the parents and those who have been working with the child, will make recommendations about the appropriate educational setting for the child. A document called an *évaluation* is drawn up, similar to a statement in the United Kingdom, which outlines the proposed educational provision. Parents are not legally obliged to accept the recommendations and can insist that their child attends an ordinary class in an ordinary school. Usually parents have been drawn into discussions and decision-making from the beginning of the evaluation process and have contributed to the final recommendations for the future placement of their son or daughter, so it is unusual for them not to accept these recommendations.

I visited two schools to gain some first-hand information about the way in which the system of selection and segregation works.

One is a large primary school on the industrial outskirts of Paris. The other is a special school in a tree-lined suburb of Paris for young people aged 14–20.

L'ECOLE PRIMAIRE RÉPUBLIQUE

The *Ecole République* is a large primary school, built in the 1960s. Its size and style suggest an English secondary school of the same period, rather than a primary school. There are sixteen classes in the school, thirteen 'ordinary' ones and three 'special' classes for *adaptation et integration scolaire* (roughly translated = educational adaptation and integration). These three classes have different functions – the one for older pupils has not changed since recent legislation. Pupils aged 10–11, who in the 'old' terminology have a 'slight intellectual deficiency' are in what is called an 'improvers' class' (*classe de perfectionnement*). This is currently separate but will be transformed into a CLIS so in the future these pupils can expect to participate in ordinary classes for part of the time.

The second special class is also a *classe fermée* (literal translation: 'closed class'), called a *classe d'adaptation* ('adaptation class'), but the pupils spend one-third of the time in ordinary classes. The third class – for 6–7 year olds – is in line with the new legislation. Pupils are full members of ordinary classes and are supported in them by their 'special' teacher, who works in close liaison with the class teacher. They are withdrawn in groups for extra help.

Because of the introduction of 'cycles' in primary education in which pupils can remain in one cycle for four years rather than three, classes can contain pupils covering a two-year age span.

Co-operative teaching in the reception class

I visited a *cours préparatoire* (reception class) at the Ecole Republique to see how the new reforms were working out in practice in this school.

Twenty-four children are working around little tables in groups busily engaged in making a fox, a yacht or a mask out of geometric shapes. Children talk quietly to each other and move around the room purposefully fetching scissors and paper. There are two teachers in the classroom. One is the class teacher – a young woman who has recently qualified, and the other the teacher responsible for the *classe d'adaptation et integration scolaire*, an experienced primary school teacher with 'specialist' qualifications. They appear to be teaching collaboratively and to have equal status in the classroom. The pupils ask for help from either teacher, depending on who is nearest and call them both by their Christian names, using the familiar 'tu' form to address them. The 'specialist' teacher explained that she meets with the class teacher regularly to discuss the content and delivery of the curriculum and the individual needs of the children. They plan the lessons together as far as possible and see themselves as a team.

All the children in the class need help at some time or another but some have greater difficulty than others in understanding instructions, concentrating on a particular task, organising their materials and in reading and writing independently.

The walls of the classroom show a colourful range of displays and teaching materials. There are photographs of all the children in the class and their self-portraits using traditional graphic techniques from Mali. Another wall is devoted to 'grammar' and a picture dictionary. Lists of parts of speech (*il/ils, elle/elles, mon/ma, le/la,* etc.) disembodied from sentences or pictures remind me of my own primary education in the 1950s and the 'old' reception classrooms in France of a few years ago.

A girl who has recently arrived from Bulgaria and speaks no French is working on her own. There is a separate service to support children who speak little or no French but usually children aged 6–7 join an ordinary class. Older children receive special French lessons and are withdrawn from ordinary lessons.

Classroom support

After the lesson the 'specialist' support teacher explained what the changes in her role have meant in practice.

> It is hard to lose the power! I was extremely reluctant at first. You need a very close understanding with the class teacher. I am only in this class for part of the day – the rest of the time I am supporting other children in another class. This means that the class teacher has children who are experiencing difficulties on her own for part of the time. Although I am there in the class for those experiencing difficulties, I see my role as supporting any child who needs help and so does the class teacher.

> I like the new system. It is important to differentiate in the way we teach, taking into account the needs of each individual child. This is the new style of teaching. The class teacher and I discuss the best way to help each child. My priority is to teach the children to read, write and count.

> I am in favour of mixed ability teaching, although many teachers are not.

They say it is too difficult to teach a mixed group and would prefer those with difficulties to be taken out of the class.

With the older classes I withdraw some children because they are having such great difficulty with the work, but I do the same work as the class teacher. I am able to help them follow the same work because I can adapt my teaching to suit the needs of a smaller group. Some teachers don't want me supporting in the classroom anyway so it is easier to withdraw the children. I am never asked to withdraw children who are behaving badly and interrupting the class. If I were, I would refuse.

The main priority for this teacher is the teaching of 'basic skills' but she sees the right of students to a common curriculum as uncontroversial. The experience of supporting in the classroom is new in primary education in France. There has been considerable resistance to some of the changes which are taking place, although this teacher is happy with the new system operating in the reception classes in her school.

It is possible that the importance given to 'basic skills' will come into conflict with the requirement to support pupils across the broader curriculum.

The special help network

Not all children who are experiencing difficulties are members of special classes. Some are supported by the *Réseau d'Aide Spécialisée* ('specialised help network'), known as the RAS, which is attached to a group of schools and works with individual pupils, usually on a withdrawal basis.

One of these networks is based in the Ecole Primaire République. It is made up of a group of different professionals:

1 Two teachers who are responsible for intervening 'pedagogically' through the ordinary curriculum to help children experiencing difficulty. They work within the curriculum helping children who are experiencing difficulty in particular areas. These are usually seen as being in the area of 'basic skills', which in France means literacy, grammar and maths.
2 Two *rééducateurs psycho-pédagogiques* who intervene through more 'psychological' routes to try and help pupils with their learning or behavioural difficulties. This may take the form of some kind of counselling and 'psychotherapeutic games' as well as an exploration of unconventional routes to improve motivation, learning, concentration and behaviour.
3 An educational psychologist, who seems to play the role of a kind of arbitrator, is there to advise the group on the nature of the difficulties experienced by individual children and to make recommendations about meeting their needs.

This group meets to discuss the needs of children who have been referred to them by class teachers through the head of the school. The meetings are attended by the children's class teachers and the head of the school. Parents and other professionals such as speech therapists, social workers, etc. do not attend these meetings. Professionals tend to work separately and in separate contexts which are determined by their training and expertise. The difficulties experienced by children and young people are categorised either as difficulties in learning or as emotional/psychological problems and the different 'solutions' which are presented derive from this categorisation. This approach to meeting the needs of pupils rules out in advance any possibility that their difficulties in learning and behaviour arise because of a mis-match between their culture, needs and interests and the curriculum offered by the school. Teachers understand the importance of adapting their teaching methods and providing support to meet the needs of different pupils, but the content of the curriculum is seen as something fixed and determined for all pupils in ordinary schools.

Jérome, Aurélie and Mohammed

At the meeting of the local special help network which I attended a number of children who were experiencing difficulties in a class of 7- to 8-year-olds were discussed.

Jérome is causing a lot of disruption in class when the *rééducateur* tries to withdraw him. The discussion focused on this difficulty and no mention was made of why he needed to be withdrawn. His parents did not want him to have extra help, saying that he did not need it. Jérome is 'no problem' in class until somebody tries to take him out. The educational psychologist says that the 'collaboration' of the pupil is absolutely essential if the help offered is to serve any purpose. It is decided to invite the parents to come into school to explain to them why their son needs to be withdrawn from the class. It is agreed that the teacher should 'negotiate' with Jérome to help him understand why he needs the help.

Aurélie is having difficulty with spelling. Her teacher tells the group that she has a lot to write about but she does not pay attention to how she is writing it. For example, she wrote *'il était'* as *'il e t'* using the two letters to make the word *était*. Aurélie is good at formulating sentences, although she needs further work in grammar and conjugations. She uses the imperfect tense and the simple past tense as well as the present in her writing. She is too reliant on the teacher. The more the teacher is there to help, the more help she asks for.

The group decides that the common objective must be to work on Aurélie's spelling and to help her to be more independent. After much discussion it is decided that her difficulties are those which should be addressed by the teacher rather than the *éducateur*.

Mohammed is having difficulty with reading and spelling and has some 'speech problems'. Does he have a hearing difficulty? Should he see a speech therapist? I discover that Mohammed is bilingual because his teacher mentions in passing that she finds it difficult to communicate with Mohammed's mother, who speaks Arabic, the only language used at home. The group decide to gather more information about Mohammed's needs, to invite the parents into school and to draw up common objectives for his teaching. At the moment he is being withdrawn from class by the specialised teacher and by the *rééducateur* for part of the week. There is no mention of the particular needs of bilingual children.

A number of issues struck me. First, the division of expertise between those around the table. The work of the *éducateur*, the 'specialist teacher' and the class teacher are seen as separate and distinct. There is a separation between the psychological needs of the child and the learning needs as they relate to the school curriculum. This meant that part of the meeting was spent deciding in whose domain the individual child's difficulties lay. Were they essentially learning difficulties or were they emotional and psychological? The *éducateur* and the specialist teacher have very different training and this is reflected in the way in which the issues are discussed.

Second, it was taken as a matter of course that all pupils follow the same curriculum but that teachers and those working with the child should try and differentiate in their teaching methods. At no point was there any discussion concerning the content of the curriculum.

Third, while there is an acknowledgement of some individual differences, others appear to be ignored, e.g., the cultural and linguistic factors which may be associated with bilingualism.

The aim of the intervention by the different professionals is to help a child 'catch up' so that further withdrawal sessions will not be needed. To do this there is an attempt to iron out differences between pupils as far as possible.

L'EXTERNAT MÉDICO-PROFESSIONEL

In spite of its name, *L'Externat Médico-Professionnel* is a school. It is not an easy term to translate into English, because the terminology does not correspond to any used in English. *Externat* means 'day school' or 'day centre', *médico* can be translated by 'medical', *professionnel* by 'vocational training'. In English this would give us 'Non-residential Medical Vocational Training School' and it might be assumed that it was a centre for training doctors. In fact, *L'Externat Médico-Professionnel* is a small non-residential special school for fifty young people aged from 14 to 20, some of whom may require some medical attention in school for a variety of conditions (hence '*médico*'). All of these young people have been assessed and categorised as having difficulties in learning. Most attended special schools or other establishments during the primary years. Some, however, attended ordinary primary schools but were moved out of the ordinary system when the process of sorting and setting began in their colleges at the age of 13 or 14.

Setting

The fifty students are divided into eight different classes. Five of these classes are for students aged 14–16 and are organised into different levels according to perceived ability, usually measured by the administration of IQ tests. The remaining three classes are for training students for employment and preparing them for life in the community.

The curriculum

In the classes, levels 1–5 students spend approximately half the day in formal school lessons and half the day doing practical activities in workshops or sport, swimming or other recreational activities.

The school has no contact with ordinary schools and students leave without any formal qualifications.

The formal curriculum for all levels is based primarily on reading, writing, grammar and arithmetic. Students take homework home every day which is usually a task such as practising the writing of sentences copied from the board.

Class 3, for example, follows the following timetable in the morning (see Figure 9.1):

Monday. Correction of homework (30 mins); dictation (30 mins); Class reading together *Le Journal des Enfants* (children's newspaper) and vocabulary work (1.5 hours).

Tuesday. Correction of homework (30 mins); arithmetic; preparation of dictation (1.5. hours).

Wednesday. Correction of homework (30 mins); library (visit to local one) (30 mins); conjugation (1.5 hours).

Thursday. Correction of homework (30 mins); sport (2.5 hours).

Friday. Correction of homework (30 mins); grammar (1.5 hrs); reading and written expression (1 hour).

The *directrice* explained to me that the pupils need to learn the 'basics' in a highly-structured timetable. The only interruption in this diet is the collective reading of the *Journal des Enfants*. In the edition dated 8 October

Lundi	Mardi	Mercredi	Jeudi	Vendredi
Corrections devoirs	Corrections devoirs	Corrections devoirs	Corrections devoirs	Corrections devoirs
Dictée	Numération Mécanisme opuniloire Raisonnement	Bibliothèque	Sport	Grammaire
Journal des enfants and vocabulaire	Preparation dictée	Conjugaison		Lecture et expression écrite
Repas			Recreation	
Corrections devoirs	Corrections devoirs	Corrections devoirs	Corrections devoirs	
Dictée	Vie pratique Prise en charge personnalle	Bibliothèque	Conjugaison and grammaire	Club Equitation
Raisonnement operatoire et mises en situations	Preparation dictée	Lecture du journal des enfants and vocabulaire	Vie pratique – documents administratifs	
Piscine	Synthèse			

Figure 9.1 Morning timetable for Class 3

1993 pupils were able to read about the European Parliament in Brussels, an earthquake in India, a car rally in Egypt and – relegated to page 2 – the news that the 400 employees at Buckingham Palace will no longer receive a free bar of soap every month.

This timetable is not quite as rigid as it at first appears. Teachers clearly encourage class discussion in a relaxed and democratic atmosphere. Students express their ideas and personal experiences and reflections. The writing, grammar, spelling and vocabulary exercises are often pulled out of more interesting material based upon discussions of visits, reading and films. Here is a brief example of a discussion after a visit to one of the rare vineyards in the Paris region.

Teacher: We are going to write a piece together as a class about the grape picking at the local vineyard which we visited. Then we will illustrate the text.
         What did we notice this morning when we visited the vineyard? What similarity did we notice between the harvesting of grapes and the harvesting of raspberries?
Student 1: You have to stand between the rows.
Teacher: And what did they use to cut with?
Student 2: Secateurs.
Student 3: Then they put it in a basket and put that in the lorry.

This discussion was later used as a basis for a collaboratively authored text which was written on the board by the teacher and copied by class members.

In the afternoon the members of class 3 will pursue one of the following activities:

Horticulture
Upkeep of buildings
Housecraft
Craft

The students all participate in maintaining the life and the fabric of the school both in the literal and figurative sense. In 'horticulture', the young gardeners dig and plant and clear the paths. In 'upkeep of buildings' cleaning and minor maintenance work is undertaken. In 'housecraft' the students shop and cook, clean the cooking area and wash the school linen. Craft periods enable students to make dolls, coil pots, etc. which are sold to raise funds for the school. The aim, the *directrice* explained, is to help young people learn independence and confidence and acquire skills which will help them achieve these. Learning to write a letter and manage a weekly budget could make the difference to many of these young people between living independently and being dependent. It is also important, she said, that the students feel that they are part of the community and that what they have to offer is valued.

Figure 9.2 School lunch

'Plat du jour'

The rigid, repetitive, 'medicinal' nature of the formal curriculum was brought into sharp contrast with one aspect of the informal curriculum at the school at lunchtime.

This is a very important part of the daily curriculum in the school which is shared by all its members. The meal was remarkable for its imagination, balance and diversity. While we were eating the cook came round the tables to see if we were enjoying the meal, stopping at one table to give a group of young people the recipe for the *poisson à l'échalote*.

Lise

The students at the *Externat Médico-Professionnel* were keen to show me their work. One girl introduced herself and talked to me about her interests:

> My name is Lise. I think the closest English name would probably be 'Lisa'. I'd really like to go to England and visit Oxford. Apparently there's quite a good university there. But Manchester would be interesting too. That's in the North with lots of factories and so on. I'd really like to see the way people live in big cities in the north of England, but I don't expect I'll get the chance.

Lise is 16. She has Down's Syndrome. She has a lot of interests and a busy social life. She loves reading, jazz, rock 'n' roll and *la musique anglaise*. I asked her about the work she was doing:

> I'm writing the acronym which corresponds to each expression. For example: *La Société Nationale des Chemins de Fer Français* (the national railway system in France): that one is 'SNCF' . . . which is always on strike and gets on my nerves!

I asked the *directrice* if she thought Lise found the curriculum stimulating enough for her at the *Externat*. No, she said. She had been reluctant to take her but had been persuaded to on the grounds that Lise is 'too friendly and trusting' and other students might take advantage of her in a large secondary school. In addition, she needed extra help to develop her fine motor skills. I reflected on the large number of young people who are being 'protected' in segregated settings and on the task of changing ordinary schools so that all pupils can join.

DISCUSSION

Education in France in the 1990s is in a period of rapid change. There are signs that in primary education there is a real attempt to teach pupils flexibly and these may mean that fewer children are excluded from ordinary classes in primary schools in the future, although there may not be a reduction in the number joining special classes when they reach the secondary phase. There are few signs yet of major changes in the content of the curriculum. There appear to be no plans to dismantle the massive system of special schools and institutions which remain outside the education system.

The kind of support currently being offered in primary schools takes a variety of forms. There is a focus on working on 'basic skills', but as 'specialist' teachers spend a greater proportion of their time in ordinary classes working collaboratively with class teachers, they will find themselves increasingly involved in teaching and supporting pupils across the curriculum. This is already happening in reception classes.

There remains a very large group of young people who will continue to be excluded, those who are regarded as having difficulties in learning which would make ordinary schools as they at the moment 'non-beneficial' and those who have difficulties which are regarded as psychiatric. In the words of a member of staff at a teacher training college, 'the dividing line between those who will be included and those who won't is drawn according to whether the child or young person is seen as being able to benefit from a normal school experience or not. If not they will stay in a specialist school or institution.'

REFERENCES

Holyoake, J. (1993), 'Initial teacher training: the French view', *Journal of Education for Teaching: international research and pedagogy*.

Kerviel, S. (1991), 'Ecole primaire: la grande reforme', *Le Monde De L'Education*, September.

Magnier, J. (1990), 'Les structures d'éducation et de soins spécialisés', *Handicap, famille et société*, Paris, Institut de l'enfance et de la famille.

Thelot, C. and Esquieu, P. (1993), *Géographie de l'Ecole*, Paris, Ministère de l'Education Nationale et de la Culture.

FURTHER READING

Daunt, P. (1991), *Meeting Disability: A European Response*, Cassell, London.

O'Hanlon, C. (1993), *Special Education: Integration in Europe*, David Fulton, London.

Labregère, A. (1990), *L'Insertion de Personnes Handicapées*, La Documentation Française, Paris.

Lafay, H. (1990), *L'Intégration scolaire des enfants et adolescents handicapés*, La Documentation Française, Paris.

Sharpe, K. (1992), 'Educational homogeneity in French primary education: a double case study, *British Journal of Sociology of Education*, 13 (3).

Chapter 10

Early childhood services in Italy, Spain and the United Kingdom

Helen Penn

This comparative study was undertaken for the European Childcare Network, which disseminates information to European Union member states about the relationship between services to young children and equal opportunities in employment. Helen Penn found significant variations between services in the three countries, with services in the UK being noticeably the worst. The quality of services to young children was directly linked to the job satisfaction of the adult workers. Where the ethos was confident, constructive and relaxed, children with a wide range of abilities and interests could successfully be included.

INTRODUCTION

The European Childcare Network is one of a series of semi-formal advisory groups set up by the Equal Opportunities Office of the European Commission. It is made up of 'experts', one from each member state. The job of the Childcare Network is to provide information across member states about the relationship between the provision of services to young children and equal opportunities in employment. The Network has published a number of studies, including a discussion document on 'Quality in early years', and is currently working on producing guidelines on targets in provision for member states.

Through the exchanges facilitated by the Network, it has become apparent both how much early years services across member states differ from one another in their values and in their organisation and yet how much they have in common. This comparative study arose out of those exchanges and the wish to make more systematic comparisons. It was funded by the local authorities in Spain, Italy and the United Kingdom who took part in the study in each country. It focuses on the staffing for day-care nurseries for children aged 3 and under in one particular area. It looks at how publicly-funded nurseries are staffed, at the levels of initial and in-service training, at the pay and conditions of service and management structures and at the ways in which staff describe the work they do.

The staffing of nurseries, the pay, conditions and training of the workers, are according to some American research (Phillips *et al.* 1991) the single most important determinant of quality in early childhood services. However, American services are mostly in the private sector, where pay and conditions are problematic. In Europe services are mostly publicly provided or publicly funded, and it is accepted that workers in the services will have standardised pay and conditions, negotiated by unions within a local authority framework.

Current debates about management philosophy in nurseries (Richman and McGuire 1988) have emphasised the importance of 'ethos', defined as the extent to which the manager or officer-in-charge involves herself (or himself) in the daily life and detailed planning of the nursery and the extent to which the manager is able to support and give practical advice to staff. The recent European Commission (EC) discussion document, *Quality in Services for Young Children* (Balaguer *et al.* 1992), also gives 'ethos', defined as the extent to which the work of the nursery is integrated and coherent, as an important determinant of quality.

In some countries nurseries are organised on a collective basis, without a hierarchical management system. The idea of collective working seems to have a number of different roots, but one study at least has dated the arrangement back to the 1960s, when collective working patterns in nurseries were seen as part of a wider radical movement for social change (Saraceno 1977). There were experiments in collective working in nurseries in Germany, Portugal, Denmark, France, Spain, Italy and, to a much lesser extent, Britain (Penn 1992). This basic principle behind collective working is the belief that the more egalitarian the arrangement between the staff, the more the children will value co-operation and socialisation; the more devolved the management, the more staff will be able to take decisions for themselves, the more autonomous and independent the children.

This project looks at four nurseries in each of two local/regional authorities where collective working has been adopted throughout the publicly-provided service: the commune of Barcelona in Spain, and the region of Emilia Romagna in Italy. As a comparison, four publicly-funded day nurseries in a local authority in England, which are hierarchically run, with several tiers of management, have also been included in the project. The aim of the research project was to make comparisons between staff attitudes and to see whether collective working did result in more coherent and integrated planning and lead to more autonomy and self-direction in the co-operation and socialisation amongst the children.

METHODOLOGY

Comparative research is notoriously difficult, since one is never comparing like with like. The structure of local authorities is different in each country. In addition language difficulties complicate any arrangements, and the accuracy of the translation can be critical. Partly for this reason, partly because I was working in an unresearched area, and partly because the project crossed the boundaries between child development and social policy, I used some quantitative, but mostly qualitative methods.

I was the sole researcher and the research was also consultancy; that is, as an experienced practitioner myself, I was making practical suggestions to the local authorities concerned, based on the material I collected. The extent to which research is neutral and value-free is in any case a matter of debate and the case has been made that research which is closely allied to policy and practical outcomes is as valid as research which is undertaken within a traditional academic framework and is unrelated to such outcomes (Farquar 1992).

The selection of the nurseries in the project was not random, and indeed could not have been, given the complications of funding and the priorities of the local authorities, who contributed to the project and who nominated the nurseries. Each local authority was asked to select 'average' nurseries, with some geographical spread across the authority.

The research involved collecting various kinds of data. First of all I collected and analysed whatever official documentation was available about the services. This included statements of aims, policy documents, procedures for advertising posts and employment of staff, details about support and advisory staff in the local authority, committee reports, leaflets to parents, admissions procedures, data on levels of service provided and on absence rates and turnover rates of staff over a year's period.

Second, I asked all staff in each nursery to complete a questionnaire, giving details of their background, training and work experience and their attitudes to the job.

Third, I undertook three to four days' observation in each nursery, covering opening hours to closing hours (although not necessarily consecutively), and I observed at a staff meeting. This part of the research was the least systematic and the observations were not at timed intervals, nor were they videoed or taped. The approach was ethnographical, that is, listening, watching and trying to build up a pictures of the meaning of the events which took place.

I observed, as unobtrusively as possible, interactions between children, or between staff and children, or between staff and parents, particularly where such interactions seemed problematic. At the most suitable moments and in the most neutral way possible, over lunch or coffee, I tried to ask staff, for example, 'Can you tell me why you did that?' I listened to group discussions at mealtimes or at other times when members of staff got together, and I sometimes exchanged views with them about what I had seen in other places, comparing it to what they themselves were doing. The idea was to try to understand the unofficial rules and implicit priorities as well as the explicit ones which guided the daily practice. As Huxley (1934) has remarked: 'Thanks to language all our relations with the outside world are tinged with a certain ethical quality; before ever we start our observations, we think we know what it is the duty of reality to be like.'

Because of the different systems of services in each country, it was easier to focus the observations on 2–3-year-old groups, because there was more similarity between countries in the format of services offered at that age than once children had started nursery school. The observations were carried out April–July 1993, when most of the children were 3 or nearly 3, although the age-grouping systems differed between nurseries. But I visited each of the group rooms in each of the nurseries, to gain an impression of the nursery as a whole. In one or two cases the staff were so acutely aware of and uncomfortable about being observed, that it was not possible to continue with that group at that time and some other arrangement had to be made, either a later visit or another group.

Fourth, in each case I fed back my results and impressions to the administrators and/or trainers who had commissioned the work, and asked them to confirm or explain the observations I made. In each country I had several meetings, both as the work progressed and when I offered a summary of it at the end of the period.

ITALY

Policies

The city states of northern Italy are wealthy, homogenous, with strong historical and cultural traditions. All those in the sample were communist (PDSOE) controlled. Co-operatives and collective ways of working were well established in many walks of life. There was little socially-segregated housing and no visible evidence of poverty. There was no vandalism or graffiti. All the children in the sample seemed healthy and well cared for. Few came from single-parent families. All children had Italian as a first language.

The nurseries were each architect-designed, spacious, inside and out, with considerable attention to detail – light, shade, colour and furnishings and equipment. They were very attractive places to be in, even if not always efficient. They all had streamlined kitchens, however, for food is an important part of life. One of the nurseries had the standard of cuisine of a very good restaurant.

In the region of Emilia Romagna 30 per cent of children aged 3 and under attend the Asilo Nido (literally translated as 'the nest'). Full-time nursery education is available for all children aged 3–5 with wrap-around care for working parents who require it. The main criterion for admission to the *asilo* is that the parents are working, and parents pay fees graded according to income. It is unusual for non-working parents to use an *asilo*. Waiting lists are very small (i.e., in one of the communes with approximately 3,000 children under 3 there was a waiting list of 100 – all other children requiring day care having been placed. It was a measure of the commitment of local administrators that they considered this figure unacceptably *high* and that nothing less than meeting *all* demands would do.)

All children are age-grouped and the *asili* have one entry, in September. The age group is an important concept and it is somewhat rigidly applied. Children with disabilities have priority although usually they come only if their parents work and extra members of staff, usually one per group, are employed to help them integrate. The kinds of disabilities I saw included hearing loss, sight loss, and Down's Syndrome, but there were no children with motor disabilities in the sample. Children with social difficulties are not recognised as a separate category. The approach is non-pathological. It is assumed that all children are basically affectionate, playful and capable of learning. In the Italian sample of 200 children there was only one instance of disturbed behaviour, a violently aggressive and attention-seeking girl, but staff did not see her as having a particular problem, only as being in need of settling in for a bit longer.

The dominant educational ideology in the sample nurseries was that of free play and non-interference by adults. This ideology was derived from a Hungarian model, that of 'Loczy' (Falk 1975), in which the intention is to enable children to be as autonomous and self-determining as possible. Whilst staff were usually very responsive, but in an undemonstrative way, to children's own initiatives, they rarely attempted to direct them and seemed uneasy when they had to do so. There were a few attempts at group activities, which were didactically organised, and toilet-changing, preparation for mealtimes, or going inside or outside, usually involved a lot of lining up and waiting.

In one of the nurseries, where this pedagogy was combined with an excessive emphasis on physical hygiene and cleanliness, this meant that at times during the day there was literally nothing for the children to do. All the toys were cleared away, the floors were immaculate, the furniture was stacked away and the children wandered around aimlessly and scrapped with one another. When toys were put out, they were poured in a heap into the centre of the floor and there was grabbing and pushing to get hold of them. The staff justified their approach by remarks such as 'We have to let the children fantasise.' However, where this philosophy of non-intervention was more sensitively interpreted, there was a planned environment, with a wide range of toys and activities and an alertness and responsiveness to the children's conversation and actions which was remarkable.

Staffing

In much of Europe access to work in the public services is through the Concourse, this is, a public examination followed up by interviews. At each concourse 200 or more applicants take the examination and then 50 or so are selected to be interviewed by a panel. In Emilia Romagna, for the nurseries, the panel was made up of trade unionists, administrators and academics. The period of interviews lasts several days although each interviewee is given twenty minutes and the successful applicants are allocated to their posts. Those who fall just short of appointment are allocated to the supply pool and may spend several years as a supply until they get a permanent post. Once appointed, the applicant receives a fully-protected job contract.

The training for work in the asilo is usually a vocational, school-based training of two years post-16. However, there are many routes to obtaining this qualification. There were also some graduates and some teachers in the present sample of staff.

The staff were organised into collectives, that is, everyone held an equal responsibility and received equal pay, according to length of service. The staff worked two or three to a room, according to the size and age of the group, on a shift system which was worked out between each group. The staff ratios varied throughout the day, everyone being on duty at lunchtime, but few people being in the rooms during the afternoon nap period.

The staff had twelve weeks' holiday and worked a thirty-six-hour week of which six hours were devoted to in-service training, meetings, etc. Staff had a separate lunch at the nursery, when the children were asleep.

The administration of the nursery, admissions, finance, maintenance and other matters were handled centrally by the local authority. A co-ordinator was responsible for each group of six to ten nurseries. His/her job was to oversee the pedagogic routines, arrange in-service training, and deal with concerns about individual children, although this role differed from local authority to local authority. In effect the co-ordinator was perceived as the boss and was listened to with deference, although he/she had no formal authority. The staff met weekly to discuss the week's work. Some meetings were formally organised, with an agenda and set business; others were more rambling discussions.

There was considerable variation between the nurseries in the sample. Each small commune or local authority organises its own system, sets its own traditions and there is no overall regional or national system of inspection or standards. Turnover and sickness rates at the nursery where there was attentiveness and responsiveness to the children in a planned environment were very low (less than 2 per cent of staff time lost through sickness in a year). At the nursery where the children scrapped and wandered about they were much higher, more than 15 per cent, and then the operation of the supply system became a critical factor. However, the staff of all of the nurseries expressed themselves on the questionnaires as being mostly satisfied with their work and valued the collective way of working very highly.

The fact that there was such a difference between the nurseries, despite similar catchments, educational philosophies, and staffing practices, emphasises the complexity of a situation where adults and children come together in a learning and caring environment. There was not a direct relationship between collective working and quality of care; within the enabling framework of one of the best-funded and generous levels of service in Europe, it is the overall organisation, its coherence, range and attention to detail, which appears to matter most.

SPAIN

Policies

Over the last fifteen years Spain has been a society undergoing rapid transition, with a socialist government after many years of dictatorship. Barcelona is a large and cosmopolitan industrial city, with a considerable historical, cultural and socialist anarchist tradition. The language of the city is Catalan, not Spanish, and the resurgence of Catalan culture and nationalism after years of suppression is a dominant feature of city life. There is an immigrant population, mainly from Andalusia in the south of Spain and a small percentage from North Africa. There is some housing segregation, but most inner-city areas are socially mixed. In the areas where the sample nurseries were situated there was a little, but not very much, visible evidence of poverty, and occasional graffiti.

Spain has introduced major educational reforms over the past ten years, based on a programme of discussion and research with practitioners. The basic education system is now defined as covering children aged 0–16 and everyone who works in a nursery has to undertake a three-year training as a teacher. Tertiary education has also been reorganised, so that teacher training is age appropriate and new courses for those working with 0–6-year-olds have been introduced. Various kinds of in-service training and modular courses have been introduced to allow those who have been working in the services to acquire the qualification the law now requires.

Services for young children can either be organised as day nursery schools for children aged 0 to 6 or as day nurseries for those aged 0–3, with separate school-based nursery classes with wrap-around care for children aged 3–5. In Barcelona, the provision for children aged 0–3 was organised separately. About 8 per cent of children in this age group attend and waiting lists are sometimes very long. Children are admitted on a priority basis, taking into account parents at work, income levels, and social and physical need. It is unusual for parents of children attending not to work. Most nurseries have several children with disabilities. Staffing ratios are altered to accommodate them and there are visiting specialists services. Children are admitted once a year, in September and are age-grouped, but less rigidly than in Italy.

The dominant philosophy is one of education and learning. It is assumed that young children are capable of autonomy and independence and of awareness of their cultural heritage. There is considerable documentation produced by the local authority and within the nurseries about educational practices. The language of the nurseries is Catalan, whether or not Spanish is a first language at home, and most children by the age of 3 are bilingual.

Barcelona is a densely-populated city and two of the nurseries were housed in converted premises, a flat and a small house, with children having to ascend or descend spiral staircases to reach roof-top yards. By UK or Italian standards these premises were unsafe and contained many hazards for small children. However, the staff viewed the premises as a positive opportunity for children to learn to be autonomous and self-regarding and to exercise self-control. The third nursery was purpose-built, to a very high standard, with a clever use of light and space and water and with a generous kitchen where children and staff could come and sit. The fourth nursery was a spacious conversion of a private house. As in the Italian nurseries, mealtimes were important for children and for adults, and the food was fresh and of a high quality. The cooks were either trained or had in-service opportunities and were responsible for budgeting and ordering the food.

Staffing

Eighty per cent of the staff had trained as teachers. In addition, training was regarded as being continuous. All nurseries appointed their own consultant trainer to develop their own training programmes and evaluation and monitoring systems and were given the time and money to do so. The local authority had its own educational research department, which included early-years researchers, who helped nurseries develop and monitor their work. The sample nurseries each had a small library of books and videos on current child development and pedagogic issues. The level of sophistication of the material used and produced by the nurseries was considerable. Children were likely to be familiar with paintings by Miró and Picasso, artists native to Barcelona, and to have some knowledge of classical music – a performance of the *Magic Flute* had recently been given for nursery children and many children could identify the tunes.

The staff appointments system and hours of work were similar to those in Emilia Romagna. The groups of children, particularly the youngest, tended to be smaller (six children), but staff–child ratios also varied throughout the day, a team of staff being responsible for a group of children.

The collective included a supernumerary member of staff who acted as 'secretary' of the nursery for a two-year period, to deal with financial and administrative matters. The staff elected this postholder from amongst the collective, but everyone was keen to stress that the post carried no seniority or extra pay. Four advisers from the local authority liaised with a group of nurseries but their role was advisory and supportive rather than directive, unlike Italy, and they were not responsible for in-service training. The Spanish collectives, therefore, had more autonomy than the Italian ones.

Within this context, there was again considerable variation between nurseries. Two of the nurseries, ironically those in the worst premises, had encouraged their children successfully to become autonomous and even quite young children were capable of longer periods of sustained, co-operative and inventive play. One of the nurseries was an exceptionally happy place, with the staff valuing their work at the highest possible rating and with much laughter and affectionate caresses between staff, between staff and children and between children themselves. Staff in the other two nurseries valued their work less highly and had more grumbles, about each other, about the work they did and how it was organised. Again this was reflected in the sickness and turnover rates.

UNITED KINGDOM

Policies

The four UK day nurseries were in a northern industrial city where unemployment is high, over 50 per cent in some areas. There was considerable visible poverty. Housing was socially segregated and the nurseries were all situated in working-class areas. Two were on estates where there were many semi-derelict, vandalised and burnt-out properties. Graffiti, vandalism and theft were common in all the nurseries and they all had elaborate security arrangements. One had a permanent night-time security guard. Although the city struggled with its civic image, there was no consciousness amongst nursery staff of a rich cultural heritage as in Barcelona and northern Italy.

Admission to the nurseries was exclusively on the basis of social need and linked closely to other social services. Most places were sessional and although they were open all year and from 8a.m. to 6p.m., most children only attended three or four sessions or half-days per week. Places for approximately 1 per cent of children in day care are available nationally, and in this city the percentage was fractionally higher. Until fairly recently no places had been available for children under 2 because of a belief that children were best off at home with their mother. In three of the nurseries baby places for under-2s were now available, but staffing ratios were very high: one adult to two children at all times. Children were admitted throughout the year, whenever there was a vacancy and as there were only three or four groups to cover the age range 0–5, all nurseries had some kind of mixed-age grouping.

Waiting lists were not long and one of the nurseries had vacancies. The admissions process, in which parents had to be assessed for the severity of their 'problems', may have discouraged applicants. The city had a relatively generous level of full-time nursery education places for children aged 3–5, in a parallel but completely unrelated system and this may have been a more attractive option to parents who were free to choose.

Many of the children who attended the nursery were unkempt, dazed or severely traumatised and had a history of abuse. In one nursery, not one child in a group of 3-year-olds in the sample had any linguistic competence – most were monosyllabic or did not speak and there was little social or co-operative play.

Few parents worked, and being at work had not in itself been a criteria for admission. Places were free, although regular take-up of allocated places was often less than 50 per cent. Very recently the local authority had decided to sell a limited number of places to working parents, but it had not been possible to sell places in the nurseries in the worst areas.

Although all the nurseries were purpose-built, with one exception they were not well designed. The accommodation was cramped and noisy and access to the outside, for various reasons, including the vandalism and the weather, was very limited even in summer when the research took place. There was no opportunity for rest or sleep during the day, except for the babies, who slept in their rooms. The children were cooped up in the rooms, with little opportunity for free movement. Each nursery had its own kitchen, but much of the food was processed, and there was little fresh fruit or vegetables.

The educational philosophy was confused and many staff found it difficult to distinguish or prioritise their work. There was no documentation at any level about educational practices, merely daily timetables within the nurseries listing rotation of activities. Many staff saw their main role as 'working with families' or 'providing a role model for mothers', although in practice they spent most of their time with the children and very little of their time with adults. Much of the activity was with table-top toys, that is, various kinds of plastic sorting games and puzzles and the children's attention span was poor, and dependent on adult intervention. One of the nurseries relied heavily on television and videos. Only one nursery had a sustained attempt to introduce multicultural materials, although this was also the only nursery which had black children on roll. The main educational framework used was the Portage system, which offered staff a ready-made account of developmental stages and a means of assessing children's progress. The expectations of what the children might achieve, or what the staff could do to stimulate the children's creativity, sociability or curiosity, were limited.

Staffing

Most staff had had two years' post-16 training as nursery nurses and some had further social-work-based training. They were appointed by interview to a particular nursery. They worked a thirty-nine-hour week (now reduced to thirty-seven) with a half-hour lunch break. The nurseries were open throughout the holidays and staff had twenty-five working days' holiday a year, to be taken by negotiation. None of this time was allocated to in-service training, but the nurseries did manage to hold weekly or monthly staff meetings at the beginning or end of the day, when children had not yet arrived or had gone home.

The nurseries were run hierarchically, with a supernumerary officer-in-charge and supernumerary deputy officer-in-charge managing a group of six to nine nursery nurses. The officer-in-charge offered 'supervision sessions' to her staff, that is, a fortnightly or monthly interview to discuss work problems, careers development, etc. The officers-in-charge, in turn, had supervision sessions with their manager in the social services department. Many staff referred to the views of 'management' as being separate from their own priorities and concerns. The nurseries did not have their own budgets and had relatively little financial or administrative autonomy. The time of the managers was mostly taken up in dealing with social services about particular children and parents, with casework meetings, preparations for court hearings, and admissions interviews. None of the managers concerned herself (or himself) exclusively with educational issues.

In this very different context, there was also a considerable difference between the nurseries. The nursery in the best premises and in the least stressed of the four areas, had some long-serving (more than twenty-five years) competent and relaxed staff. The activities for the children were more varied. They played outside more often and they had access to a big hall with large soft bricks and mattresses on which to tumble about. This nursery had also attracted the most fee-paying children, some of whom were very articulate and lively children and who offered a friendship and stimulus to some of the more traumatised children. The staff at this nursery valued their work highly.

The nursery that was badly vandalised and broken-into (half of it was boarded up and the grounds were checked daily for used needles, broken glass, condoms and other debris) had a demoralised work-force, chaotic routines and a high level of staff sickness. The other nursery in a semi-derelict area was rigid and controlling towards the children, but they did offer the children a secure and predictable framework and routines. At both these nurseries, not surprisingly, staff were more ambivalent about their work.

CONCLUSIONS

Altogether there were 128 staff in the research sample across the three countries. There were similarities between them. They were the same age, each staff group averaging from 32 to 39 years of age. The oldest staff were to be found in Barcelona, the youngest in northern Italy. The average length of service for each nursery varied, ranging from two years (UK) to eleven or twelve years (Italy/UK/Spain). Further, however, in each country, despite very different circumstances, there were staff who valued their work very highly. In each country, too, there were highly-sensitive and responsive staff and unresponsive and abrupt staff, although generally there were more incompetent staff in the UK.

The staff in each country were paid at roughly similar rates, in the range £7,500 to £10,000 per annum and had secure conditions of employment. The working conditions of the staff in Italy and Spain were much more favourable, with fewer hours, more holidays, and time offered for regular in-service training. The work friendships were stronger, and the pleasure in work was greater but their collective practices, although highly valued, did not always appear to be directly related to outcomes.

Because of the different catchments of children in the nurseries it was difficult to make any generalisations about children's progress. The Spanish day nurseries were undoubtedly the most educationally orientated and had the most varied range and carefully-planned educational activities, but teachers' individual skills and competences varied widely.

SUMMARY

In each of the three studied countries there are major differences in the provision of publicly-funded day-care services to young children. The strong regional/local input into developing the service in northern Italy and the national and local input in Barcelona have led to services of a generally high quality. The more depressed services in the UK have less to offer children. The contrast between how children of the same age in publicly-funded day care spend their time in the UK nurseries compared with the Italian and Spanish nurseries is extreme and is an indictment of the British system (see also Penn 1993).

The national/regional/local policies and educational philosophies set the scene for what the nurseries can do. It is possible to provide a good service, even when the odds are stacked against it, as in one of the UK nurseries. It is also possible to provide a bad service, even when circumstances are favourable, as in one of the Italian nurseries. But generally the economic well-being and vitality of the local community, the overall framework and financial and developmental investment by the local authority and national government, the availability of places, the staff training, their pay and conditions of work and the condition of the premises make it much more likely that nurseries will be able to fulfil what they set out to do.

REFERENCES AND FURTHER READING

Balaguer, I., Mestres, J. and Penn, H. (1992), *Quality in Services for Young Children*, European Commission Childcare Network Discussion Paper, Brussels.

Bloom, P. J. (1991), *Organizational Climate in Childcare Settings*, in B. J. Fraser and H. Walberg (eds), *Education Environments*, Pergamon, New York.

Falk, Judit (1975), *Institut Loczy: Un foyer pour nourissons pas comme les autres*, Le Coq-heron, N.53, Dupont, Paris.

Farquar, S. J. (1992), 'Quality is in the eye of the beholder', PhD thesis, University of Dunedin, NZ.

Huxley, A. (1934), *Beyond the Mexique Bay*, Chatto & Windus, London.

Manlove, Elizabeth (1992), *Conflict and Ambiguity over Work Roles*, Paper presented at the American Educational Research Association Annual Meeting, San Francisco.

Penn, Helen (1992), *Pre-Fives: The View from Strathclyde*, Scottish Academic Press, Edinburgh.

Penn, Helen (1993), 'Careless society', *Guardian Education*, 7 December, p. 4.

Phillips, D., Howes, C. and Whitebook, M. (1991), 'Child care as an adult work environment', *Journal of Social Issues*, 47 (2).

Richman, N. and McGuire, J. (1988), 'Institutional characteristics and staff behaviour in day nurseries', *Children and Society*.

Saraceno, Chiara (1977), *Experiencia y teoria de las comunas infantiles*, Editorial Fountanella, Barcelona.

Chapter 11

Parents and schooling in the European Union: a case study from Denmark and Germany

Harry Daniels

Since 1988, the HELIOS programme of the then European Community, in association with the European Association for Special Education (EASE), has supported an international study of the quality of life of disabled students and those who experience difficulties in learning. The role of parents in decisions which affect the education of their children is discussed in the context of securing the best possible quality of life. But the values and traditions of different countries have led to very different approaches. In Denmark the emphasis is on parental involvement at every stage of decision-making, and the aim is for the inclusion of all students into a single educational mainstream. In Germany, there is a highly specialised education system and a minimal role for parents in the structures of decision-making. Harry Daniels discusses what the possibilities are for the implementation of the principle of subsidiarity in these circumstances and argues that a shift from a 'free' to a 'social' market is the way to guarantee the rights of all parents.

INTRODUCTION

Parents' organisations provide an intriguing example of a mechanism by which public policy and private interest may be brought into a direct relationship. In the current climate of supposed decentralisation of decision-making and devolution of funding in education, the future respective roles of local, national and indeed supranational parent bodies in policy formation with respect to children with special educational needs (SEN)[1] comes into question. What will subsidiarity bring for parents?

Systems for balancing parental influence against teacher influence, for ensuring financial accountability, and reserving final decisions to elected politicians have been established in many European countries. For example, Boards of Governors (England and Wales) and Elternbeiräte (Germany) incorporate elected parent representatives in consultative and decision-making committees established by law to assist in various aspects of the government of schools (Beattie 1987).

Bristow (1988) argues that in England and Wales, the post-war legislation of the Education Act of 1944 expressed the notion of 'partnership' as its central organisational and operational value and encouraged a description of educational provision in England and Wales as 'a national system, locally administered'. Interestingly parents as parents were and are unrepresented in any formal way at local authority level. Parent–Teacher Associations (PTAs) in England and Wales have tended to concentrate their efforts at the school level and they rarely try to exert pressure on either local or national government (Bristow 1988). These changes in the locus of control over schooling have involved real and rhetorical shifts. Arguably the real shift has been towards a massive centralisation whilst the rhetoric has been that of parental charters, choices and responsibilities.

This chapter will consider some aspects of the balances achieved between public education policy development and the interests of parents of children with SEN in two European countries. In doing so it describes some aspects of a multidisciplinary exchange and research programme involving specific regional groups in Denmark, Germany, Italy, Spain and the United Kingdom. The project is funded through the HELIOS programme of the European Community in partnership with the European Association for Special Education (EASE). The HELIOS programme is concerned with the promotion of vocational training and rehabilitation, economic integration, social integration and independence of handicapped people and was adopted on 18 April 1988. (For full details see Commission of the European Communities 1992.) The focus of the project discussed here is on the quality of life experienced by children and young people with identified special educational needs in a variety of educational contexts. The practices of integration into mainstream settings in education and community contexts are compared from a wide range of perspectives.

The parental representatives from Germany and Denmark were interviewed and provided background information for the preparation of this chapter. Karin Zah (Reutlingen, Germany) and Gunhilde Madsen (Rosenholm, Hinnerup, Hadsten, Denmark) are members of well-established parents' groups in their respective regions. They are both engaged with local and national debates concerning parental participation and integration. Both made contributions to the ISEC international conference held in Cardiff in 1990.

The opportunity to discuss the content of this article with them was invaluable as it helped to alleviate some of the difficulties inherent in European intercultural comparison. The obvious linguistic barriers to communication serve to amplify the underlying conceptual differences as expressed in terminology and assumptions governing specific practices. In that the author has worked in collaboration with the interviewees for almost five years it has been possible to identify some of the sources of confusion and interference in communication. The process of tuning in to cultural differences and respectively attempting to explicate that which is tacit in one's own cultural practices and to comprehend the subtleties of those of others is complex. Above all it requires a setting in which those who are attempting to communicate feel able to abandon the temptation to promote national identities at the expense of accuracy. Large conferences sometimes provide venues for acts of national rhetoric, which at times bear little relation to reality. The experience of long-term collaboration has allowed for the exchange of experience of some of the reality.

THE EUROPEAN INTEGRATION NETWORK (EIN)

The European Integration Network comprises groups of representatives who work in specific regions of each member state. They include:

1 teachers from schools and school psychologists;
2 social service and health workers;
3 municipal and school administrators;
4 parents' organisations;
5 professional organisations;
6 elected members of local administrations.

The exchange programme has involved two or three meetings a year held in the participating countries in rotation. It has consisted of visits, observations and topic-focused seminars/public symposia which were used to raise awareness of the wider political and ideological issues involved in the practice of integration in each area. Topics such as 'The impact of decentralisation of financial control on integration into the school and community' and 'Multidisciplinary decision-making processes in integration' are recent examples. These experiences fostered an increasing interest in the quality of life of children and young people with SEN. This was linked to a growing concern for the development of community-orientated professional work with a particular interest in self-help groups and their participation in decision-making.

FAMILIES OR COMMUNITIES?

As the project has grown it has become a strong source of support for local integration policy development. It has provided a vehicle for the local interpretation of European pro-integration recommendations. However, these interpretations vary significantly from group to group. Hence, when issues of support strategies were debated at a recent seminar in Denmark the Spanish and Italian groups argued that the most important and stable element in a child's life was the family; thus all public policy should aim to support the family in the process of integration into society. By contrast, the Danish position was that the community was responsible for all its members and that community-based support, albeit alongside family support, was in the disabled person's long-term best interest. Indeed, one administrator stated that a concern held by colleagues was that some parents felt that as the community demanded high levels in taxation it was also accepting high levels of responsibility. It is through the analysis and debate of this and other such contrasts that EIN hopes to develop a broad perspective on the development of the breadth of European principles and practices.

DEFINITIONS

Integration in Germany is understood in terms of measures designed to improve social and occupational interaction in adult life. This is most frequently found in special schools which see themselves as preparing children for integration into adult community life. In Denmark pupils are defined in terms of the special consideration and/or support that they need to maintain a position as near as possible to the mainstream educational experience of their peers. Whilst these two definitions do not demand necessary differences in practice they have resulted in very different patterns of provision. The German system has a long tradition of specialist education which has developed alongside a highly differentiated structure of mainstream schools. Figure 11.1 provides a diagram of the basic structure of the German education system as of 1990. This may be contrasted with the more comprehensive structure of the Danish system shown in Figure 11.2. Comparison of Figures 11.1 and 11.2 at secondary level reveals a difference between the one type of school (*Folkeskole*) in Denmark and the four types of mainstream school in Germany (*Hauptschule, Realschule, Gymnasium* and *Gesamtschule*). This is paralleled by the highly-differentiated structure of special categories of children and schools in Germany.

DENMARK

In Denmark co-operation between the home and the school is seen to be of fundamental importance. Parents have considerable powers with respect to their children's schooling. For example, parents have the right to psychological and educational advice as to their child's needs but it is they who choose whether they want their child to go to a *Folkeskole* or a special school. Parents have a majority on school governing bodies and have extensive rights to visit classrooms.

As long ago as 1959 Denmark pioneered the principle of 'normalisation', incorporating it into a Federal Act regulating residential services (Scheerenberger 1987). The distinctive and crucial aspect of the evolution of the

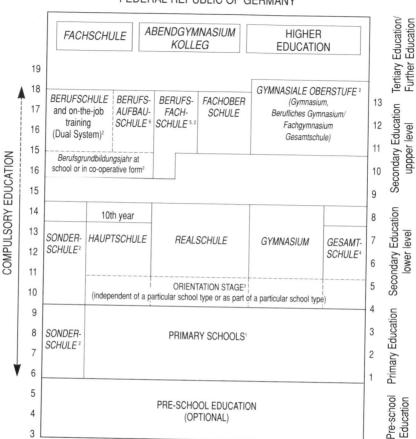

FEDERAL REPUBLIC OF GERMANY

Figure 11.1 Basic structure of the Federal Republic of Germany's education system in September 1990

Within this common framework, special features exist in the individual *Länder* of the Federal Republic. The situation in the 5 *Länder* on the territory of the former German Democratic Republic that joined the Federal Republic on 3 October 1990 is not taken into account here owing to the political developments and the ongoing reforms in education.

1 In some *Länder*, special types of transition from pre-school education to primary school exist (pre-school classes, school kindergarten). In Berlin the primary school comprises 6 years: there is no separate orientation stage.

[box] = not described in the text

- - - - - - - = division in the level/type of education

— · — · — · — = alternative beginning or end of level/type of education

2 Different forms of special education – general and vocational – depending on the disability in question.

3 The orientation stage exists in all *Länder* with the exception of Bavaria where it is tested in several pilot experiments and Berlin where years 5 and 6 are part of the primary school.

4 In some *Länder* the comprehensive school is a regular type of school alongside *Hauptschule*, *Realschule* and *Gymnasium*. In the other *Länder* it is an optional or experimental type of school.

5 Full-time vocational schools differing with regard to entrance requirements, duration of courses and leaving certificates.

DENMARK

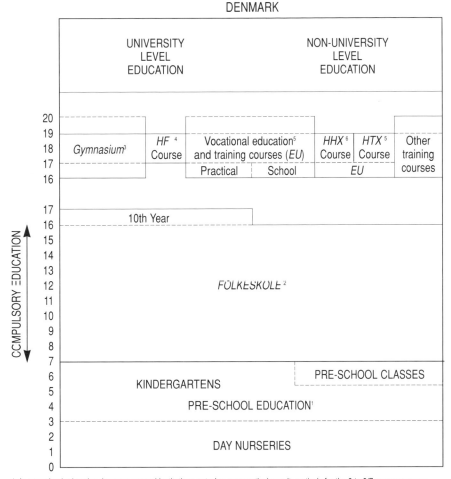

1 In pre-school education there are several institutions catering consecutively or alternatively for the 0 to 6/7 year age range.

2 The *Folkeskole* comprises an optional pre-school class, nine years of full-time compulsory education and a supplementary optional tenth year. It provides general education at primary and lower secondary levels; the Danish education system does not differentiate between primary and lower secondary education.

3 The *Gymnasium* provides a three-year course of general education at upper secondary level, after the ninth or tenth year of the *Folkeskole*, with the final examination qualifying for university entrance.

4 The course for the *HF* (higher preparatory examination) is a two-year general course, after the tenth year of the *Folkeskole* with the final examination qualifying for further and higher education.

5 The basic vocational education and training courses (*EU*) last between three and four years with approximately two-thirds of the time spent in a company. A typical course consists of a first 20-week school course or practical training in a company of similar length, followed by a second 20-week school course. After that the course alternates between practical training and school.

6 The courses for the *HHX* (higher commercial examination) and the *HTX* (higher technical examination) are three-year based courses comprising one year of vocational training (usually followed with the first-year pupils of basic vocational training) and two years of theoretical training.

☐ = not described in the text

--------- = division in one level/type of education

— — — — = alternative beginning or end of level/type of education

Figure 11.2 Basic structure of the Danish education system

Danish system has been the way in which parents have been centrally involved in the design and development of the SEN decision-making practices. A national association of parents had been established in 1951. In December 1953 the national association of parents sent a note to the Minister of Social Affairs, who was responsible for services for children and adults with severe learning difficulties, requesting the appointment of a committee to discuss the problems of these services.

The parents' association was the immediate and most powerful reason for the review of the Danish service at that time. In 1969 a parliamentary decision was made that the teaching of the 'handicapped'[2] was to be extended in such a way that the children should be taught in an ordinary school environment as far as possible. The Danish government set up a committee which, in 1971, recommended a cohesive structure of all special teaching provision within the primary and lower secondary school, covering all special educational facilities, including teaching in residential care institutions and special pedagogical assistance for children below compulsory school age.

The parental lobby was determined to bring a number of perspectives to the policy-formulation process. These included what they termed a 'lifetime perspective', arguing that respite care, counselling and support to parents before the child enters school is a prerequisite of avoiding segregation. They also introduced arguments about the elusive concept of 'quality of life' to the general political analysis of decision-making about provision for children and adults with special needs. This concept was applied to school as well as everyday contexts, one result being a parental voice in pedagogic issues. The school curriculum was examined from this perspective and recommendations were made by the parents' association about individualised teaching. The suggestion was made that 'teaching must be individualised and primarily set out from the prerequisites and needs of each child'.

Perhaps the single most significant aspect of the practices that arose from this style of consultation process was the placing of parental approval as the final level in decision-making processes. The principles of placement for 'handicapped' pupils have been restated as follows:

1 *Proximity*: The child should attend school as close to home as possible.
2 *As little intervention as possible*: The child should not be offered more support or special education than absolutely necessary.
3 *Integration*: Instruction of the handicapped child should take place in an ordinary and normal school if at all possible.
4 *Efficiency*: Measures must be taken to ensure that the child derives maximum benefit from the subjects taught at school and thereby develops its own ability and talents to as large an extent as possible.

5 *Motivation*:   It is essential that the special education established is in accordance with what the teachers involved and the parents think is most suitable for this given child.

(Hansen 1992)

Evaluation studies

In 1985, following a request from LEV (the Danish parents' association) to the Ministry of Education, the Royal Danish School of Educational Studies and the Pedagogical Research Institute were asked to evaluate the situation of children with severe learning difficulties (MR) in ordinary schools. The formal background was an amendment in 1980 shifting responsibility for the education of MR students from the Ministry of Social Affairs to the Ministry of Education. The concrete background was anxiety expressed by parents who felt that their MR children were being pressed too hard in ordinary classes.

The main purpose of the family-based aspect of this study was to explore the total 'ecology' of these students in home, school and leisure-time arrangements, the impact of the disability on the student and the family, the problems encountered by the family before school-age and after, the pre-requisites of coping, the support acquired and missed, the level of the child's social competence, the social relations, the co-operation and means of communication between home and school as experienced by parents.

The findings indicate that parents constitute the most important resource for the children as well as their only constant support. Parent counselling and education, respite care, and co-ordination of family support are often insufficient. Danish teachers need more supervision and in-service training as well as time for co-operating with parents and colleagues. The study points to the importance of working for quality of life for persons with MR, to the importance of focusing on strong points and acceptance in order to reassure MR students as they develop their identities. The lifetime perspective pervades the thinking and attitudes of the parents.

Parents and professionals

The establishment of the parents' association led to public debate which both criticised the existing system and demanded a reformed service. This, in turn, led to increased opposition among the majority of professionals. The debate was essentially one of questions of balance of power within decision-making processes. Thus the Danish situation is not devoid of conflict – rather the balance of power which creates the setting for the conflict is unfamiliar in many national contexts. Parents' organisations in Denmark continue to operate at a national level. The actions of local community parents' groups tend to be tuned to the needs of particular communities and schools rather than to the formation of national policy. The general perception is reported to be that of satisfaction with the national framework which has created a context which enables parents to have a more effective voice at local community level.

GERMANY

Germany has a well-organised system of educational, vocational and residential services designed to provide cradle-to-grave care for its citizens with disabilities. Almost all of these services are provided in separate, centralised settings. No more than 3.5 per cent of special school students ever transfer to general education and less than 5 per cent of sheltered workshop employees ever move into competitive employment. German schools continue to place a high priority on student homogeneity. Currently, there are ten separate types of special schools in the Federal Republic (Murray Seegert 1992).

Germany's government is highly decentralised. Each state has developed different regulations with regard to students with disabilities, although it would appear that there is a party-political accent to local policy. The SPD tend to favour integration more than the CDU and this appears to be reflected in the close mapping of the complexion of local control with integration policy. Because there is no federal law supporting integration, applications for mainstream placement have to be decided individually in some states. For example, Kniel (1987) examined motives and decisions of seventy-four German parents of handicapped children in choosing different pre-school settings. His results indicated that choice of an integrated or segregated pre-school is largely determined by family background and information-seeking behaviour and reflects specific family needs.

One German parents' group sees integration as compatible with a more general reform effort aimed at making schools less competitive. *Gemeinsam leben – Gemeinsam lernen: Eltern gegen Aussonderung* (Living Together – Learning Together: Parents Against Separation), the group that leads the initiative to integrate children with severe and multiple disabilities, has a significant number of members who are parents of non-disabled children (Zah 1988).

In Germany parents are encouraged to participate at local school level but not to organise at national level. Parents' groups feel they have to make a political and empirical case for influencing decisions. They have very little effect at national level. At school level parents have extensive rights to participation in their local schools. Thus the social organisation of parent participation must be seen in specific legal and cultural contexts.

An analysis of the different types of German secondary schools suggests that they differ in the way they allow parents to participate in their children's schooling. Oswald *et al.* (1988) discussed the kind, degree and timing of parents' management of their children's school careers which may reflect institutional characteristics of schooling. They examined the relationship between parental management and an institutional characteristic of schooling, the school charter. They considered the managerial actions of a sample of 238 parents with students in three types of West German secondary school with distinctly different charters: the *Gymnasium*, *Realschule* and *Gesamtschule*. The analysis indicates that parents' actions about their children's schooling vary, depending on the school's charter.

The central hypothesis was that school charters and the way schooling is organised around school charters will influence the degree and kind of parental management of adolescents' schooling. Parents of students in the two traditional types of secondary school tended to undertake formal contact with the school. The *Gymnasium* and *Realschule* parents attended parent–teacher association meetings, and the *Gymnasium* parents became parent–school representatives.

The articulation of family–school relations is influenced by the institutional organisation of schooling in a particular educational system. These institutional rules and arrangements set the framework for parental actions about schooling and help define the kind and degree of effective parental management. *Gemeinsam leben – Gemeinsam lernen: Eltern gegen Aussonderung* (Living Together – Learning Together: Parents Against Separation) operates at a national level to provide an exchange of information between the different federal *Länder* (local authorities), and to co-ordinate the activities and publicity work on subjects of overriding and topical importance. In this way it tries to change the large-scale institutional rules and arrangements which set the framework for possible parental actions in Germany. It sees itself as being dependent upon academic evaluation of model experimental integration schemes at the local level for empirical evidence to support its political / social policy case. In order to do this it seeks the active support of the teacher trade unions and university-based research.

For example, at local meetings, parents of children without SEN often raise the question of whether their children would be put at a disadvantage in an integrated school class. Evaluation reports of an integration experiment which suggested that children without SEN achieved at least as much, if not more, in an integrated class proved to be the most effective response to this kind of question.

In summary, the German experience is that of a state which has not incorporated parents into the early stages of consultation in the policy-formation process. As a consequence the activities and actions of local community groups are constrained and curtailed by virtue of the position that parental opinion has been allocated in the decision-making process about individual provision. It is in this context that a major aspect of the operation of parents' organisations has been geared towards the formation of a national lobby in order to promote the ideal of a national framework which allows for what is seen as a more equable distribution of power and participation in specific community issues.

SUBSIDIARITY AND POWER

On the basis of the review of parental activity in Denmark and Germany it is clear that the concept of subsidiarity is inextricably associated with that of power. It seems clear that many aspects of parental involvement within education are, understandably, reflections of self-interest rather than interest in some democratic ideal as manifested in parental representation. This is evidenced within the SEN lobby in two ways. First, it is symptomatic of many parents' groups and voluntary bodies that they represent the interests of particular groups or groupings of people with disabilities and/or associated difficulties. This is most obviously the case in the UK where even lobby activity in both Houses of Parliament is sectional rather than generic to the SEN case. Clearly the most powerful sections of the SEN lobby achieve most influence. Indeed, it is doubtful whether some students categorised as having SEN ever achieve formal representation. Second, in the context of devolved decision-making, whether or not it is referenced to the concept of subsidiarity, it seems that only the most powerful local 'voices' are heard in local community decision-making processes. Hence in Germany parents struggle for national safeguards and structures which allow them to act within their local settings. In Denmark where such central structures are in place, local activity can proceed in a protected and supported context.

It seems inevitable that the concept of subsidiarity will remain influential in social policy development over the coming years. The concept itself is in need of some development if potentially-disadvantaged groups within society are not to be further marginalised. Following the primary thrust of the notion of subsidiarity it is logical that parents should be central figures in the education of their children. If this is to be the case then structures for collaboration in decision-making are required for all sections of the parental community and issues of minority rights must receive attention at a central level. In short the 'rules of engagement' for local debates and negotiations need to be written. That is not a plea for a return to centralist dictat at a detailed level. Rather it is a suggestion that international 'spaces' require some structure if equity is to be an outcome. Cast in terms of the current political jargon of the free market this implies that there is a need for the protection of less powerful sectors if progress is to made. The move from a free market to a social market would be one step on the way to ensuring that children who experience difficulty in schooling do not become 'goods' which are 'surplus to requirements' and that their parents retain their consumer rights. One strategy may be for parents' organisations to form networks that extend beyond their immediate local circumstances in order to gain a more powerful voice.

NOTES

1 The term SEN is used here as it is the one which has achieved legal status in the UK.

Within the HELIOS programme of the European Commission, the World Health Organisation definition of 'handicap' is used as a reference point:

Social disadvantage for an individual resulting from a deficiency or a disability which limits or prevents the accomplishment of a role considered to be normal (related to age, sex, and sociocultural factors).

There are many issues of confusion and obfuscation with respect to terminology within the European Community. Despite their limitations terms which have attained official status will be used throughout.

2 'Handicapped student' is the official term used in the Danish educational system (Danish Ministry of Education 1989).

REFERENCES AND FURTHER READING

Akalin, O. (ed.) (1985), 'The special school system in the Federal Republic of Germany', *Bildung-und-Wissenschaft* 9–10.

Beattie, N. (1987), 'Parents as a new found land: reflections on formal parent participation in five polities', Paper presented at the Annual Meeting of the American Educational Research Association, 27–31 March, San Francisco, CA.

Bristow, S. (1988), 'Reporting to parents: the implementation of the 1986 Education (No. 2) Act', *Education Today* 38 (1).

Commission of the European Communities (1992), *Report of the Commission on the Progress with Regard to the Implementation of the Policy of School Integration in the Member States (1988–1991)*, Brussels.

Danish Ministry of Education (1989), *Handicapped Students in the Danish Educational System*, Ministry of Education, March, Copenhagen.

Hansen, O. (1992), *Special Education in Denmark: Statements, Notes and Figures*, Mimeo.

Kniel, A. (1987), 'Choosing a preschool for handicapped children – factors in parents' decision-making', *International Journal of Rehabilitation Research* 10 (2), pp. 210–14.

Murray Seegert, C. (1992), 'Integration in Germany: mainstreaming or swimming uphill', *Remedial and Special Education* 13 (1), pp. 34–43.

Oswald, H., Baker, D.P. and Stevenson, D.L. (1988), 'School charter and parental management in West Germany', *Sociology of Education*, 61 (October), pp. 255–65.

Scheerenberger, R.C. (1987), *A History of Mental Retardation: A Quarter Century of Progress*, Brookes, Baltimore, MD.

Sonnenschein, P. (1984), 'Parents and professionals: an uneasy relationship', in M.I. Henninger and E.M. Nesselroad (eds) *Working with Parents of Handicapped Children: A Book of Readings for School Personnel*, University Press of America, Lanham, MD, pp. 129–39.

Zah, K. (ed.) (1988), *Treffen der Bundesarbeits-Gemeinschaft Eltern gegen Aussonderung von kindern mit Behinderugen*. Arbeitsgemeinschaft Integration Reutlingen, Reutlingen, pp. 19–26.

Chapter 12

Inclusive education in Spain and Greece

Christine O'Hanlon

Throughout the European Union there is a rhetoric of support for the inclusion in mainstream education of children and young people with disabilities and those who experience difficulties in learning. However, cultural and economic differences between countries have led to marked variations in policy and practice. Christine O'Hanlon argues that we have not paid sufficient attention to developments in southern Europe, and her chapter is a comparative discussion of developments in Spain and Greece. Spanish policy has been reconstructed, since the death of Franco, on the principle of equality of opportunity and there is a strong political will to implement plans for inclusive education. Greece, on the other hand, has not passed legislation to back up its rhetorical support for inclusion. There are enormous economic and geographical barriers to overcome, as well as the persistence of a defect model of disability and difficulties in learning.

INTRODUCTION

Across Europe, there is an imperative, driven by the desire for political correctness, to back the rhetoric of inclusive education. Countries have defined their school policies in terms of laws which aim to include those children and young people whom the education systems of particular countries can support without undue financial strain. Innovatory practices that I have seen in Germany and the Netherlands, for example, are well planned and unsparingly resourced and there is first-rate provision for *all* the pupils.

Countries in southern Europe, which have come into the European Union later than the founding countries in the north, are generally less wealthy but they are attempting to keep pace with the policies and practices of their new economic partners. In Spain, Andalusia, Catalonia and the Basque region, there are successful innovatory programmes working within limited budgets. However, in contrast to the attention paid to northern Europe, little interest has been shown by educators in the UK in developments in the south.

There are barriers to the communication of educational ideas and practices between the countries of northern and southern Europe, particularly where English is not the effective second language, and this leads to an ignorance of issues facing other countries which may be relevant to those facing our own. There is so much to learn from the sharing of our successes and failures in the practice of inclusive education in the wider context of Europe.

In this article I want to illustrate through personal experience and the analysis of other sources of information the extent of inclusive practices in Greece and Spain. 'Inclusive' in this context is used to refer to the deliberate attempts by educationalists in different countries to increase the participation of all students in mainstream schools. Relevant questions include: how full a picture of the situation in southern Europe do we have in the UK? What can we learn from government statistics? Are children in rural areas properly served? Who has a say in policy-making in each country? Is the climate which supports inclusive education mainly a financial one?

The administrative strucutures of Spain and Greece

Greece is situated in isolation from other EC countries in the south-east of Europe. Greece shares its borders with Albania, Macedonia, Bulgaria and Turkey, and has a population of approximately 10.25 million. The educational system is centralised and most of the administration, organisation, curricula and teacher employment is directly controlled by the Ministry of Education. The education system is divided into three levels:

1 Primary education includes pre-school education from 3.5 to 5.5 years and the primary or elementary school for children aged 5.5 to 11.5 years.
2 Secondary education includes the *Gymnasium* for pupils aged 11.5 to 14.5 years, and the *Lycea* for pupils aged 14.5 to 17.5 years.
3 Higher education is provided by technical institutions and universities.

Education is compulsory between the ages of 5.5 years and 14.5 years. National education is free and includes free provision of books irrespective of the social or financial status of the student.

Special schools, since the early 1970s, have been run by the Ministry of Education and now number approximately 185 (between fifteen and twenty are privately run). There are also about 500 special classes and programmes in ordinary schools. In addition there are about 3,000 children under the care of the Ministry of Health and Social Affairs. There are also large numbers of children, unaccounted for in official figures, and in private schools.

Spain is situated in the south-west of Europe and has a population of about 39 million people. Spain shares its borders with Portugal and France.

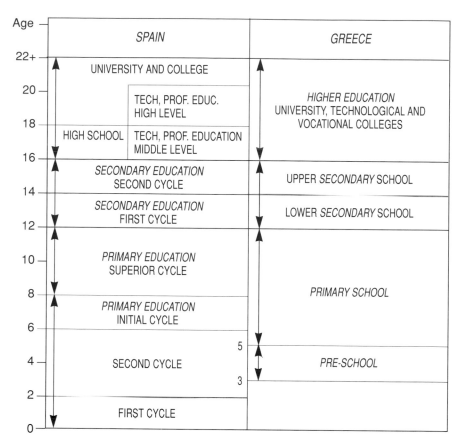

Figure 12.1 The structure of education in Spain and Greece

The education system is centrally governed. The state regulates both investment in education and the overall structure of the system. About 75 per cent of schools in Spain are state controlled, 10 per cent are run by the church and 15 per cent are privately run.

Compulsory education in Spain lasts for ten years from 6 to 16 years. There are three phases of education:

1 The primary stage from 6 to 12 years.
2 The secondary stage from 12 to 16 years.
3 The higher level of technical and professional education from 16 to 18+ years.

Spain has a high dependence on private schooling particularly in pre-school and in special education. In pre-school education, out of the total of 843 schools, 564 are privately owned and run. In special education, out of the total of 215 schools 130 are privately owned and run (Ministry of Education and Science 1989).

Similarities and differences between Spain and Greece

Spain and Greece are both southern European countries and therefore they have a number of features in common. They both have a determination to succeed with a policy of inclusive education and they both have a population in rural areas which is difficult to monitor and provide for. There is a high proportion of the population in the Athens area of Greece and in the big cities, e.g., Barcelona and Madrid, in Spain. The result of this is that most experimental inclusion projects and programmes are centred in the cities and the rural areas are often neglected.

In many other respects there are wide differences between the two countries in their progress in developing inclusive education. Neither Spain nor Greece would be considered a rich country in EC terms. They both have over 40 per cent of the under-25s unemployed, although this may need to be qualified by the fact that 74 per cent of the same population in Spain are in full-time education, whereas there are 66 per cent in full-time education in Greece (CEC 1991). There are also similarities in the creation and devolution of government policy in a European context. Both Spain and Greece are governed centrally, from Madrid and Athens respectively. Spain is made up of seventeen autonomous communities which are self-governing from the educational point of view. Greece is divided into thirteen regions (peripheries) and the head of the education affairs department is appointed by the government. However, the administration of local affairs is conducted by local councils, the municipalities and communities, headed by the mayor and the president of the community, who are elected every four years. In Spain the autonomies are directed by national legislation which is administered within the autonomies by education departments. In eleven of the autonomies education is administered directly by the Ministry of Education, while the management of the schools is undertaken by the education department of the autonomy. The Ministry of Education and Science (MEC) in Madrid co-ordinates the administration of the education policies in both private and public schools throughout the autonomies. In relation to practices in education there are great differences, not only between one community and another, but also within the same community within Spain.

SPAIN: DEVELOPING INCLUSIVE POLICIES AND PRACTICES

Spain like most countries in Europe has responded to the inescapable imperative of integration or the inclusion of pupils with special needs in mainstream education, because of the collective desire to develop equal-opportunity policies for all its citizens. This new imperative has been addressed in the autonomies as a result of two significant laws. The first was the 1982 law which recommended the social integration of young people with 'handicaps'. The second and most influential law was the Real Decree 334/1985 on special education. As a result of this law many children were transferred from special to mainstream schools all over the country and since then more funds and personnel have been redirected from the special to the ordinary educational sector. Therefore the costs of the transfer were balanced by the redeployment of resources. There is, however, a problem in finding out the full extent of the shift towards inclusion because of the way that national statistics are recorded. There is therefore a problem too in finding out exactly how many children are defined within the country as having 'special educational needs' because records are related to the type of school attended rather than the needs of individual pupils. Pupils are recorded according to the type of school they attend; thus we can define pupils in particular or special schools as a percentage of the total school-going population. Only 1.2 per cent of the total population attending educational establishments including higher education are designated within the special school sector (O'Hanlon 1993). This is a low percentage but reflects similar practice elsewhere in Europe.

However, what is hidden from us in official government figures is the number of pupils with special needs who may be in mainstream or ordinary schools. For the researcher it is not simply a matter of counting the numbers of pupils in attendance at certain schools, as is the case with finding out the number of students with special needs, i.e., if all students with special needs attend special schools we can see and compare national statistics. The manner of recording the figures in European countries makes the investigation of inclusion in mainstream education very difficult. We need to specify individual student's differentiation, to make the point that inclusion in mainstream schools is taking place. We need to define categories of children linked to the differential nature of the pupil's needs, in order to show that this or that category or child is now included in mainstream education, otherwise it cannot be proved that there is more or less inclusion taking place. Where categorisation is used, it is simply a matter of counting the numbers of children within certain clearly-defined conditions to come up with a table like Table 12.1.

This is the kind of information that is traditionally recorded in most countries in Europe, and which can be used as comparative data.

It can be clearly seen from Table 12.1 that 62 per cent of pupils in special education are considered to have 'mental handicaps' while 7 per cent of pupils are considered to have 'emotional difficulties'. When these children are included in ordinary schools their categorisation goes too, because in inclusion the factors that made the pupils suitable for special education are now the factors that are being minimised to ensure the successful acceptance

Table 12.1 Pupils in early education centres according to the type of handicap

Mental		Vision		Hearing		Motor		Autistic		Emotional		Others	
No.	*(%)*	*No.*	*(%)*	*No.*	*(%)*	*No.*	*(%)*	*No.*	*(%)*	*No.*	*(%)*	*No.*	*(%)*
52,973	(62)	1,300	(1.5)	5,230	(6.1)	5,113	(6.0)	1,716	(2.0)	5,967	(7.0)	13,140	(15)

Source: O'Hanlon 1993

of these pupils in mainstream schools. There are a number of issues related to the new move towards inclusive education which make it difficult to judge the extent of its use in both Spain and Greece. Another factor which is difficult to ascertain is the amount of private schooling. There are a substantial number of private schools in both countries and they are partly under the control of the education authorities. There may also be a number of children who are hidden or are not accounted for in official documentation. Therefore it is difficult to make comparisons from country to country based on the official documentation produced, particularly in the countries we are examining.

Although Spain has a centrally-controlled educational system there are a number of independent autonomous communities in Spain which need to be examined more closely to understand their practices and policy in relation to pupils with special educational needs in recent years.

The Basque area of Spain, which is an autonomous community, responded to the national 1985 legislation by setting up a committee to produce guidelines in relation to pupils with special educational needs, to be followed up by the Department of Education. As early as 1982 the Basque Country designed a Special Education Plan which proposed radical changes in the philosophy and structure of the special education services existing at that time. The plan began with the view that the ordinary school was the main reference point and proceeded to design a structure for the transformation of the ordinary school system. As a result of the committee's deliberations there have been a number of significant changes to schools in the Basque region:

1 Many special classes have been set up in primary schools to encourage social/educational inclusion in schools.
2 Regional special co-ordination centres have been established to help to organise special support services.
3 A network of multidisciplinary teams has been established to disseminate the support work.
4 Resource centres for blind and visually-impaired children have been set up to support integration into mainstream schools.
5 Specific teacher training, initial training and continuing education

programmes have been carried out for the members of the multi-disciplinary teams.

6 Class sizes have been reduced in schools with numbers of special needs pupils.

7 Support staff, such as classroom assistants and speech therapists, have been increasingly provided in ordinary schools.

8 Different financing arrangements have been made for units specially designed for pupils with special educational needs.

9 School enrolment guidelines have been prepared for parents to give the necessary information and advice about available school alternatives to provide a basis for more inclusive education.

(Basque Government 1989)

In spite of the progress made, the Basque Committee considered that there was much more which needed to be addressed in relation to further improvement in the situation. They provided the following criticisms among their comments:

- Information should be provided to improve the sensitivity and attitudes in schools and in the community to pupils with special educational needs.
- A follow-up system is needed to ensure the implementation of the plan.
- Present resources are insufficient to deal with the wide range of needs which have arisen.
- Architectural barriers will take time to amend, but will need to be removed.
- Administrative procedures in relation to grants and subsidies need to become more flexible.
- The future of special schools is uncertain. In special schools numbers are decreasing and the pupils' needs in those schools are becoming more severe.
- The resources for inclusive education have not always served the best interests of the pupils they are intended for, e.g., pupils have been wrongly segregated from ordinary to special classes in some schools.
- Public agencies and institutions have not been co-ordinating their facilities through a coherent community policy.
- New users of the services provided have not been sure about how to use them, so that they have not been used in the most profitable manner to date.

Notwithstanding these initial problems in the implementation of the plan, the Basque Committee then proceeded to take action by contacting the various institutions, groups and people directly concerned to present different opinions and to present joint recommendations for improvement. Contributions were sought from the Department of Education, government departments, the local authorities, parents' associations, voluntary associations, educational research groups and universities. The committee also consulted the MEC in Madrid, other autonomous communities, and authorities and institutions in other European countries. During the course of a year a report was drawn up for the department to study, with details of resource implications, their estimated cost and a prospective calendar. The committee produced the report entitled 'Improvements to be made in the education system for students with special educational needs', along with guidelines for putting the improvements into practice. Included in the report are themes related to the reforms proposed by the Spanish Education Reform Bill (1987) which address the quality issues within the curricula through the integration and inclusion of special needs pupils. The four themes are:

- Initial teacher-training programmes and continued professional development.
- Innovative curricula, new methods and ways of teaching in the comprehensive school.
- The development of support systems through educational teams for schools.
- A continuous process of guidance and counselling for pupils, teachers, schools and families to meet the particular needs of each student in increasing and improving their personal and social self-sufficiency.

The Basque Committee realised the importance of integrating the principles of inclusive education into the recent reforms of the general education system in Spain, which included the increase of the school-leaving age from 14 to 16 years, and the reorganisation of secondary and vocational education. Their guidelines were designed to complement the curriculum reforms.

What we are illustrating in this example is the consultative process that the Basque government went through to ensure a general consensus before putting forward more firm proposals for supporting inclusive education.

In Andalusia and in Catalonia similar initiatives have been taken to accelerate inclusive education. As a consequence of circular no. 3 in May 1985, the provincial department of Education and Science in Malaga formed a working group for school integration in Andalusia (Delegacion Provincial de Educacion y Ciencia 1987). The group was made up of professionals, representatives of voluntary associations, and provincial delegates. The functions of the group were to construct an integration plan for the province of Malaga and to elaborate the criteria to put the plan into action. The working group in time developed into a provincial commission for integration in special education, to co-ordinate the activities of schools participating in the integration plan, to develop plans for its expansion and to co-ordinate and disseminate the experiences of integration that resulted from the plan. What followed was an elaborate and detailed planned initiative to bring about inclusion of pupils with special educational needs through two provincial orders. The first was the Order of 25 March 1986 for integration in 1986/87, and the second was of 27 April 1987 for the establishment of funds and resources in 1987/88. Both of the above initiatives now have been implemented and the results are anticipated imminently. Again in Andalusia there was a consultative process which involved parents and all interested professionals in the plan to proceed with new and innovatory practices in relation to inclusive education.

However, in Catalonia the consultative process has been more extensive and involves the evaluation of the initiatives previously undertaken. There has been a published evaluation of the ten years of the Law of Social Integration of Special Needs, carried out by the Departament de Benestar Social of the Generalitat de Catalonia. The report examines the present results of the 1982 law and its implications for the future. It reminds us that the national law in Spain called for the *normalisation* of services, the *sectorisation* of units in geographical areas and the *individualisation* of the teaching adjusted to the characteristics of individual pupils. It examines the need to specify exactly the professional costs of inclusive education and evaluates the contribution of special schools, their teachers, psychopedagogic assessment teams, special resource centres and educational programmes. Two clear conclusions to emerge are that:

1   The proportion of pupils with special needs receiving education in ordinary schools has increased during the last ten years from 1982 to 1992. Effectively in all courses in 1981/1982, the number of pupils taught in special schools was 7,935, or 0.71 per cent of all school children, while the number of pupils with special educational needs in ordinary schools was 15,429, or 1.39 per cent of school children. In comparison, in 1991/1992 the number of pupils in special schools was 4,893, or 0.55 per cent of school children, while the number of pupils with special educational needs in ordinary schools was 12,940, or 1.45 per cent of school children between the ages of 6 and 16 years. There has been a decrease of 0.16 per cent in special school pupils and an increase of 0.06 per cent in the special needs population of the ordinary schools.

2   There has been a considerable increase in the professionals needed to provide services to schools. There has also been an increase in the number of special teachers needed to teach in ordinary primary schools. In 1981/82 there were only fifteen professionals in the assessment and psychopedagogical teams, whereas in 1991/92 there are now 453 professionals – a massive increase of 30 times the original number! The special teachers in ordinary schools increased from 550 in 1981/82 to 1,304 in 1991/92 – an increase of between two and three times the original establishment.

(Corretja *et al.* 1992)

The evidence also points to the need to increase training facilities for teachers and professionals in the support of pupils with special educational needs and for the possibility of co-ordinated professional training.

From the evidence above we can be assured that in the Spanish educational context time and effort are being put into the implementation of provision for inclusive education, which has increased substantially in recent years. There is a plan for further review in the planned evaluation and follow-up. There is open debate on the subject at all levels, which includes parental representation, and there are plans for improving educational practice based upon rigorous and critical planned research and evaluation.

In the last ten years Spain has made remarkable progress in espousing the inclusive rhetoric in action. I have been in schools where inclusive education was operating successfully with the enthusiastic support of everyone in the school. Parents, teachers, assistants – everyone concerned was happy and positive about the inclusion of students with special needs and was determined to make a success of the situation with as little fuss as possible. Schools were proud of their inclusive stance and felt it was only a matter of time before the procedures for total inclusion would take place throughout the whole country. The schools involved in inclusion programmes did, however, give the impression of being committed pioneers in a new movement! I have been given the unlimited time of the Minister of Education in Catalonia and his staff in explaining the efforts being made in the region on behalf of children with special educational needs. I have consulted with psychopedagogical teams and have been in every form of school or centre which is involved with the development of greater inclusion in education. The overall impression made on me through these experiences is that the Spanish people are proud to share their efforts on behalf of their students in an effort to learn what they can in their quest for more equal educational practices. They show a generosity of spirit I have never encountered in any other country in Europe.

GREECE: OVERCOMING A RHETORIC–REALITY GAP

The official rhetoric in Greece, as in Spain, is that the Ministry of National Education through the Directorate of Special Education is in full support of integration or inclusive education. In the booklet published by the Ministry of National Education and Religion in Athens (Nicodemos 1992), it is clearly stated that 'The Ministry's educational policy and philosophy concerning the education of children and youth with special needs *is clearly integration oriented*, not only in theory but also in practice.'

There is, however, no enabling legislation to support the views expressed. Greece has had a different history from Spain and is one of the most recent countries to join the EC. Greece acts as a bridge between East and West which is today openly building its hopes upon the generosity of the

EC. Greece has been struggling to emerge in the last two decades from a largely agrarian society to a more industrialised one, but it cannot easily overcome the fact that it has the lowest income per head in the Community, the lowest productivity, the highest inflation and the biggest external debt (*The Economist* 1993). Their record in education, and in special education in particular, is something to be obscured from critical eyes. Spain is physically and economically a much larger and stronger country than Greece. The population of Spain is more than three times greater than that of Greece. Greece also has a peculiarity in its extensive coastline and hundreds of islands which are spread in the Aegean and Ionian seas. This physical geography gives rise to particular problems in the care and education of children with special educational needs. Therefore children in rural areas pose problems in being included in the recording of figures and in the targeting of much-needed resources in education. In Greece it is difficult to ascertain the number of children receiving special education and therefore even more difficult to estimate the numbers of pupils with special educational needs in ordinary schools. The ministry documentation states:

> We have no specific statistics concerning the number of children with special educational needs and learning difficulties but we accept the international 10 per cent of the population being handicapped, and consequently we consider there are 180,000 children of school age with special educational needs.

> (Nicodemos 1992)

Therefore it is even more difficult from an outside perspective to ascertain the extent of the needs, and to assess the government's success in meeting the needs because they are hidden.

The same document affirms that the needs of the education system are still numerous and great and the overall impression of the education of children with special needs is that the situation is not quite, but almost, in hand and efforts are being made against a tide of unsympathetic opinion within the country which is struggling to keep up a positive image, in view of the new wider European audience.

In Greece in 1990/91 the total number of children involved in special education programmes organised through the Ministry of Education was about 12,500, while the teaching personnel were about 1,200 at primary and secondary level. Even allowing for the fact that there were another 200 support staff for the pupils, the ratio of pupils to professionals was approximately 90:1. There were also approximately 3,500 pupils receiving special help from units run by the Ministry of Health and Social Security. Most of the special educational provision is in Athens and there is a genuine difficulty in meeting the needs of the rural population. Bardis (1993) states fourteen problems in managing integration in rural Greece which include:

- Social prejudice and ignorance in society.
- Teacher resistance to teaching pupils with special educational needs.
- Permanent pupil placements in special education because there is no periodic review of pupils.
- Inadequate numbers of school advisors.
- Inadequate numbers of teachers for pupils with special educational needs.
- Few services for pupils in the rural areas.
- Parents' resistance to special help because of the stigma.
- The arbitrary nature of the diagnosis of special educational need.
- Lack of support services for special school leavers in rural areas.

He emphasises, through many specific examples, the general lack of educational support facilities for children with special educational needs in rural areas. In most Greek villages there are no special education units of any kind. In the greater urban environs of Athens there are 150 special education units and only 300 others in cities and small towns throughout the rest of Greece.

The Ministry of Education (Nicodemos 1992) claims that, in the spirit of integration, the majority of children with special educational needs attend ordinary schools. These children are involved in special programmes either individually or in small homogeneous groups, according to their needs and difficulties, usually for approximately one hour per day. Special programmes are extended to special schools, homes or children's hospitals, if there is an obvious need. The identification of special learning difficulties is undertaken by teachers in co-operation with parents. When the 'handicap' is more prominent or severe, the assessment of need is undertaken by the medico-pedagogical service. This name 'medicopedagogical' itself indicates the assessment priorities which are in operation, i.e., the disciplines of medicine and teaching. Psychology has long held a very marginal position in the Greek education system (Demetrios 1990). There is no academic or professional training for educational psychologists in Greece, so Greek psychologists come from a variety of psychological backgrounds. The aversion to the discipline of educational psychology arises from its primary association with psychopathology in childhood. Parents and teachers of children with special educational needs therefore wish to avoid this association which is linked to stigma.

The Greek education system is in a process of change, transforming itself into a more responsive system in the European and international context. Many of the Greek schools, particularly the special schools, are private. The quality of educational response to the child is largely dependent upon the opportunities provided by the family's financial and geographical situation. This comment can be made to a lesser degree of educational opportunities in Spain and in some other parts of Europe, like the UK. However, there is a number of other significant differences between Spain and Greece.

The word 'integration' is used in a very positive way by the Greek authorities. On close examination it appears to be more a form of mainstream inclusion with few resources or support services.

There are a number of children who receive no help because the quality of the help does not warrant the child's removal to a 'school' or unit, and also because in some rural areas transport and services are totally absent. These children spend most of their time at home.

The political and collective will to make a real success of inclusion is not apparent in Greece, nor is there the atmosphere of total acceptance of children with special needs or confidence in the value of their contribution to the educational community. Unlike the Spanish authorities, the Greek Ministry of Education looks to the old Soviet Russian model of functional intervention for 'handicapped' children and for the development of school and social integration.

The Ministry of Education in Athens acknowledges the long journey that needs to be taken to achieve the status of adequate provision for children with special educational needs. The following recommendations are seen as essential in any future direction and as a way out of the present insecurity:

- A radical revision of the current special education legislation.
- A research study to indicate the need for the revision.
- An increase in the special educational services and, in particular, help for school-leavers.
- An emphasis on curricular needs of pupils with special educational needs.
- The expansion of special educational units to include new technology, school counsellors, psychologists, speech therapists, occupational therapists, special teachers and educators.
- The development and expansion of training and education of special teachers and support staff.

Government funding for the above recommendations is essential in order to make a substantial difference and to ensure the establishment of an organisation and support system country-wide to meet the needs of all children, particularly those in more remote areas. There is also the need for clear legal imperatives to underpin the move towards inclusive education.

I have also consulted with the minister responsible for special education in Greece and have visited many schools and educational centres. The schools that have been offered to me as examples of good practice, I have subsequently found, have been predominantly privately-run establishments. The teachers I consulted were critical about the education system and about the lack of political effort on behalf of students with special needs generally, and in particular in the move towards inclusive education. The educationalists in Greece who wish to make progress in this area are being restrained by an unsympathetic public and a negative environment for increasing the participation of all students, with support, in mainstream schools. It appears at present to be a situation where increased inclusion is claimed as increased but unsupported schooling, especially in the more remote rural areas.

CONCLUSION

I have argued, with the use of available evidence and personal experience of inclusive education in both Spain and Greece, that where the political will exists to implement the changes necessary to succeed in offering equal opportunity policy and practice in a national context, it can be achieved in spite of financial constraints. I have attempted to do this through the comparison of the Spanish and Greek situations which show marked similarities and contrasts in both their policy creation and in school practices. Both countries have economical problems, a large rural population, and a high number of students in private schools. They also exhibit different priorities in their focus on pupils with special needs. Spain concentrates considerable resources on the improvement of education for all its school population which openly espouses a committment to positive discrimination in favour of students disadvantaged in the former segregated school system. There is a large political will on the part of educationalists and the general public at large to make sure that inclusive education is given the best possible organisation and support. Inclusive education is important to the Spanish. It is flown as a banner of freedom in Europe as a symbol of equal opportunity, and needs little persuasive argument in its favour in educational circles. The Spanish sense of reclaimed freedom which exploded after the Franco regime, and the sense of purpose that it engenders in any moral or human cause for justice and equality gives the integrational/inclusive activities an added imperative. There is no doubt in my view that Spain will lead Europe in its example and energy in successfully including children in mainstream schools in the latter decades of this century and the beginning of the next. The only thing which may hinder it now is the economical situation in the country. However, in spite of the financial difficulties the progress and the collective will to succeed are steady and firm.

Another significant factor about Spain which sets it apart from the Greek situation is the fact that most of the policy direction and rhetoric is openly acknowledged to a US or a UK source. The Warnock Report and the Fish Report are repeatedly cited as important and leading documents in an international context. In Greece the educational examples from policy and practice are taken from the old Soviet education system and still show evidence of the themes of defectology in the child rather than the focus on the school and the social situation of the child to enable the child to overcome whatever disadvantages he/she may have accrued through the social and locational accidents of birth. In Greece, in spite of the inclusive rhetoric, there is generally a lack of public support at present for the necessary imagination and planning to create the conditions for widespread inclusion of *all* students in public education. The consultation process necessary to bring about democratic change in a national educational context takes time and planning, as has been shown through the procedures used in the autonomous communities in Spain. The Spanish progress has taken many years to achieve, yet they have learned the need to build in evaluation strategies to the ongoing practices of developing better inclusive education. This will ensure a base for future improvements.

REFERENCES

Basque Government (1989), *Comprehensive and Integrative Schooling*, Central Publications of the Basque Government, Salamanca.

Commission of the European Communities (CEC) (1991), *A Young People's Europe*, Official Publications of the European Communities. Luxembourg.

Corretja, M., Sloe, J. and Ruiz, R. (1992), *10 Anys de la Llei d'Integratio Social dels Minusvalids (LISMI) a Catalunyà: Present y Futur*, Generalitat de Catalunya, Department de Benestar Social, Barcelona.

Delegacion Provincial de Educacion y Ciencia (1987), *Puerta Nueva Anexo 1* (June), Malaga.

Demetrios, P. S. (1990), 'Forum: special education in Greece', *EASE*, 11(1), pp. 33–7.

Departament d'Ensenyament (1991), *La Reposta a les Necessitats Educatives Especials dels Alumnes a l'Ensenyament Infantil y Obligatori*, Generalitat de Catalunya, Barcelona.

The Economist (1993), *Greece: A Country of the Edge*, 22 May.

Estadistica de la Ensemanza en Espana 1986–87 (1989), Madrid Centro de publicationes de Ministerio de Educacion y Ciencia, Madrid.

Nicodemos, S. (1992), *Bulletin of Information in Special Education. School and Social Integration*, The Ministry of National Education, Athens.

O'Hanlon, C. (1993), *Special Education: Integration in Europe*, David Fulton, London.

Spanish Education Reform Bill (1987), Madrid Centro de publicationes de Ministerio de Educacion y Ciencia, Madrid.

Chapter 13

Teacher unions, special education and Europe: a study in international policy-making

Paul Bennett

Around 3 million teachers across Europe are members of an international teacher trade union. The world-wide Education International (EI) takes responsibility for Europe as a whole and particularly the countries in Central and Eastern Europe, while the European Trade Union Committee for Education (ETUCE) concentrates on relationships within the European Union. ETUCE working committees focus on higher education, equality of opportunity and teacher education. The discussion of issues relating to special educational provision are seen as an extension of equality of opportunity. One example is concern with the relative professional status and conditions of service of teachers of students identified as having special educational needs. Another is the unequal attention paid to provision for students with different kinds of perceived learning requirements. The UK government is often out of line with other European countries, for example, on its attitude towards trade unions. Using the consolidated voice of an international union may be a way for national groups to exercise greater influence.

THE EUROPEAN CONTEXT

Teacher trade union structures in Europe and globally have undergone a major transformation in recent years, partly as a result of the political realignment which has taken place in the world since the late 1980s, and partly as a result of the continuing development of the European Community's role in respect of social and educational matters. In January 1993 the two major teachers' international organisations outside the old Eastern bloc, the World Confederation of Organisations of the Teaching Profession (WCOTP) and the International Federation of Free Teachers' Unions (IFFTU), merged to form the Education International (EI). The process of integration of these two large bodies is still continuing, and it is significant that the new world body will set up its new headquarters in Brussels, which is the focus of European decision-making and of European trade unionism.

This new organisation, with approaching 20 million members world-wide and 3 million members in Europe, represents a potential key player in education policy-making at world and European levels.

This global realignment has had significant spin-off effects in Europe, one of the regions of the new EI. Until the merger took place, the two internationals mentioned above and a third small international of Catholic teachers, the World Confederation of Teachers (WCT), all operated alongside each other in a mix of collaboration and competition. All three were represented on the European Trade Union Committee for Education (ETUCE), until the ETUCE constitution was changed in June 1993, to reflect the EI merger. Teachers' unions in Europe were represented on the ETUCE Executive Board via the three internationals. Since the adoption of the new constitution, the teachers' unions have been represented in their own right, by election at the annual Assembly, subject to safeguards for the position of the WCT.

The EI operates through its Executive and Congress at world level and through a pattern of regional and sectoral bodies. The inaugural meeting of the EI European Region took place in May 1993, and an important part of the discussions regarding the work of the EI in Europe was concerned with the distinctive roles of EI European Region and the ETUCE. A broad division of responsibility on the basis of the EI European Region being concerned with a broader political perspective across Europe as a whole, with a particular emphasis on assistance for Central and Eastern Europe, contrasting with the ETUCE's prime concern for relationships with the European Community, was agreed. This reflects the fact that the ETUCE, over a number of years, has built up a detailed expertise and range of policies concerning the European Community and its education and training activities, which EI is not immediately in a position to replicate. However, it is clear from the way in which the European Community itself is developing, that its policies will have a direct or indirect impact on the wider Europe, including the European Free Trade Association (EFTA) countries and, increasingly, Central and Eastern Europe. This change in the geopolitical pattern will undoubtedly need to be reflected in the interrelationship between EI European Region and the ETUCE, and is likely to lead in a few years to a realignment of the responsibilities.

THE ETUCE

The membership of the ETUCE in 1992 was 2.85 million: of these, the great majority were in the thirty-eight organisations in the constituent bodies which formed the EI. A small proportion are in the WCT or are in no world international teachers' body.

The new preponderance of a single international within the ETUCE, together with revised financial arrangements, is likely to lead to a number of those organisations outside the EI reviewing their position. Also the relationship between the EI and WCT at European level is likely to evolve.

The two main institutions of the ETUCE responsible for policy development are the annual Assembly and the Executive Board, elected by the Assembly. In addition, the officers of the ETUCE (the President, three Vice-Presidents, the Treasurer and the General Secretary) act on behalf of ETUCE between Executive Board meetings. Over the years the ETUCE has developed a good working relationship with the European Commission and in particular with the Task Force. Also, it is developing a range of dialogues and contacts with the Council of Ministers, the Council of Europe, the Organisation for Economic Co-operation and Development (OECD), the International Labour Organisation (ILO), and the United Nations Educational, Scientific and Cultural Organisation (UNESCO). It is also developing dialogues on specific issues with members of the European Parliament. When appropriate, it makes approaches to individual national governments, for example, in expressing its concern on the suspension of collective bargaining for schoolteachers in England and Wales, to the UK government. It is noteworthy that a number of the ETUCE's interventions in respect of individual countries have related in recent years to the action of UK governments. Also it must be said that the British Secretary of State for Education, when President of the Council of European Education Ministers in 1992, did not meet ETUCE representatives – a break in a long-established practice in which the current President of the Education Ministers does participate in such a meeting. Such a UK meeting was set up but cancelled at short notice. The ETUCE operates as an Industry Committee of the European Trade Union Confederation (ETUC) and works closely with that body's committees responsible for education and training issues. Also, of course, the ETUCE has a regular dialogue with its own members. Now that the ETUCE has appointed a full-time General Secretary for the first time, it is hoped that the dialogue with the members, including collation and dissemination of information on a regular basis through bulletins and newsletters, will greatly increase. The ETUCE has a major potential role to play in respect of the early warning of member organisations about European-level developments which affect them. The close relationship between the ETUCE and the EI, with its much larger resources, should help in the whole area of information, research and publicity.

THE ETUCE'S WORKING COMMITTEES: HIGHER EDUCATION, EQUAL OPPORTUNITIES AND TEACHER EDUCATION

The ETUCE has developed an effective method of working in certain key areas through Working Groups (two of which have now been incorporated into the structure as permanent Standing Committees). The two Standing

Committees are responsible for advising the Executive Board on higher education and equal opportunities issues and have greatly deepened the ETUCE's capacity for policy formulation and influence in these areas. They have both organised very successful colloquia which have had a significant impact both on the thinking of the European Community institutions (which have also participated in these events) and in advancing the thinking of the ETUCE and its affiliates. A third body, the Teacher Education Working Group, is currently working on a major policy document on teacher education in Europe, which it intends to complete in the first half of 1994 and to use widely within the European Community institutions, and with national governments and individual institutions.

THE HIGHER EDUCATION MEMORANDUM

Perhaps the most significant single initiative undertaken by the Higher Education Working Group is its contribution to the debate within the European Community on the European Commission Memorandum on Higher Education published in 1991. In advising the Executive Board, and in organising and participating in the two colloquia on the Memorandum, the Higher Education Working Group (as it then was) had a clear major input to the debate on the Memorandum and on its outcomes. This is clearly shown by the many references to the ETUCE contribution in the summary documents prepared within the Commission. The Higher Education Working Group was enabled to have a significant impact on the drafting of the Memorandum itself through its links with the Liaison Committee of European University Rectors and informal contacts with the Commission. Certainly some of the original proposed themes of the Memorandum as it was published were softened and other elements strengthened, in line with expressed ETUCE thinking. Building on the success of the ETUCE within the Memorandum debate, the ETUCE is now seeking to develop the dialogue, and to influence the thinking of relevant members of the European Parliament. This is obviously a potentially important dimension for any European lobbying organisation.

This example is particularly important, as this work was undertaken while the much larger debate on the Maastricht Treaty was continuing and was shaping European Community policy irrespective of the Maastricht process. The ETUCE lobbied strongly before the Maastricht debate began in order to seek an extension of the educational provisions of the Treaty of Rome (Article 126) in order properly to reflect the work which had been done over the period since 1956, which was widely regarded has having gone well beyond the formal meaning of the original Treaty of Rome provisions, with the help of sympathetic European court rulings. The outcome of this lobbying, and the much wider pressure which was applied to the European institutions and to national governments, was the significant increase in the scope of the education provisions contained in the Maastricht Treaty (Articles 126 and 127).

This only represents the tip of the iceberg of the issues dealt with within the Higher Education Working Group/Standing Committee. The range of other issues covered includes performance-related pay, quality, assessment, funding, equal opportunities, research and research staffs, mobility of higher education staffs, etc. It is to be hoped that the knock-on effects of the EI merger will make it easier over time for the ETUCE and its constituent bodies to work more readily on substantive issues, as the previous teacher union politics elements of international/European trade union meetings tend to be internalised or reduced in relative terms, and the discussion of substantive policies can increase in proportion.

EQUAL OPPORTUNITIES

The ETUCE Equal Opportunities Working Group has again done substantial work in a number of areas relating in particular to equal opportunities for women teachers. This work has included a survey of part-time teachers among member organisations of ETUCE, and a pamphlet on equal opportunities, published in 1992, which was funded by the European Commission, published in nine Community languages and widely disseminated throughout Europe. The UK's National Union of Teachers played a major part in the writing of this pamphlet. The pamphlet set out to make practical proposals for the development of equal opportunities in the education system, making the links between equal opportunities for young people and for their teachers, and highlighting possible actions not only for educational institutions and governments, but for teachers' unions too. For example, the pamphlet says:

> Since 'attitude' problems have remained so intractable it would be helpful for national governments and employers to get together to fund initiatives to support teachers through grants for in-service training on equal opportunity issues. Clearly unions have a major role to play here in negotiating with their employers to support these initiatives. They might also be asked to introduce schemes of advertising with positive images and encourage visits to schools by successful women who can provide role models for girls and influence the way they view their future careers.

In addition, the ETUCE Executive Board undertook to hold a major conference in Antwerp in February 1993 concerning intercultural relations, as part of its response to the growing tide of racism and xenophobia in Europe. This colloquium was widely regarded as a great success and the basis for further work on this important set of issues. The ETUCE is now actively considering the establishment of a new Standing Committee to look at transcultural and anti-racist issues.

The Teacher Education Working Group has been set up on an *ad hoc* basis to prepare several major documents and reports on teacher education, for consumption by the European Community institutions and national governments and by the ETUCE and its affiliates. It is hoped that this work will mark a significant development in the ETUCE's thinking on teacher education. The work will address vital issues like the status of teachers and of teacher educators, the compatibility of teacher education with other higher education qualifications, mobility of teachers, and the need for initial and in-service education to be developed as part of a package, including both academic and practical elements and induction and lifelong learning. The Teacher Education Working Group will clearly have important things to say regarding the standing of the teacher in society. Like other ETUCE work it is expected to attract European Community funding, which plays an important part in the on-going work and in the dissemination of the findings of such groups. The role of the European Commission in funding many of the bodies who are lobbyists to it and which may find themselves from time to time saying unpopular things to the European Commission is a complex and sensitive one. The ETUCE has always been conscious of the need to preserve its independence and capacity to represent teachers' views fully, taking the stance that, as the most representative organisation for teachers in the European Community, its opinions cannot be ignored.

SPECIAL EDUCATION ISSUES

The three Standing Committees or Working Groups of the ETUCE, and the Executive Board itself, place considerable emphasis on equal opportunity issues and the extension of opportunity and therefore do attempt regularly to reflect special needs interests. This is an area in which different national practices and even definitions of special need clearly need to be resolved or at least understood as a starting point in any European-wide dialogue. Also the themes of subsidiarity, diversity and respect for individual national cultures and norms can be highlighted very starkly by reference to an issue such as special educational provision.

While respecting subsidiarity and diversity, there is clearly scope for introducing concepts of best practice in the areas of equal opportunity and special educational need, and seeking to raise all countries' practice to these levels. It is clear that the status of teachers of children with special educational needs varies widely from one country to another, as well as the degree of involvement of teachers in diagnostic and counselling work associated with the education of these children. Also, the limited degree to which the European Community has recognised special educational needs requires more detailed pressure for a comprehensive policy. While the Community has developed policies on physical disability, it has been less effective on less immediately obvious aspects of learning difficulty. As well as an educational issue, this is a collective bargaining matter, since many teachers of students with special educational needs are relatively disadvantaged in terms of salaries or career structures, compared with teachers in mainstream education.

DEVELOPMENTS FOR THE FUTURE

Within the work described above, there is a wide range of elements which are in the process of evolution. Perhaps the largest of these is the whole question of the future size of the European Community and its relationship with the broader concept of Europe as a whole. The European Community itself seems certain to continue to expand, with a number of EFTA and other countries in the process of making application to join the European Community. The expansion of European Community programmes to cover EFTA and some other countries of Central and Eastern Europe, as well as the establishment of special programmes like TEMPUS to meet their needs, also greatly increases the scope and diversity of European Community activities. These expansionist trends, although in many ways welcome, will clearly have implications for the pace and direction of change within the European Community. Meanwhile the Community institutions will be grappling
with their increased powers over educational issues – while a major review of existing European Community programmes is being conducted and European politicians and bureaucrats are emphasising that the Community does not have the money to deliver major new programmes.

The process of reviewing existing programmes and seeking to codify them in the context of Maastricht is already well under way. This begs the question of how far relatively small European Community programmes can affect the lives of many millions of young people and adults within the European Community. It is important for the ETUCE and other European-orientated educational union structures to keep abreast of these developments and to maintain the progress already made in influencing the European Community institutions. As usual, it is seeking to hit a moving target.

The pressure within the European Community during and following the Maastricht debate centring on subsidiarity raises a number of questions, not only for the European Community and national governments, but for the European teachers' trade union movement. Some progress has been made in opening dialogues between European-level trade union bodies and national governments, although the British experience has been relatively unsuccessful in this respect. It seems certain that there will be an increased dialogue between national and Community level on issues like education and training. The ETUCE is working to increase its input to the European Trade Union Confederation (ETUC), of which it is the education industry committee. This provides a more extended opportunity to influence European Community policy-making through the Social Dialogue process. The application of Article 126 and Article 127, on education, vocational training and youth, will require detailed and sustained pressure by lobbyists such as the European Trade Union Movement, particularly in the light of subsidiarity. The recognition of the importance of education for mobility within the Community as a central objective, and the similar importance of training in European languages, should act as catalysts for progress even within a relatively restricted climate.

While subsidiarity is a central plank of the Maastricht Treaty, it is equally true that European institutions will themselves be seeking to maintain or extend their powers, and Maastricht gave some additional power to the European Parliament, which it is reasonable to expect that it will wish to use. If the European Parliament takes on more of the characteristics of a national parliament for Europe, it is likely that it will be the subject of greater and more continuous pressure from bodies like the trade unions. Certainly other institutions like the European legal structures, are already proving their worth, particularly in the context of the United Kingdom, whose government so regularly finds itself out of line with its neighbours or with a common agreed European Community position.

CONCLUSION

It is easy to forget how much progress has been made in a relatively short time in the development of common European policies and goals. The fact that the European level itself is changing so radically, and that European institutions will therefore require some breathing space to digest these geopolitical changes, should not obscure the underlying fact that a significant change has taken place in policies, practices and assumptions of governments, decision-makers, opinion-formers and citizens, regarding European solutions to social and economic questions. There are clearly wide-ranging differences which still exist between one country's practice and another's, and the UK Government's intransigence on many issues is a case in point. However, a sustained European-level pressure for a common approach and for the sharing of best practice, is likely to effect gradually decision-making processes at European, national and subnational levels. The teacher trade union movement in Europe must be part of this process.

Chapter 14

Special educational provision from a Czech Republic perspective

Marie Cerna

Special educational provision in the Czech Republic is characterised by an interdisciplinary approach which focuses on the early identification of 'defective development'. Educational settings are highly specialised and movement between special and mainstream schools is rare. Disabled students and those who experienced difficulties in learning have been largely invisible and teachers have had very little autonomy. Since the 'Revolution' of 1989 and the collapse of communism there has been a revival of what Marie Cerna describes as 'humanism', an approach which stresses individual rights and responsibility and which implies a radical overhaul of the education system. She discusses how far the gap can be closed between the structures and attitudes inherited from the Soviet past and the spirit of the new reforms.

INTRODUCTION

Special education in the Czech Republic has a rich tradition. Based on democratic principles, special education received significant attention, especially between the two World Wars, both from people within education, health and social services and from academics. Professionals from various fields, particularly medicine, education psychology and sociology, developed special educational theories derived from biological and philosophical bases. This interdisciplinary approach is the guiding principle in current special education theory and practice.

IDENTIFICATION AND CLASSIFICATION OF LEARNING DISABILITIES

Classification is based on the categorical approach. It covers the following categories:

- speech impairment;

- hearing impairment;
- visual impairment;
- physical handicap and health impairment;
- social maladjustment;
- mental handicap and learning disability;
- multiple handicaps.

Children requiring special care (the term used during the past forty years) are diagnosed and identified as early as possible by paediatricians, who observe and assist in assuring all children's current physical and mental development, look after their nutrition, and carry out all prophylactic measures. This includes handicapped infants, toddlers and pre-school-age children. Paediatricians seek out congenital defects, defects of genetic origin, chronic diseases and other handicapping conditions. There are additional health services, especially psychological and early rehabilitation intervention.

For attendance at school, mostly special schools, children are selected by pedagogical and psychological advisory centres that provide educational diagnoses, suggest suitable educational measures, and direct the special curricula. The centres are also expected to offer advisory and consultancy services to the children, parents and teachers.

Children recommended for special education are entered into a register by local/regional school authorities, who then have the responsibility for providing the necessary services. Placement in a special school is discussed with the parents, although their permission is not a prerequisite for admission. The situation is changing slowly towards more parents' involvement in education and their rights to make their own decision as concerns the selection of a proper school for their child.

Under the previous system, different types of special schools existed: special kindergartens and special elementary schools for all the categories listed above; special secondary schools for students with hearing impairment, visual impairment and physical handicap; special vocational schools for the above-mentioned three; and auxiliary schools for the mentally handicapped and students with multiple handicaps.

When a child is admitted to a special school, attendance is mandatory. During their attendance children are observed regularly and their performance evaluated continuously in order to verify the placement. If warranted, a transfer to another special school or class is possible, but rarely is a learner returned to an ordinary school.

Upon completion of elementary schooling, students matriculate into special secondary schools, differentiated according to the type and degree of impairment.

Current assessment practices reflect allegiance to the concept of defective development. Professionals utilise a deficit model, assessing what is wrong with the child. Psychologists provide individualised intellectual assessment. They stress informal procedures and techniques. Qualitative differences are accentuated more than quantitative indicators. Psychological assessment aims at gaining insight into the children's abilities, together with the quality and character of responses in a testing situation. This emphasis probably underscores the long-standing Soviet bias towards intelligence testing. A more recent element, greater credence given to the personality of the youngster and his/her social environment, also characterises what we call psychodiagnostics. Projective techniques, in-depth classroom observation, interpretations of overt behaviour, and analysis of responses to situations of daily living are common elements of the evaluation process.

Forty years of communist educational ideas left Czech special education with a residue of concepts that focused on individual defects. The recent opening to Western ideas exposed special education to the fruit of decades of research and innovative thinking. One can expect that it will take some time for the specialists to filter and absorb the wealth of ideas, and then to see changes reflected in Czech special education.

CHANGING ATTITUDES TOWARDS DISABILITY

During the last forty years the Czech Republic has had both positive and negative experiences with special education. Proclamations and generally acceptable legislation, on the one hand, strongly contrasted with the segregation and isolation of persons with handicaps, on the other. This is particularly true of people with severe handicaps, for whom the social care institutions were established, mostly far from their home communities. It looked as if there were no handicapped people in society.

After the Revolution of 1989, the principles that handicapped persons, including children and their families, have the same basic rights as other citizens was widely agreed upon. Equal education is one of these rights. Unfortunately, society is still far from translating this principle into practice. We are sure that we shall make progress only if we continue to insist on basic rights for all, stressing the right of handicapped students to inclusive education. Not to do so would be to accept second-class citizenship for handicapped people, for families with a handicapped child and for the professionals who work with them.

Priorities for school-age handicapped children

The perception of people with handicaps, and public attitudes towards them, are changing rapidly after the Revolution, as a result of the present emphasis on the value of every individual human being, on the discovery of each person's ability and on the recognition of the possibility of the development of his/her capacities. The goals are socialisation, normalisation, integration into society, and emancipation in order to incorporate the persons with handicaps into the world of work and social activity.

Prevalent ideas stress democracy and humanity as the philosophical basis for everyday life, and are fully acceptable to the majority of Czech citizens. These ideas are also supported by many programmes on TV and radio and in other mass media. More and more people meet persons with handicaps on the streets. Many people, especially the young, are involved in voluntary organisations that have programmes for handicapped children, youths and adults.

Although current policy is more favourable towards people with handicaps, we urgently need to:

1 develop a positive vision of how people could lead more fulfilling lives;
2 promote coalitions of interest among public agencies, professional staff and relevant voluntary organisations;
3 establish advice, consultancy and training resources to support local initiatives;
4 develop partnership between professionals from different fields and between professionals and parents of children with special needs.

The co-operation between the association of parents of children with mental handicaps, the Czech Association for Help to the Mentally Handicapped, and the professional Psychopedic Association (PSAS) serves as an example for the last point mentioned above. The two organisations developed mutual co-operation on an equal basis. They organise joint seminars, conferences and projects.

One of their recent projects is a night school for mentally-handicapped adults, established in 1991. The thirty students, all over 18, are leavers from special schools or persons excluded from obligatory school attendance, but who can benefit from further education.

The curriculum content focuses on social behaviour and skills, education for citizenship, and self-advocacy. Computer teaching and basic English language are also included. Although the programme faces many obstacles, there are hopes that after a trial period it will become part of the adult education system in the Czech Republic.

PARENTAL INVOLVEMENT AND SUPPORT FOR PARENTS

When educating students with special needs, it is impossible to be successful without establishing a strong partnership between parents and professionals. The role of the individual parent and of parents' associations, together with other voluntary organisations, is becoming more important with the current changes in education.

One of the organisations that supports special education and plays a significant role in its improvement is the Czech Association for Help to the Mentally Handicapped. The Association has been developing its activities for more that twenty years. During that period it was practically shut off from the rest of the world. Due to the current political atmosphere and the new democratic social conditions in the country, it is no longer forbidden to develop new activities. Currently, the organisation is involved in educational reform, establishing its own facilities and entering into partnerships abroad, as with the German *Lebenshilfe* and many others.

The Association's original mission was to bring parents of mentally-handicapped children together; to provide them with relevant information about social, health and educational services; and to help them meet the individual needs of their children. The Association has also been serving as a centre for guidance and consultation. It has organised many leisure activities for people with mental handicaps: sports and physical education, dancing lessons, swimming, skiing and other recreational activities. A great boom in the Association's activity came after the Revolution: the number of members increased roughly ten times, and the Association established eight facilities for the education of children and adults with mental retardation that provide the clients with non traditional cultural, educational and social services and individual support.

'Non-traditional' cultural, educational and social services means all the new methods and forms that are now being implemented in current special education. Traditionally, the clients in state institutions, such as state hospitals and so-called social care institutions, were (and many still are) just being fed and taken care of by people without any concept of the real care they needed and without any support. Non-traditional means also new, modern ways of supporting people in their personality development.

The Association closely co-operates with professional organisations, such as the Psychopaedic Association and other parent associations both in the Czech Republic and abroad. It is also a member of the Czech Council for Humanitarian Co-operation and a member of the Federation of the Associations for People with Disabilities. In 1992, the Association became a member of the International League of Societies for Persons with Mental Handicap. As a heritage from the past, a distance still exists between family and school in general. The majority of teachers are afraid of the parents, and the majority of parents do not fully believe the school. During the communist period harmony and co-operation between school and family was broadly declared, but it did not exist in practice. Co-operation from the school side focused mainly on giving parents information about the academic progress and behaviour of their children. Parents were expected to maintain good conditions for children's home study. The proclaimed harmony and co-operation represented, in fact, a subordination of the family to the aims of official education. Families were isolated, without any possibility of affecting education and school policy.

Generally, it is clear that the situation must change rapidly. Parliament took the first step when it passed the State Administration and Self-Government of Schools Act.

The term 'self-government of schools' covers financial management, budgeting and educational and school leadership.

The Act covers the role of parents, respecting their claims as well as the claims of teachers, students and other people interested in education. School–family partnership is a vital and urgent challenge in our current education system. The conviction prevails that parents should play an important role in school so that they can exercise their full rights.

INTEGRATION INTO MAINSTREAM SCHOOLS

The first priority for school-aged handicapped children is to ensure that they have access to schools. This is a matter of rights and of legislation. To restructure the school in general towards more democracy, freedom and independence is the most essential part of Czech current effort. New educational reform is being prepared and the first proposals of the Ministry of Education have already been published for a broad discussion among teachers and other people interested. The new proposals of the Ministry of Education as concerns the public school are different from the State Administration Act. They refer more to the content of teaching, curricula and educational reform, but do not cover management issues.

Going step by step, starting with our basic (elementary) school, a 'public school' for children aged 6 to 11 has been prepared. Selected schools will test new proposals in the school year 1993/1994. The proposals for this 'public school' proclaim democratic ideas, including the statement that the public school will be open for everybody, but not for those who require extra special care. It is imperative that the proposal be corrected to include programmes integrating students with special needs into the schools. Several independent bodies, such as professional groups and teacher organisations, have offered their own proposals. Private and church schools provide students with their own programmes. Everything is on the move, creating a new situation in the field of special education in the Czech Republic.

The policy of integration has generated a diversity of responses from parents, teachers, and administrators. While some people receive it as progressive, possessing substantial benefits for the children concerned, others express a completely opposite point of view. The NIMBY (Not In My Back Yard) feature became an attitude of many teachers in ordinary schools. Some special schoolteachers, afraid of losing their jobs, argue against integration, claiming that it will not provide handicapped students with the proper educational environment. There are also parents who are not committed to integration. In addition, people are worried about dismantling hundreds of special schools and institutions and dispersing the children and the staff into ordinary schools.

Resistance to change is understandable when a tried system of provision is being replaced by the unknown. Whatever opinion people hold, a new democratic school system must offer special children learning experiences that enable them to enjoy life to the full.

POLICY AND PRACTICE – THE CZECH DILEMMA

The policy of normalisation needs to be adopted as a general social policy in the Czech Republic, pertaining to education, employment possibilities, community living, social activities, etc. and should be fully reflected in the legislation. The first steps have been taken already – for example, relatively favourable legislative conditions for inclusive education or the community-based living arrangements – but the greatest challenges lie ahead.

In many national school systems a significant gap exists between stated policy and actual practice in special education. In the Czech Republic, ironically, such a gap does not exist, since reforms have not yet penetrated even into levels of policy.

Current issues include:

1 changing the public perception of and attitude toward fellow citizens with special needs;
2 increasing parental involvement and participation in the education of the child with a disability;
3 mandating the integration of students with special needs into mainstream academic and community environments;
4 adopting the principles of normalisation as a social policy;
5 influencing society to provide accessibility to buildings, employment and areas of recreation for all the people with special needs.

Teachers, especially, can play a significant role in the development of social policy by improving their teaching/educating skills. 'Professionalism' in teaching means, in substance, 'humanism'. It is manifested in the teachers' skill to evaluate objectively the education process, to analyse the success of their activity, to generalise the acquired experiences, and to compare them with their knowledge of educational theory. The teacher–professional excels also in establishing and maintaining optimal pedagogical communication. S/he appropriately motivates the students to the desirable activity, supports the development of their activity, creates a favourable emotional atmosphere and prevents the development of a psychic barrier which renders it impossible for students with special needs to use their capacity to the full.

Developing a real professionalism in teachers is important. A teacher–professional–humanist stands up to the growing demands of the democratic society that has been developing in the Czech Republic since the Revolution of 1989. It is agreed that the mission of the contemporary teacher is not merely to teach and provide guidance, but to accept responsibility for the economic, cultural and social development of society and the promotion of positive human relations both inside and outside the community. Thus the activity of the teacher assumes cultural and humanistic dimensions.

Similarly, the role of the modern school was defined as early as in the 1920s by an outstanding Czech educationalist, Vaclav Prihoda, who said:

> The school cannot be reduced to the education of youth. The school is a general cultural and people-educating institution that embraces all human behaviour, craving for the improvement, cultivation and refinement of the whole society. Through its general cultural, social and societal service the school becomes the most efficient tool of a more perfect humanity and a perfect humanitarian unity.

(Prihoda 1924)

The Czechs are proud of their cultural tradition and heritage. In the field of education it is Jan Amos Komensky (Comenius) whom they trust, even nowadays. The following quotation admirably relates to the democratisation of education, education for all:

> Nor it is [sic] any obstacle that some seem to be naturally dull and stupid, for this renders more imperative the universal culture of such intellects. The slower and the weaker the disposition of any man, the more he needs assistance, that he may throw off his brutish dullness and stupidity as much as possible. Nor can any man be found whose intellect is so weak that it cannot be improved by culture. . . .
>
> Again, just as some men are strong as children, but afterwards grow sick and ailing, while others, whose bodies are sickly and undersized in youth, develop into robust and tall men; so it is with intellects. Some develop early, but soon wear out and grow dull, while others, originally stupid, become sharp and penetrating. In our orchards we like to have not only trees that bring forth early fruit, but also those that are latebearing. . . . Why, therefore, should we wish that in the garden of letters only one class of intellects, the forward and active, should be tolerated?

(Komensky 1632)

REFERENCES

Komensky, J.A. (1632), *Didactica Magna*. English version, Matthew Keatinge (1896), reissued by A. & C. Black (1957) (see also Sadler, J. (ed.) (1969), *Commenius* (Collier–Macmillan, London)).
Prihoda, V. (1924), *Racionalisace Skolstvi*, Perspektivy, Orbis, Prague.

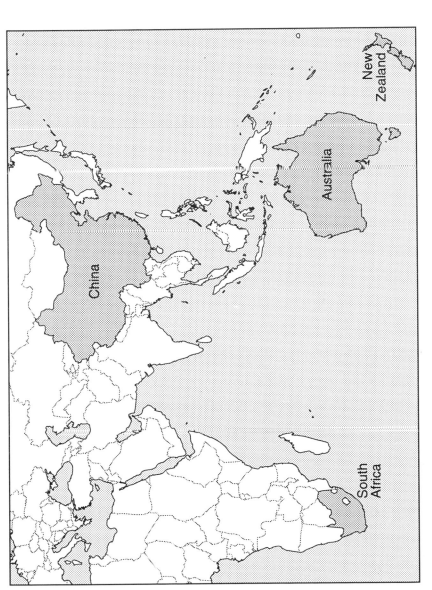

Map 2 New Zealand, China, South Africa and Australia

Chapter 15

South and north: special educational provision in New Zealand, Britain and the United States

Ross Wilson

Ross Wilson is the chief executive of New Zealand's Special Education Service, which was formed in the late 1980s and manages the resources for the full range of special educational provision, inside and outside the mainstream. He spent three months of 1993 touring Britain and the United States to study developments in policy and practice and see if there was anything he could usefully translate back into the New Zealand education system, which was undergoing a series of reforms similar to those taking place in the UK, for example, the devolution of budgets from local authorities to schools. Wilson observed that inclusive education requires planning, legislation and an approach to teaching and learning based on classroom activities and individualised support.

INTRODUCTION

In April and May 1993 I visited Vermont and Michigan in the United States, and England, Wales and Scotland to look at developments in the provision of special education services. This was very timely in that the nature of changes taking place in the wider New Zealand education system were also taking place, or had already taken place, in Britain and the United States. In this chapter I shall begin with a brief account of education services in New Zealand and then go on to discuss some of the common trends which I observed in all the countries I visited.

Education for children with special needs in New Zealand

There have been, for many years, specialist services and extra support for children and young people in the New Zealand education system. This springs from the Education Act 1877, which declared that education between the ages of 7 and 14 (now 6 and 16) would be compulsory, free and secular. Peter Fraser, when Minister of Education in 1937, said that education would be of a type for which the child was best fitted, no matter what the nature of a child's learning needs were. Since the end of the Second World War a considerable expansion of the range of specialist and support services for children with special needs has taken place, sometimes on an *ad hoc* basis. However, they have all been state-funded, usually through central agencies, principally the Department of Education.

In New Zealand since 1989 the education of children and young people with special needs has been primarily the responsibility of boards of trustees of schools and early childhood centres in partnership with parents. The Ministry of Education develops and advises on policy relating to their needs and allocates resources, and the Special Education Service provides advice, guidance and support for the benefit of these children and young people (Education Act 1989). Thus there is now a three-part structure for special education in New Zealand.

The provision of special education services is managed in this way in the context of the overall educational administrative reforms set out in the Report of the Picot Committee (1987) which emphasise local control, bulk funding of financial grants to institutions, accountability for service provision to local communities, increased competitiveness for educational service providers and improved choice for 'consumers (e.g., with more relaxed school zoning regulations as provided for in the Education Amendment Act 1991).

The New Zealand Government is committed to a continuum of provision for learners with special needs – special schools, special units or classes in regular schools, and the placement of children with special needs in regular classes, though it is acknowledged that there is not, at the present time, equity of access to each provision.

The Education Act 1989 gives all children with special needs the same rights as all other children. This enables them to enrol at their local regular school but does not provide for an automatic entitlement to additional resources. Such resources are available from the central Ministry of Education on the advice of the Special Education Service and may include an additional teacher, teacher-aide, equipment or transport assistance. The students Individual Educational Plan (IEP) will usually identify if and what type of additional resources are required but, unlike a UK 'educational statement', gives no legal rights to additional resources.

The Special Education Service

The Special Education Service is one of a number of new organisations established as part of the 1984–90 Labour government's reforms of the administration of education in New Zealand (Report of the Picot Committee 1987; and Lange 1988). It is the major body providing specialist educational support services to children and young people with special educational needs and arose from the 1989 amalgamation of the majority of professionals providing such services in New Zealand. These include educational psychologists, speech and language therapists, advisers on deaf children, early intervention teachers and advisers, and visiting teachers.

The writers of both the *Administering for Excellence* (Report of the Picot Committee 1987) and the *Tomorrow's Schools* (Lange 1988) reports recommended that the Special Education Service be made contestable. That is, after a short period of time the service would not be funded directly by government for its services, but would sell its services to institutions who would be given government funding in their bulk grants to buy these services. Similar proposals, with mixed and unresolved results are taking place in Britain and the United States.

In all, four sets of recommendations to make the Special Education Service contestable have, for a number of reasons, been rejected by central government.

This issue (of contestability) continues to present itself as part of the continuing reform of state-sector activities (Treasury Briefing Papers to Incoming Government 1990), and while various approaches to this have continued as part of the current government's agenda, no workable model has been found.

There is no history of alternative providers in this area of specialist provision of services. A small number of private providers do exist (mainly educational psychologists and speech therapists) but they are dependent on private funding, mainly from parents or very specialist government departments or agencies (e.g., family court work, social welfare work, Accident Compensation Commission). Some of these agencies are now favouring the consistency and quality provided by the Special Education Service.

The possible future

A 1991 document entitled *Education Provision for Learners with Special Needs in New Zealand: A Statement of Intent* has proved to be more of a discussion document on how to allocate resources than a policy for special education.

The Special Education Policy Implementation Team, set up by the 1990 National Government, has spent two years consulting parents, teachers and community and professional groups around New Zealand in an attempt to provide for the more efficient and effective use of special needs resources. Their main recommendation is that local resources should be allocated by local committees and that some resources will continue to be allocated at a national level. These include resources for the Special Education Service, the Correspondence School and national residential schools for students who are blind or deaf, have mild and moderate intellectual disabilities along with family difficulties, or who are emotionally disturbed.

A decision by central government to allocate all or more of special needs funding to a range of alternative service providers, or parents (for example, in the form of vouchers), or to educational institutions to spend however they choose, may reduce the total money available within the current pool for the purchase of such services if learning institutions choose to spend this money on other priorities. Such money, even if tagged or targeted to 'special needs' may also be spent within the school on internal resources such as teacher-aides or computers. This possibility must be considered alongside the objective of placing greater decision-making power in the hands of those primarily responsible for the education of children – education facilities and parents.

The government's aim has been to provide equal access to services no matter where a New Zealander lives. Alongside this sits the view that competition improves productivity, efficiency and effectiveness and provides choice for the consumer. Such a view is discussed in Crocombe, Enright and Porter (1991) In the non-profit state sector there is a prevailing viewpoint that competition is the best mechanism to achieve value for money (Sexton 1990). This is motivated by the continued recognition of the needs of children and young people experiencing educational and developmental difficulties as being legitimate and requiring special resourcing in an economy that can find little 'new' money to support growth in this area. This holds true for all of education in the 1990s, not just special needs education.

The Special Education Service (or any other service with national coverage – rural and urban and throughout New Zealand), employing highly qualified and experienced staff, has certain quality control and distribution costs to be met. Its claim to being in the field at all is that such services as it provides are not easily obtainable without extraordinary provision. Bryson (1988) says, 'If there is nothing unique or distinct about the (public) organisation, perhaps it should not exist', and 'If the private or non-profit sectors fail to meet an important social or political need, perhaps a government corporation or agency should enter the field (1988, p. 53).

The Special Education Service as an organisation provides stability and a yardstick for measuring the quality and effectiveness of other competing services. Johnson and Scholes (1989, p. 67) say, 'the most stable markets tend to be the ones with dominant organisations within them'. Specialist advice, guidance and support services will always be required to some extent or another. There will always be some people who fall outside the capacity of normal provision to have their needs met. Caring societies like New Zealand will make special provision for them.

INTERNATIONAL COMPARISONS

Inclusive education

The Warnock Report (1978) states that all schools have the responsibility to identify and meet pupils' needs, and all children with special educational needs should be educated alongside their peers as long as their needs can be met and it is practicable to do so. In Britain the 1981 Education Act requires local education authorities (LEAs) to:

- identify children with special needs;
- place children in ordinary schools where possible;
- make additional provision where a child's needs cannot be met by an ordinary school alone;
- work closely with parents;

In the United States since 1975, Public Law 94-142 mandated that a continuum of special education programmes and services be available to meet the unique educational needs of all students with disabilities. Inclusive education is part of this continuum.

The two overriding impressions I gained about inclusive education during my visits were that:

- it needs to be carefully planned and legislated for; and
- it works best when classroom programmes are activity-based and teaching is individualised.

In the London Borough of Newham it was clear that the Chair of the local education authority (LEA), supported by other councillors and council officers, had encouraged a planned approach to the progressive closing of separate special facilities and the inclusion of all children into regular schools. New people, with special skills, had been employed to ensure that this worked.

All the changes were quite transparent with the direct translation of one specific set of resources into another. Parents knew exactly what was to take the place of services being curtailed (for example, the replacement of a local school for the deaf with a hearing advisory, support and itinerant teaching service). It was clear that rights were being protected and more appropriate assistance was being offered. I saw the beginnings of this approach in Salford, where a new education officer had been appointed to effect similar changes. This was the process used in the former Wellington (NZ) Education Board district, and although in Wellington there is some unfinished business in respect of the retention of senior positions, there have been no significant problems with this transition.

In Michigan it was clear that the Washtenaw Intermediate School District had also carefully planned the movement of a large number of children with special needs into regular schools. Publicly-available literature set out what was to be achieved, and how and when. The last children still in a separate facility, those we know as 'psychopaedic', with profound disabilities, are still to change, with some question about whether the health or education sector should be responsible for their funding. In Rochester the move to inclusion had moved steadily forward, with the considerable support of the Superintendent of Schools and the Director of Student Services.

I visited numerous regular classrooms and saw students with various disabilities ranging from profound to those resulting in no real educational handicap. Those who appeared to be most successfully included were invariably in classrooms where a lot of planned individual activities were taking place, where the teacher (and any other adult in the room) moved around interacting with the children, who were invariably engrossed in their own tasks, and where the dynamics operating took the attention off the disability and on to the learning task. Galloway (1990) says that there is an explicit relationship between 'effective schools' and the successful education of children with special needs.

In both Britain and the United States, where students qualified for paraprofessional support (teacher-aide), it was usually more generous than is the case in New Zealand.

Strong features of successful inclusion were a stated commitment to its philosophy by the most senior administrators in the district, a transparent plan for its implementation and an accessible and expert support service, usually provided from outside the school.

Parental and student choice

> When I was addicted to the social services no one thought I could do or know anything. Now Kate is in the normal community I am also treated like normal.
>
> (Quote by parent to me in Stockport, UK)

The Warnock Report (1978) states that parents, and as far as possible the children and young people with special educational needs themselves, have the right to share in the decisions about how their needs are met.

One of the most rewarding experiences I had on my visits was to the Stockport home and school of an 11-year-old girl with a severe disability. The parents, supported by staff from the Bolton Institute of Higher Education, a parents' support group and local Health Service psychologist, had successfully integrated their daughter into a caring and sensible primary school and were now negotiating, with mixed results, for her to attend her local secondary school. Although the law allowed for this enrolment the school was resorting to a number of tactics to delay or divert it. (A recent letter and photograph sent to me by the mother of this student show her now happily attending the secondary school of her choice.)

It became clear from my visit that it is not parents who have the freedom to exercise choice; it is the schools, despite legislation that would appear to guarantee right of access. There is both overt and covert resistance to ordinary enrolment in Britain and this appears to have been exacerbated since central funding of support services was replaced by schools receiving their formula-based share of special needs funding. Increases in truancy and suspensions were reported by almost every local education and school official I talked with. It seems schools are reluctant to spend *their* money on what they perceive as 'problems' they did not create.

These patterns seem to be similar in New Zealand. There has been significant comment about truancy, children 'disappearing' from the system as they move from their school, which ceases to be responsible for them after twenty-one days absence, the abolition of truancy officers, redefining the role of the visiting teacher and so-called 'kiwi' (informal) suspensions.

Parents of children with special needs report the difficulties they have in enrolling their children in regular schools despite their legal right to do so, and politicians, many of whom become unnecessarily embroiled in the day-to-day operation of the education system, in a manner that they would not contemplate for the health sector, come up with their own proposals about how such children should be educated.

Cost/benefit analysis of different provision

> Most teachers don't even know what our children look like. It's like putting your money on a horse you've never seen.
>
> (Further quote by parent to me in Stockport, UK)

Pollock and Klipp (1991), discussing the Washtenow (Michigan) Inter-mediate School District, make a series of theoretically-supported assumptions and best-guess, but reasonably accurate, costings. These show that students educated in inclusive settings cost marginally less to educate than students educated in a segregated setting. This provides for total one-to-one support by a teaching assistant (teacher-aide), reduced transport costs, similar therapeutic and consultant (support services) and similar general education costs.

The study also reports on the much-improved employment chances of students educated in regular facilities. They are more likely to obtain supportive, rather than facility-based, employment (usually workshops) with significantly increased earnings potential. This is similar to the evidence found by the Disabled Persons Assembly in New Zealand: that almost no young people entering the workplace from segregated education facilities obtain outside employment, whereas many having the same educational needs but from regular schools are successful.

Pollock and Klipp argue and provide data that suggest that when questions of cost are asked in relation to different types of educational provision it is important to look at the improved life and employment chances as well as actual, up-front costs.

Thomson and Ward (1993) outline a theoretical approach to addressing issues of cost effectiveness in provision for special educational needs. They ask three questions: how can outcomes be defined, how are costs to be determined, and how can effective provision be evaluated?

A summary of the literature suggests that indicators of successful outcomes include employment, economic self-sufficiency, personal independence, role-taking in the family, role-taking in society and uptake of post-secondary education. By constructing an 'educational status level' based on these factors the true added-value of different types of programmes and placements and the marginal benefit gained by young people can be determined.

Even with reducing resources and increasing costs a purely economic model of assessing costs will prove untenable for educators who also have educational outcomes in mind.

Other aspects not possible to quantify are human rights issues related to the right to choose not to be excluded from mainstream society, improved quality of life within a regular community, language and social skills learning and increased independence. As well as benefits to the learner with special needs, the rest of society gains in tolerance and compassion for people with differences.

Thomson and Ward state that:

> It is recognised that education authorities, in varying degrees, have developed costings models for all sectors in education but none have adapted these models to take account of the differential quality of educational experiences, far less reached agreement on such contentious matters as differential outcomes.

In New Zealand, although we now have much more accurate data on the costs of various types of education, no real analysis of comparative costs in relationship to educational and vocational outcomes has been undertaken. There is some limited anecdotal information related to changed operations at the Forbury Resource Centre in Dunedin. This suggests that more students with special needs can be served by the same amount of resource when they are in regular schools. However, there are, no doubt, a number of factors not properly included.

Wedell (1993) says that a greater regard for cost-effectiveness of services could lead to more considered use:

> However this does not imply that special needs services can be operated on market-economy principles. Forcing specialist services to depend on purchaser–provider relationships with individual schools makes them too

sensitive to the ability of schools to afford them. Quality services for pupils' special educational needs can be quickly lost, but would take a long time to rebuild.

In this paper I am not arguing for the closure of segregated facilities, although, provided special units within schools are retained and advisory services are appropriately resourced, I believe that it would be educationally possible to do so. What is needed is parental choice based on fair treatment and equitable provision of resources.

I am also suggesting that resources must follow students as they move into the mainstream of education. In Britain the Audit Commission and Her Majesty's Inspectorate (1992) have estimated that if resources had followed special needs students into regular education £53 million would have been released in 1991/92 for their support. The New Zealand government has recognised this issue by transferring NZ $5.5 million to regular schools from special residential schools in 1992, and $2.5 million from special day schools in 1993.

Centralised versus devolved funding

There is currently much debate taking place in Britain, the United States and New Zealand about the devolution of special needs funding to schools. In Britain it was the 1988 Education Act introducing local management of schools (LMS) that forced the debate in this area, rather than any altruistic movement towards mainstreaming. In New Zealand it was *Tomorrow's Schools* (Lange 1988) and the continuing follow-up to these reforms that is still leaving open the question of what you give to schools and what you hold back, and for what purpose.

Thomas (1992) argues for the complete removal of any body between (in Britain) the Department for Education and schools, claiming that co-ordinating bodies and support services soak up funds better used directly by schools to reduce class sizes and to make schools responsible for catering appropriately for all children. He suggests that by removing responsibility from schools and giving it to a separate body you encourage the development of parallel regular and special education systems, breed dependence on a central authority, marginalise children with special needs and soak up funds in administration that would be better spent on the direct teaching of children.

The same arguments continue to be advanced in New Zealand and are unlikely to be resolved unless the right questions are asked. Thomas asks the wrong questions:

Do existing decision-making and resource-allocating systems facilitate effective education for *all* children?

Or do they centralise decision-making, disempower schools, deskill teachers and alienate parents?

Questions that need to be asked are:

What degree of special education need falls so unevenly as to require some supplementary resource input or support from a more centralised source than the school or early childhood centre?

How can this resource or support best be given and its use monitored in ways that empower and give responsibility to the school or early childhood centre?

There needs to be an analysis of what support parents and schools need from outside agencies. Recent debate in New Zealand, including the Special Education Policy Implementation Team (SEPIT) rounds of consultation, demonstrate that specific advice, guidance and support outside those which the school or early childhood centre can provide are needed. A 1987 House of Commons Select Committee on Education concluded that special needs provision was too complex to be left to the responsibility of individual schools (Wedell 1993) and now advocates legislation to require local authorities to provide the type of support services the Special Education Service provides.

Funding cuts in the United States seem to be signalling the demise of 'intermediate' layers in the administrative system, as they have in New Zealand. Washtenaw Intermediate School District in Michigan is turning from an administrator of segregated special facilities to a provider of specialist support services, using the same resource base, for regular schools (Washtenaw County 1990).

In Britain, there is a powerful political move to reduce (and emasculate) the LEAs, which are now much more limited in size and function. They have largely moved from a controlling to a supportive (and market-orientated) role and in one case at least (the London Borough of Hillingdon) there are plans to amalgamate the Education and Social Services departments to provide for better economies of scale and more flexibility.

An irony in the United States and Britain is that the most 'progressive' education authorities in the 1960s and 1970s, that built up elaborate and costly special education infrastructures, are now stuck with the political consequences of getting learners out of them before they are dismantled.

In the LEAs I visited, two areas where some central resourcing is still held to be essential is for larger-scale property maintenance and renewal, and for children and young people with significant special learning needs. The 1993 Education Act in Britain will require LEAs to make provision for specialist support services for learners with special needs, even those attending grant-maintained schools which are quite removed from LEA influence.

The concept of 'top-slicing' as practised in Leeds was useful in enabling school headteachers to have some say in how much special needs money is kept at a central level. There the LEA already had a well-regarded history of consulting with and involving schools in making decisions that affect them. At the time of my visit no schools in their area had opted for grant-maintained status and officials attribute this to their previous record of good consultation.

Every year Leeds LEA receives recommendations from representative groups of headteachers on the percentage of total school funds they want retained by the LEA for special educational needs purposes. The majority decision is accepted by all. In this way headteachers have a realistic expectation of what they must meet from their school budget and what level and type of need can be reasonably expected from the retained central resource.

Even though some central services may be retained for sound educational reasons, the direct responsibility for students has been taken away from central authorities and given to locally managed or grant-maintained schools. This is as it is in New Zealand with boards of trustees now having responsibility for students. For this reason the existence of some central support service (but not 'ownership' of the students) is consistent with the *Tomorrow's Schools* philosophy.

Postscript

With the 6 November 1993 election, the National Government's previous huge majority has now been reduced to just one seat, with two minor parties and the official Labour opposition having the potential to influence change in New Zealand. Many political commentators suggest that though there will not be an undoing of the significant political and economic changes that have taken place in New Zealand since 1984, there will be a weakening of the 'new right' free-market philosophies that were introduced by Labour and expanded by the National Government. The electorate has clearly signalled its displeasure as these philosophies moved to introduce more extreme changes in the social services.

The Editor of the NZ *Listener* sums up the prevailing mood

Appreciative as New Zealanders are of lower debts and mortgage interest, there appears to be a demand for less mathematics and more vision, for fewer balance sheet statements and more discussion about humans – employed or not. Like households, governments must pay attention to what is in the purse, but then build a life outwards from there – not remain buried in the coinage.

(*Listener*, 27 November 1993)

From what I have seen in the United States and Britain, the point has been reached where the treatment is apparently sound but the patient is probably dying because of the side-effects. I have tried to identify some of these side-effects in this report. With any luck the success we have had in New Zealand with the changes brought about by *Tomorrow's Schools* will not now entice us to proceed too much further down the same track to an illogical conclusion.

REFERENCES

Audit Commission and Her Majesty's Inspectorate (1992), *Getting in on the Act. Provision for Pupils with Special Educational Needs: the National Picture*, HMSO, London.

Bryson, J. M. (1988), *Strategic Planning for Public and Non-profit Organisations*, Jossey Bass, Wellington.

Crocombe, G. T., Enright, M. J. and Porter, M. E. (1991), *Upgrading New Zealand's Competitive Advantage*, Oxford University Press, Oxford 1991.

Department of Education and Science (1978), *Special Educational Needs, the 'Warnock Report'*, HMSO, London.

Galloway, David (1990), 'Support for learning in Tower Hamlets: Report of the Consultant in Special Educational Needs to the Chief Education Officer', unpublished report.

Johnson, G. and Scholes, K. (1989), *Exploring Corporate Strategy*, Simon & Schuster, Hemel Hempstead.

Lange, David (1988), *Tomorrow's Schools*, Government Printer, Wellington.

Listener, 141 (2799), 27 November 1993, NZ Listener Ltd, Auckland.

New Zealand Government. *Education Act 1989*, Government Printer, Wellington.

New Zealand Government, *Education Amendment Act 1991*, Government Printer, Wellington.

New Zealand Government, *Human Rights Act 1993*, Government Printer, Wellington.

Pollock, Blair and Klipp, Glenn (1991), 'A benefit cost analysis of inclusive education in Washtenaw Intermediate School District', unpublished report.

Report of the Picot Committee on the Administration of Education in New Zealand, *Administering for Excellence* (1987), New Zealand Government, Wellington.

Sexton, Stuart (1990), *New Zealand Schools. An Evaluation of Recent Reforms and Future Directions*, New Zealand Business Roundtable, Wellington.

Thomas, Gary (1992), 'Local authorities, special needs, and the status quo', *Support for Learning* 7 (1).

Thomson, G. O. B. and Ward, K. (1993), 'Cost effectiveness and provision for special educational needs', to be published in *Mental Handicap Research*.

United Kingdom Government, *Education Act 1981*, HMSO, London.

Warnock, M. (1978), *Report of the Committee of Enquiry into the Education of Handicapped Children and Young People*, HMSO, London.

Washtenaw County (1990), *Inclusive Education in Washtenaw County*, Washtenaw Intermediate School District brochure.

Wedell, Klaus (1993), *Special Needs Education: The Next 25 Years*, National Commission on Education, London.

Chapter 16

Reforming special education in China

Patricia Potts

After the death of Mao in 1976 there was a turning away from the aim of a vocational curriculum for all students towards the reconstruction of higher education for a selected minority. During the 1980s, this elitism was tempered by a renewal of commitment to mass education. The aim of universal attendance, together with changing attitudes towards disabled people and those who experience difficulties in learning, has led to the extension of special educational provision across China. The scale of the project is huge and the demand for qualified teachers urgent. The Chinese approach is pragmatic and learning support is seen as a specialised task, wherever it is provided. So far, there has been little reform of the mainstream itself, which remains highly centralised and competitive.

INTRODUCTION

With the death of Mao in 1976 and the end of the Cultural Revolution, China, under the leadership of Deng Xiao Ping, turned away from the aim of a vocational curriculum for all students everywhere and concentrated, instead, on the reconstruction of higher education for a selected minority, looking to the West, particularly the United States, for a scientific and technological model.

During the 1980s, a number of factors combined to raise the profile of provision for disabled students and those who experience difficulties in learning. First of all, universal elementary education was reaffirmed as an aim of the post-Mao government. To counterbalance criticism of the return to an elitist education policy, a law to establish nine years of compulsory education was adopted at the Fourth Session of the Sixth National People's Congress in April 1986 (see Pepper 1990, p. 188).

However, access to school has been impossible both for many disabled children and for others considered to be ineligible because of their low level of attainment. Provision for urban blind and deaf students is long established in China, but, until the 1980s, provision for physically-disabled students and those who experience difficulties in learning, was minimal. The aim of universal attendance by the end of the century includes access for disabled children and increased provision for those who experience difficulties in learning.

Second, the position of disabled adults has been discussed more openly than before and the task of increasing their economic and social opportunities has been related to the provision of appropriate education. For example, the magazine *Women of China* devoted its December 1986 issue to disability and special education. The movement gained visibility and authority when Deng Pufang, son of Deng Xiao Ping and a wheelchair-user as a result of being thrown out of a window by Red Guards in the late 1960s, led a campaign for what he described as humanitarian reforms (Deng Pufang 1989).

In 1988 the government published a *Five-Year Work Programme for People with Disabilities* and in December 1990 the Law of the People's Republic of China on the Protection of Disabled Persons was adopted at the seventeenth meeting of the Standing National People's Congress. The contribution of disabled people and the work of supporting them are described in positive terms, although disability itself is still seen as a defect:

> People with disabilities have the desire and the right to participate in social life and most of them have certain abilities to do so. Facts have shown that people with disabilities are also creators of material and cultural civilisation and constitute a force for social progress.
>
> Humanitarianism is one of the tenets underlying the thinking in the Chinese society and a norm governing human relations. To do a good job in the work for people with disabilities and promote their welfare constitutes a bounden duty of the whole society and a hallmark of social progress and human civilisation. The whole society should, displaying humanitarianism, understand, respect, care for and help people with disabilities and safeguard their legitimate rights and interests.
>
> *Five-Year Work Programme* 1988, paras 4 & 10)

> A disabled person refers to one who suffers from abnormalities or loss of a certain organ or function, psychologically or physiologically, or in anatomical structure and has lost wholly or in part the ability to perform an activity in the way considered normal. The term 'disabled person' refers to those visual, hearing, speech or physical disabilities, mental retardation, mental disorder, multiple disabilities and/or other disabilities. The criteria for classification of disabiliities shall be established by the State Council.
>
> (Law on the Protection of Disabled Persons 1990, quoted in Stone 1993, p. 25)

In the context both of the aim of full attendance at school and of the 'open door' policy in relation to other countries, pressure from new organisations such as the China Fund for the Handicapped and the China Disabled Persons' Federation had led educators in China to pay attention to special educational reform and to seek support from a wide range of sources. In 1988 China hosted its first major international conference on special education and established two major research centres in Beijing: the Division of Special Education within the China Central Institute of Educational Research, and the National Special Education Research Centre at the Normal (teacher training) University. Government leaders and others attending a national conference in November 1988 passed a resolution to spend 23 million yuen a year for five years on the development of special education (Chen Yun Ying 1990).

I shall begin with an outline of the Chinese education system. Then I shall discuss some examples of new approaches to special education. I shall conclude by asking how far Chinese educators can go in the 1990s to achieve their aims.

UNDERSTANDING THE CHINESE EDUCATION SYSTEM

The human scale of things in China is hard for Westerners to appreciate. The government booklet 'Facts and Figures' for 1990 lists 122.42 million children in primary schools, 38.69 million in junior secondary schools, 13.25 million in senior secondary schools, over 2 million undergraduate students and 93,000 graduate students. You will notice the sharp drop in places as students get older. There is great pressure, particularly on rural junior secondary schools (Chen Kai Ming 1990) and on universities (Fu Yawen 1986). The present exclusiveness of the higher education sector is not just the result of lack of resources, however: enrolment in universities was cut by 30,000 in 1990:

> The size of the general Higher Education system was checked in order to improve quality.
>
> *(Beijing Review* 1990, p. 57)

But for those who do gain entry to higher education, there are, in the 1990s, irresistible distractions, particularly in the context of the low status and pay of anyone employed in education (Zhang Guanghin 1992). The government is encouraging private businesses. People are giving up their 'iron rice bowl' of a job for life and using their *guanxi*, or connections, to embark upon the risky course of making their own money. This phenomenon is called *Xia hai*, or 'going down to the sea':

> There are reports of millionaires among Chinese university students. I've heard stories of professors who have had to abandon their lectures because of the noise of pagers going off all over the classroom as students keep in touch with their business contacts. . . .

Right now everyone – middle school students, teachers, university professors – are involved, it's become a kind of flood.

(Lin Jin Rong, in Hoyland 1993; see also Unger 1994)

School students all over China follow the same curriculum, use the same textbooks and have substantial amounts of homework. The organisation of primary and secondary schools is the same, with up to about 1,000 students grouped in classes of forty. The standard teaching method is lecturing to the whole class and assessment is by timed examination. There is a complicated pattern of status relationships derived from examination results. For example:

Nowadays all secondary schools are classified into state key secondary schools, provincial (or municipal or autonomous regional) key secondary schools, county (or district) key secondary schools and ordinary secondary schools on the basis of teachers' quality and school-running conditions. For example, in Shanghai, there is one state key secondary school, 20 municipal key secondary schools, 40 district key secondary schools and hundreds of ordinary secondary schools. Generally speaking, the teachers' quality, school-running conditions and student prior attainments in a state key school are superior to municipal key secondary schools. The teachers' quality, school-running conditions and student prior attainments in municipal key secondary schools are better than district key schools and the rest may be deduced by analogy, because the kind of schools students can enter depends on the scores they gain in heatedly competitive school entrance examinations.

In the evaluation of teaching quality by CESE (Certificate Examination of Secondary Education) results, Shanghai makes a list of schools according to their classification and in order of each school's examination results and at the same time publishes average grades and average pass rate of Shanghai, each district, each school and each subject. If a school performed worse or better than it would be expected, it will lose or gain the title of key school, and it will be lowered or promoted in its status. For example, if a municipal key secondary school has performed worse than it might be expected for three years, it will lose the title of municipal key secondary school and will be lowered to be a district key secondary school. Conversely, if a district key secondary school has performed better than it might be expected for three years, it will be promotoed to be a municipal key secondary school. This policy encourages schools, teachers and students to perform very well in CESE and impels them to overtake each other in competition.

(Wang Binhua 1993)

Shanghai has around 14 million people. Despite the enormous size of Chinese cities, however, 80 per cent of the total population still live in the countryside, where attendance at school may be difficult, either because of distance, because of the cost of paying for the necessary boarding accommodation or because of the loss to a family of their children's earnings. Further, as the structure of the old commune system is breaking down and responsibility for collecting taxes for education has been devolved, not only is funding for schools subject to local corruption, but there is no longer any possibility of the subsidising of the poorest areas by more prosperous neighbours. Nevertheless, attendance at the primary level is probably over 90 per cent (Chen Kai Ming 1990).

Irving Epstein (1993) argues that the official rhetoric, which links compulsory mass education and modernisation, does not sufficiently acknowledge either the individual right of children to an education or the experience of other East Asian countries, where it was not until there was a demand for skilled workers that education became economically vital. The result is a gap between policy and rural economic practices which continue to rely on child labour:

> The township has failed to acquire a degree of legitimacy commensurate with that afforded to the commune; as a result, a reliance upon child labor is quite visible and . . . is promoted by changing rural conditions that are part of an international political economy. . . .
>
> Since the initiation and enforcement of compulsory basic education policies demand a level of shared commitment that extends beyond the instrumental and informal character of rural politics, it is difficult to imagine how current educational inequities will be effectively redressed in the short term.
>
> (Epstein 1993, p. 234)

Another problem for rural education is the catch-22 situation of teachers. *Minban*, or community-sponsored, teachers were recruited from the local peasant-farming population in large numbers during the Cultural Revolution. They are paid by means of local revenues, a national subsidy and a plot of land. They are registered as resident in the countryside. *Gongban* teachers are on the government pay-roll, can be recognised as qualified teachers and can work in urban areas. Upgrading the professional status of the *minban* teachers would involve giving them permission to move to the urban areas, which is contrary to Personnel Ministry policy:

> No solution of the teacher supply–demand problems seems possible in the near future. On the one hand, there is a great shortage of qualified teachers, on the other, many committed and qualified minban teachers have not been given recognition and as a result many unqualified minban teachers have no incentive to become qualified.
>
> (Chen Kai Ming 1990, p. 7)

The Chinese education system, therefore, despite the uniformity of content and teaching style, encompasses significant regional differences and complicated selection procedures, both within and between schools. Priorities for the 1990s include the achievement of universal literacy, the improvement and extension of initial and in-service teacher education and the reduction of truancy from secondary schools.

NEW APPROACHES TO SPECIAL EDUCATION

The scale of the project

In 1987 the government commissioned a sample survey to project the number of disabled people throughout the country. The categories used were: hearing and speaking disabilities, mental retardation, physical disability, visual disability, mental disorder and multiple disabilities. Out of a total population of 1,054,44 million, there were estimated to be about 51.64 million disabled people. Out of 307.4 million children aged 0 to 14, 8.17m were estimated to be disabled (Xu Yun 1992).

The largest category was hearing and speaking disability. It has been estimated that, in 1987, there were school places for 42,432 deaf students, as compared with 12,286 'mentally retarded' students and 2,899 blind students (Armfield 1992, p. 33). In Shandong Province there were places for 10 per cent of blind children aged between 7 and 15, 12 per cent of deaf children and 8 per cent of 'low IQ' children (Chen Yun Ying 1990). Only a few years later the provision across the country for children categorised as mentally retarded had increased dramatically, from 131 special schools and 599 special classes, to 856 schools and 2,651 classes (*Beijing Review* 1990).

Reforming teacher education

Dr Chen Yun Ying is the Director of the Special Education Division of the China Central Institute of Educational Research in Beijing, and one of her first tasks when she took up her post in 1988 was to carry out a study of existing arrangements for special education in the three coastal provinces of Liaoning, Jiangsu and Shandong and make recommendations for reform. She found that a lack of qualified teachers and suitable training materials was a major problem, particularly in view of the hoped-for dramatic increase in school places. Working on a teacher:student ratio of 1:6, Chen Yun Ying calculated that, together, the three provinces she studied would need 68,500 more teachers (Chen Yun Ying 1990, p. 2).

Chen Yun Ying's plans for the reform of teacher education include placing a higher value on practical experience than has been traditional in China. She argues that everyone who will work with disabled children should have taught in the mainstream and she recommends that a new generation of teacher educators should be taken from experienced practitioners. She therefore argues that relevant knowledge and skills should form part of the training of all teachers.

Training is seen to consist of distinct specialisms, related to the categories of disability, for example:

> Psychology of and education of deaf children, psychology of and education of low IQ children, testing of aural abilities and rehabilitation for deaf children, diagnosis and testing of intellectual and physical abilities, behaviour correction for children, vocational training for special children.
>
> (Chen Yun Ying 1990, pp. 9–10)

The list is long; teachers cannot study everything, so training has to be selective. Chen Yun Ying argues that the pooling of specialisms is the best way of raising the quality of teaching and the competencies of schools: "'not many but excellent" specialisms before we slowly but eventually work towards "many and comprehensive"' (Chen Yun Ying 1990, p. 7).

Some courses have been set up as pilots, for example, the 1988–89 professional education workshop at Beijing Normal University, which included lectures and seminars by overseas contributors. There are initial teacher trainees working towards a graduate qualification in special education in Beijing, Shanghai and Wuhan (Armfield 1992, pp. 34, 36). Chen Yun Ying would also like to utilise a distance-learning, multi-media, approach, particularly for short in-service courses (Chen Yun Ying 1990, p. 3).

Developments in practice

I have observed a range of special educational provisions in China. My first visit, in 1988, included a Further Education (FE) college for deaf students, a kindergarten, a mental health centre and three special schools: for deaf students, blind students, students in need of behavioural 'correction' and students classified as 'mentally retarded' and 'mentally handicapped' (see Potts 1988). My second visit, in 1992, included a mainstream primary school, a kindergarten, a social welfare institution, an adult training centre and four special schools: two for deaf students, one for blind students and the same school for children classified as 'mentally handicapped' that I had visited in 1988. One of the deaf schools was brand new and the school for blind students had been reopened in 1989 after being closed in the 1960s during the Cultural Revolution.

In 1992 I was particularly interested to see what sort of support was being introduced in mainstream settings and I was struck by the changes in the school for 'mentally handicapped' children that I have visited twice. Here are three short case studies, therefore, of support in a primary school, a kindergarten and a special school. The policies that Chen Yun Ying is endeavouring to implement across the country are, directly or indirectly, reflected in these developments.

Peer-tutoring in a primary school in the northern suburbs of Beijing: *gong hua zhen zhong xin xiao xue*

There are 780 children in the school, aged from 6 to 12–13 years. A few young people, however, stay until they are 15–16, the end of their compulsory schooling. The standard size of classes is forty and school hours are from 7.50a.m. to 4.30p.m. The school year is about sixty days longer than in the UK. Zhong Xin primary school is a series of separate, single-storey, brick buildings with playgrounds and trees in between and a large playground at the end.

We enjoyed a formal welcome and introductory discussion. There were eleven people in the meeting room. We were offered tea, cigarettes and decorative trays of fruit.

Our interpreter had accompanied us from the China Central Educational Research Institute in Beijing. Through him, we were told that peer-tutoring had been introduced in the school in 1989 to provide learning support within the mainstream by improving the quality of teaching and varying the pace of instruction for students who experience difficulties in learning. About forty classes in local schools are involved in what was described as an 'experiment'. An area leader supports and evaluates the experiment, for example, visiting Zhong Xin school once a week. Pressure to develop a system of mainstream support has arisen partly from the lack of special schools in the area.

Two classes in Zhong Xin school were involved in the peer-tutoring experiment. We observed lessons in a grade 2 class of forty 7- to 8-year-olds where three children had been identified as in need of additional support, on the grounds of having an IQ in the 60s. Peer-tutors were selected on the basis of their high IQs and levels of attainment to work alongside those who needed support.

The children were sitting in pairs of desks set in columns facing a blackboard and the teacher's desk. They greeted us and clapped when we entered and sang goodbye when we left. The children were reading aloud in unison from their Chinese language textbook. The noise was cheerful but deafening. The headteacher and others in our group wandered around listening to individual children, who were not in the least put off by the invasion.

It was clear that some of the children found it hard to keep up. One boy in the front, who, we were told, had a severe stammer, seemed lost, which could have been the result of articulation difficulties. His peer-tutor was sitting next to him but it was not clear what he could do to support his partner in this situation.

We had been told that work habits, such as paying attention in class and completing homework regularly were among the 'non-intellectual factors' that the experiment was designed to improve, so it may be that the tutor was seen as a role-model for the tutee and, therefore, that the experience of sitting beside him or her would, in itself, be beneficial.

During our initial discussion session, the experimental leader said that the teacher divided her time between three broad ability 'clusters', making it possible to provide more individual support than within the traditional format of whole-class teaching, and that the peer-tutoring was organised on the basis of these clusters. We did not observe any group work while we were at the school so we did not see what tutoring in this context involved.

Apart from experiencing difficulties in learning, the children in this class who had been identified as being in need of support all shared another characteristic: they had been in the class for three years already. They were over-age children who had not been promoted up to the next class because they had failed to reach the required standard as measured by the end-of-year examinations. Differences of age and physical size were therefore additional potential sources of negative feelings about learning.

The experimental leader said that the peer-tutoring system had led to positive changes for students and that all those receiving extra support were making better progress than before. Children who had participated in the experiment in its first year were now in grade 4 and doing well. He mentioned two students as not being included in the experiment any more because of their achievements. He also said that the boy with the stammer was now much more fluent.

We were told that children in grades 1–3 all followed an identical curriculum, but that, after grade 3, there was some differentiation for those experiencing difficulties. Eligibility for promotion up through these higher grades was therefore based on different standards of learning and behaviour for different groups of children.

The classteacher we observed said that it had been difficult for her at the beginning of the experiment, because of the changes she had had to make in her customary practice and because of the evaluative attentions of the experimental leader. However, she felt that he, the headteacher and the other teachers were very supportive. She told us that she loved teaching the students who needed extra support.

There was a five-minute break between lessons while the whole school did eye-exercises to music. We were told that this was to preserve good sight for close reading.

During playtime we saw familiar games, including skipping. Some of the children are 'pioneers' and wear red scarves. This is a recognition of good work and behaviour. The headteacher introduced us to a girl pioneer who was doing very well academically. One of the children who was receiving learning support was also a pioneer.

When we returned to the meeting room for a final discussion, I wrote a thank-you note in the school's visitors' book, which our interpreter translated underneath. I had some questions to ask about the peer-tutoring, but this was difficult because of the mutual inexperience of each other's education system, which made questions hard to frame and answers hard to understand. I wanted to know why there were not more children in the school who needed support, as the system was thought to be working well and as there were no specialist facilities locally. I wanted to know if the peer-tutoring experiment was making a difference to teaching, learning and assessment throughout the school. Or was it seen as a solution to the specific problem of enabling children in the early grades to gain promotion up to the next class?

I later discussed this visit with our host from the Educational Research Institute. She said we should understand that Chinese teachers are very concerned about the appearance of their classrooms and that they aim for orderliness and good behaviour. There is no tradition of classrooms in which the children are busy making their own enquiries. I then asked about group work, as we had only observed whole-class activities, like the reading lesson. Our host said that this classteacher had, in fact, undertaken some group work, but only a little. It is hard for Chinese teachers to move away from lecturing the whole class. She added that about thirty-two regions across China had so far expressed an interest in what they see as an exercise in integration. So there is a desire to respond to students' experiences of difficulties but also anxieties about exploring new approaches to teaching and learning.

Support for young children who experience difficulties in communicating: Nanjing experimental kindergarten

The study of language acquisition in young children is new in China and the provision of support for children who experience difficulties in communicating is just beginning. The job of 'speech therapist' does not yet exist.

Zhou Jin works in the Education Department at the Nanjing Normal University, a teacher-training university founded in 1911 as a women's college by American missionaries. After studying Chinese literature at the Normal University, Zhou Jin stayed on to became a teacher of Chinese language and literature to teacher-trainees. A UNICEF scholarship to the United States allowed her to begin a study of the teaching of language to young children, which involved her in looking at language acquisition and at approaches to teaching children who experienced problems. This is how she became involved in the area of special educational provision.

Since her return to China, Zhou Jin has undertaken research into language development in Chinese children, following three children from 0 to 6 years and studying 180 children at a number of different stages. She wants to produce material for teachers on what may be universal about language acquisition but she also wants to produce material which compares Chinese and English language development to see what is specific to each. Zhou Jin's work is likely to become an important component of special education training curricula.

We walked from the university to the kindergarten where, in 1990, Zhou Jin had helped to set up the provision for children who experience difficulties in communicating. There are nine classes of about thirty children, with a ratio of one teacher to ten children. The kindergarten is open from 8.00a.m. to 5.00p.m., six days a week. The children are mostly from families where the parents have had a higher education (Zhou Jin's own son attends), so it is selective by background and the catchment area is the whole city. All parents pay 30 yuan a month for tuition/administration, 30 yuan for food and 15 yuan for the 'experimental' group. Parents can ask for help with fees from their work units, if necessary.

There are six children in the experimental programme. Their difficulties are diverse: hearing loss; minor physical disabilities that make speaking difficult; difficulties that have resulted in an identification as 'retarded'. The children have their own teacher and their own room and they work at their own pace. They may join the children in the larger classes in the afternoons as they get older, more articulate and more confident. There are illustrated charts up on the walls with the names of objects given in 'pinyin', or roman letters, rather than ideographic Chinese characters, which do not contain information about pronunciation.

I asked about children with more severe problems of communication and was told that they would be in special institutions. The activities in the experimental group focus on learning the basic sounds required for entry into elementary school, where Zhou Jin will continue to provide support after the children transfer.

In the experimental group, as in the rest of the kindergarten, the children were lively and friendly, working at structured activities round groups of tables. There is no sand or water play in the kindergarten, though there are construction toys, slides and climbing frames in the playground.

As in the Beijing primary school, the aim of the support provided in the Nanjing kindergarten was to enable the children to move up into the next stage of mainstream education. It was acknowledged in both places that this access would be facilitated by a different kind of relationship between teacher and taught and by flexibility in the expected pace of learning. The wider revision of classroom organisation or curricula are topics which have not been brought into the discussion of learning support.

Guangzhou Zhi Ling special school for children identified as mentally handicapped

The school is run as a voluntary organisation and has no resources from the government. At the time of our visit there were no official inset or domestic travel opportunities for staff. Professional and financial support comes mainly from Hong Kong, which is not that far away and which presents no communication difficulties. People in southern China speak Cantonese, just as they do in Hong Kong, although in school children study Mandarin, the official language of the mainland since 1949. Zhi Ling parents have to pay a fee, so the school is selective by parental occupation, like the Nanjing kindergarten.

If Zhi Ling school had not opened in 1985, as a result of pressure from local parents, the children who attend would either be at home or in a welfare institution. This is particularly true of the children who have cerebral palsy or who have Down's Syndrome. We recognised one boy whom we had seen with his family in one of the restaurants near our hotel. Because of the voluntary, unofficial nature of the school, the children are still, in a sense, outside the education system, though there is contact through the school's management committee, which consists of principal Meng Wei Na, headteacher Mo Hui Hong, the headteachers of the two local government-run special schools, two teachers and one parent.

The school is for children aged 4 to 18 and there are between twelve and fifteen children in each class, with three adults, a far more favourable ratio than in the mainstream. There were not enough specially-adapted chairs for the children to sit up comfortably, so some children were strapped on. The younger children were working at groups of tables, while the teenagers sat in rows of desks, with the teacher at the front. Even activities such as hair-brushing are carried out in this format, sometimes leaving considerable classroom space unused. In none of the Chinese special schools or kindergartens or the welfare institution that I have visited was there any use made of the floor for children's activities, a marked contrast to practice in the UK. However, most school buildings in China are unheated in winter and there are no carpets or other floor coverings.

The students are grouped according to both age and ability. Some classes do writing and arithmetic. Older groups of students were doing puzzles. We saw English–Chinese flash cards and some children writing English numbers.

The Zhi Ling school has a large and airy circular room in a separate building for music and physiotherapy.

As in other educational settings I have visited, the staff was very stable. People rarely change their jobs, though, of course, this may change. The teachers and helpers were cheerful and welcoming. There was only one man on the staff.

After looking round the school, we sat in the meeting room for a discussion. As in special schools in the UK, there are many more boys than girls in the Zhi Ling school. We talked about the 'one-child' policy designed to control population growth and the reports we had seen of female infanticide. Principal Meng Wei Na was reluctant to draw any conclusions. According to the terms of the 'one-child' policy, families in Chinese cities can have a second child if the first child has a disability.

Developments at the Zhi Ling school between 1988 and 1992

There have been a number of significant developments at the Zhi Ling school since my first visit in 1988 (described in Potts 1989). First of all there is more support from the Hong Kong Caritas Catholic organisation, in the form of equipment and ongoing professional training. For example, there was a brand new computer especially for the children with cerebral palsy and there was a visiting teacher instructing the staff on its use. The specialist music teacher was also a recent appointment.

Second, there are more staff members with overseas experience, who can therefore speak English and read British and American educational journals. Our interpreter for the day was a graduate student on placement from Hong Kong University's Department of Social Work and Social Administration. Maggie Kwan had completed her first degree in Winnipeg, Canada, supported by her parents. She was in Guangzhou for two months and her project was to set up a parents' group. She had worked in a Family Centre in Hong Kong. This was her first visit to mainland China and she had only been at the school for two weeks.

Third, Meng Wei Na now spends her time out looking for additional resources and canvassing support. She admires the government's policy developments but says that Beijing, which is very far away, is acting too slowly. Her priorities for 1992–7 are pre- and post-school provision. When they leave the school some students go into sheltered workshops or to jobs found for them by their 'street committees' (though this system is breaking down in the 1990s), but many do not and there are, as yet, no adult day centres. People who have not been attached to a work unit are not eligible for benefits.

Lastly, we were taken out in the school's minibus to a nearby restaurant for lunch. This treat would have been impossible four years ago.

Meng Wei Na is impatient for the positive changes she desires for her students and she often feels isolated. However, the official *China Education Yearbook* for 1989 encourages private and voluntary initiatives:

We must run schools on the basis of multi-channels and multi-formats. In conjunction with the state-run schools, we must actively advocate and encourage the running of schools, donation of funds or materials and strong support from all social forces, organisations in industry, mining, forestry, exploration, collective financial organisations, private financial organisations and private individuals.

(Long Qingzu 1989, p. 117;
translated by Lillian Chia 1992)

CONCLUSION

The aim of universal school attendance and changing attitudes towards disability have resulted in the funding of major initiatives in special educational provision in China. The approach is pragmatic: where can we find a place for a child or young person and what is the best way to provide support? This means that integration is encouraged alongside an increase in segregated provision. However, there is a continuity here, for the task of providing appropriate support is seen as a specialist, child-focused one, whatever the setting. The aim is to help children catch up, to overcome what are seen as individual defects: 'Let no one fall behind' is the title of a chapter in the Beijing Review booklet 'A Nation at School' (1983).

There is limited flexibility within the mainstream. The academic curriculum of senior secondary schools and higher education, and the examinations system, constrain the possibilities of change. There is no continuous or qualitative assessment, no project work. Only in special schools can you find variations in pace, teaching methods or class size.

There is a reluctance to see how far competitive examinations at every level of the system exacerbate students' difficulties in learning and poor self-esteem. This is at odds with the recognition of disabled children's educational rights and the undoubted energy and resources that are going into the present reforms.

Suzanne Pepper suggests that there is an ambivalence in 'China about educational reform that has deep and complicated roots' (Pepper 1990, p. 21) and it has been suggested to me that the idea of a fully-inclusive education system is a luxury for the First World, that other countries cannot afford it. Chen Yun Ying sees her task in these terms:

If China could really solve all of its many difficulties and reach the pre-set target laid out in the development plans, then by the year 2000 China's Special Education work will be able to join the ranks of middle-level developed countries.

(Chen Yun Ying 1990, p. 2)

REFERENCES

Armfield, A. (1992), 'Special education in China', *DISES*, 1.
Beijing Review (1983), 'A nation at school', Special features series, *China Today* 5.
Beijing Review (1990), 'Facts and figures', New Star Publishers.
Chen Kai Ming (1990), 'Education in rural China: issues and perceptions', *China News Analysis* 1414 (July), Hong Kong.

Chen Yun Ying (1990), 'A few problems in teacher training in special education', Report of study commissioned by the Teacher Education Bureau of the State Education Commission, transl. by Lillian Chia.

Deng Pufang (1989), *The Development of Human Resources in the Field of Disability in China*, UNOV/CSDHA, Vienna.

Epstein, I. (1993), 'Child labor and basic education provision in China', *International Journal of Educational Development* 13 (3), pp. 227–38.

Five-Year Work Programme for People with Disabilities (1988–92).

Fu Yawen (1986), 'Second try', in X. Zhang and Y. Sang, *Chinese Lives*, transl./ed. W. J. F. Jenner and D. Davin, Macmillan, London.

Hoyland, K. (1993), 'Campus husslers', *China Now* 146, pp. 12–13.

Law of the People's Republic of China on the Protection of Disabled People (1990).

Long Qingzu (1989), 'Special education work', *China Education Yearbook*, Beijing, transl. by Lillian Chia.

Pepper, S. (1990), 'China's education reform in the 1980's: policies, issues and historical perspectives', University of California at Berkeley, Institute of East Asian Studies, Centre for Chinese Studies, *China Research Monograph* 36.

Potts, P. (1988), 'Special education in China', Report to the British Council.

Potts, P. (1989), 'Working report: education children and young people with disabilities or difficulties in learning in the People's Republic of China', in L. Barton (ed.), *Integration: Myth or Reality*, Falmer Press, Lewes, pp. 168–81.

Stone, E. (1993), 'Disability in the People's Republic of China', undergraduate dissertation, University of Oxford.

Unger, J. (1994), 'Taking the plunge', *China Now* 147, pp. 30–1.

Wang Binhua (1993), 'Comparing CESE in the People's Republic of China and GCSE in the UK', paper given at a seminar at the University of London, Institute of Education, International Centre for Research into Assessment, December.

Xu Yun (1992), 'Current status of special education in China', *International Journal of Special Education* 7 (2), pp. 115–22.

Zhang Guanglin (1992), 'Great demand for teachers', *China Daily*, 6 June 1992, p. 4, letter to the editor.

Chapter 17

The role of special education in a changing South Africa

Zandile P. Nkabinde

Nkabinde, Z. P. (1993) 'The role of special education in a changing South Africa', *Journal of Special Education* 27 (1), pp. 107–14.

All black students in South Africa can be said to be educationally disadvantaged as a result of racial segregation. Their experiences of political violence, poverty and physical neglect add to the complexity of their requirements for special educational services. Under apartheid, black students have been taught in classes of between forty and sixty, their curriculum has been restricted to basic literacy, vocational skills and moral education, and they represent only about 3 per cent of all university graduates. The 1976 Soweto riots were provoked by a dispute over education. As in China, the scale of the reforms necessary to build up an equitable education system is vast. For example, it is estimated that around 600,000 black students with disabilities and other difficulties are either not attending school or are in the mainstream without appropriate support. Zandile Nkabinde argues that dispelling the effects of apartheid will take a long time, that it is essential to fund all students equally and that all teachers should be prepared by their training to support the learning of students seen to have special educational needs.

INTRODUCTION

To comprehend fully the present situation in special education in South Africa, it is important to have a historical overview of the general educational system. The apartheid policy in South Africa has legally separated its 35 million inhabitants into four racial groups: whites (15.5 per cent), coloureds or people of mixed race (9.0 per cent), Indians (2.8 per cent), and blacks (72.7 per cent) (Seedat 1984). Political power and privilege have always been vested in the white minority; meanwhile, blacks continuously remain socio-politically disadvantaged (Van Vuuren *et al.*, 1985). The systems of education and special education strikingly reflect this division and class inequalities. Skuy and Partington (1990) noted that the majority of black South African students are academically retarded due to the inadequate and imbalanced educational and socio-political systems.

It is unfortunate to point out that, despite all the recent changes in South Africa, almost all black youths are still denied the right to equal and effective education (Ka Choeu 1991). White South Africans, on the other hand, enjoy one of the highest standards of education. Well-equipped schools and special education facilities are provided for white children and other minority children, whereas black South African children languish in a system that is poorly funded and generally substandard. The policy of limiting educational resources for blacks is part of the overall strategy used by the ruling elite to miseducate blacks. According to Schrire (1991), blacks in schools are subjected to the infamous 'Bantu' education system, which Verwoerd (South African Prime Minister 1958–66) acknowledged was intended to educate blacks merely to the level of menial usefulness to the white economy. A report by the Department Committee on Native Education (1935–6) summed up the policy as follows:

> The education of the white child prepared him for life in a dominant society and the education of the black child for a subordinate society. The limits of [native education] form part of the social and economic structure of the country.
>
> (Seedat 1984, p.87)

It is obvious that these circumstances, no matter how complicated, are a result of social engineering on the part of the South African government.

GENERAL EDUCATION SYSTEM

Education in South Africa is currently going through social and political upheavals. Apartheid, which has dominated South Africa for decades, with its effect on the educational system, is beginning to crumble. Nevertheless, the negative effects of apartheid and apartheid education are incalculable and will persist long after the demise of the system (Green 1991).

In terms of the current legislation, public schools in South Africa are still segregated on the basis of colour or ethnicity, except where parents in a local school vote favourably to include children of other groups. Even when such a decision is made by a local school, the Minister of Education and Training has the final say. Within the education system in South Africa, there are different departments of education with separate budgets and administrations. This is a waste in human and financial resources. Education is compulsory and free up to the end of secondary schooling for all racial groups except blacks. The state spends about fifteen times as much on each white school child as it does on each black child, with expenditures for coloured and Asian children falling in between (Regehr 1979).

Chronic overcrowding is the most visible feature in black schools. The teacher:pupil ratio, for example, is about 1:15 for whites. Estimates for blacks range from 1:40 to 1:60 (Green 1991). The 1976 Soweto riots, which were triggered by an educational issue, focused on the inequality and the lack of quality in black education. For example, there was a raise of per capita expenditure on black children (Regehr 1979). As the head of the South African Institute of Race Relations, John Kane-Berman, reported, between 1971/72 and 1987/88, state spending on African education went up by nearly 6,000 percent from 70 million to 4,097 million (Green 1991, p.12). Although the government is now spending relatively more on black education, the gap between the races remains enormous, while the black student population is exploding.

According to Gaunt (1990), of the 10.8 million working people in South Africa, 30 per cent have no education, 36 per cent have only primary education, 31 per cent have some secondary school education and only 3 per cent have university degrees or diplomas. It is conceivable that no country or nation can enjoy peace and prosperity if the greater majority of its citizens are not educated properly. White people, who represent less than one-fifth of the total population, comprise 90 per cent of all university graduates (Seedat 1984). It has been estimated that only 10 per cent of the college graduates are non-white (blacks, coloureds and Indians).

Also, teaching methods used in black and white schools differ. The teaching process in most black schools emphasises chalk-and-talk methods, leading inevitably to a reliance on rote learning (Donald and Hlongwane 1989). This, in turn, means black schools are forced to neglect the development of mental abilities, promotion of reasoning and problem-solving powers, or creative imagination. In most instances, education of black students teaches them to accept perpetual inferiority, to accept the submissive roles and to be compliant (Regehr 1979). On the other hand, the teaching processes in white and racial minority schools are designed to enable these students to exercise sound judgement and to sharpen their critical faculties (Van Vuuren et al. 1985). The present educational system for whites seems to be geared toward the growth of the individual in all physical, emotional, intellectual and aesthetic aspects (Seedat 1984). High value is placed on the development of a critical intellect.

Furthermore, curricula in all schools reflect the views of the South African minority group in power. To a larger degree, the imposition of its educational and cultural ideals is seen by many as social engineering (Csapo 1986). The learning process for black children in South Africa is still difficult as the curriculum continues to alienate black youth (Ka Choeu 1991). For example, the curriculum glorifies Western civilisation and belittles the contributions of Africans. This exercise results in the low self-image of many black students (Skuy and Partington 1990). Most black pupils also hold negative views on the emphasis on manual and moral instruction, which has been seen as supportive of the status quo and the apartheid system. The lack of emphasis on technical, mathematical, computer, natural science, and business science subjects in black schools is associated with the primary goals of education for blacks in South Africa.

SPECIAL EDUCATION SYSTEM

Under South Africa's apartheid system, special education services are offered on a racially-segregated basis, further complicating the problem of distributing the already limited human and physical resources. Although special services for children with disabilities in South Africa have the same objectives of educating the country's children with special needs, Skuy and Partington (1990) commented that hardly any communication exists between these departments. These authors argued that, because of fragmentation and lack of co-ordination, differences have emerged among the departments of education in terminology and classification of categories of special education.

Apart from differences and inequalities in the provision of services for children with disabilities, features of special education are common to all the systems (Skuy and Partington 1990). These features include the rigid labelling and classification of children into different categories of severe disabilities. For example, black children with severe disabilities, such as mental retardation, visual impairments, hearing impairments, and physical disabilities, are not served in regular schools. They are served in a limited number of clinics, provincial hospitals, and residential institutions. Currently, thirty-five special schools serve black children with disabilities (Heyns 1987–8). These facilities are mostly residential institutions and clinics for the disabled. Special schools and clinical services for children with disabilities serve primarily disabled children (Heyns 1986). As in many developing countries, church and humanitarian organisations are responsible for the establishment of these special schools for blacks in South Africa (Heyns 1987–8).

The initial focus of these humanitarian organisations is to provide basic reading and writing education for black students with visual and hearing impairments. In addition, these students are taught vocational skills, such as woodwork, weaving, basketry and agricultural skills. In South Africa, most formal special education facilities are concentrated in the big cities: the Bartimea school for the deaf and mute is in the Orange Free State, the Dominican school for the deaf is in Southern Transvaal, the Vuleka School for the blind and deaf is in Natal. Two schools for children with cerebral palsy have been opened, at Tlamelang in Western Transvaal and at Letaba in Northern Transvaal (Horrell 1968).

Additional new special schools for blacks exist throughout the republic of South Africa. One of the new schools is Kwazamokuhle. It is a project of the

Lutheran Evangelical Church in South Africa under Bishop Zulu. The school is situated near Estcourt on the Loskop road to the central Berg. The school serves sixty-eight black children with physical disabilities. Of these children, twenty-four are cerebrally palsied, twenty-five have had polio, and others have had amputations and other conditions (Hlatshwayo 1992).

Although residential facilities for children with severe disabilities are available for all racial groups in South Africa, there is still a severe shortage of such facilities for the black majority. In 1966 there were nine special schools for African children with disabilities, and the total enrolment was about 1,140 (Horrell 1968). Clearly, these facilities were inadequate to meet the needs of black children with severe disabilities. Nevertheless, the increased numbers of special schools in recent years has not met with needs for the increases in the number of children with disabilities. Donald (cited in Skuy and Partington 1990) estimated that only 0.1 per cent of African children with special developmental needs were accommodated in special education facilities in 1985. Thus, based on a conservative estimate of 10 per cent incidence of disabilities in a school-age population, at least 600,000 black children with special needs currently are not attending school or are struggling without additional help in ordinary classrooms. Considering the problems besetting African education, such as underfunding, illiteracy, violence, the teacher:pupil ratio of up to 1:60, and the fact that teachers are relatively under-qualified, it is obvious the situation has grown desperate.

Previously, black children with disabilities were unserved in regular class-rooms in South Africa. Only recently has remedial teaching been introduced in black schools, and only to a limited extent. Nothing substantial has been done to address each disabling condition in regular education. For example, an attempt has been made to use community resources, which include the Panel for the Identification, Diagnosis and Assistance (PIDA) scheme, and the Remedial Advisory System (Skuy and Partington 1990). The duties of these specialists vary. Some act as special education consultants, whereas others work as teaching assistants in dealing with learning disabilities. Most of these specialists undergo a year of training, which is inadequate. Concern among many black professionals is that such specialists are given roles and responsibilities that are beyond their training.

Generally, within the white, coloured and Asian school systems, self-contained remedial classes in regular schools do exist to serve the needs of children of at least average intelligence with learning problems (Skuy and Partington 1990). Assistance for students varies. Slow learners may receive extra help within the classroom, or they may be pulled out of a class to receive individual assistance. Such practices are common and practical in white schools, where the teacher:pupil ratio is very low. The practice is impossible, however, in black schools owing to chronic overcrowding.

Most residential facilities for children with disabilities focus on vocationally-directed education to help children with disabilities train for eventual employment in sheltered workshops (Heyns 1986). Because many employers in South Africa are hesitant to hire blacks with disabilities, many blacks who have vocational skills end up staying in residential or government facilities for the rest of their lives.

One major obstacle faced by special education in South Africa is the sheer weight of numbers involved (Skuy and Partington 1990). The implications are dismal for the quality of services provided, as well as the money to be spent on each child with learning disabilities. According to the Human Sciences Research Council statistics, 120,000 South African children have disabilities. Of these, only 26,000 are receiving specialised education (Hlatshwayo 1992). Because criteria for identification affect prevalence, accurate figures for all racial groups in South Africa are hard to establish. Kriegler (1989) suggested that, owing to the current culture of violence and chaos, nearly 75 million black children would have learning disabilities in South Africa in the near future.

Most studies dealing with black education in South Africa suggest that the majority of black students are generally academically retarded owing to the absence of quality educational opportunities. Some of the effects of long-standing inequalities in education are shown in statistics contained in the 1989 population census. These statistics revealed that 42 per cent of black children, 72.7 per cent of coloured children, 96.9 per cent of white children, and 93.67 per cent of Asians had achieved the standard-ten level (12th grade) of education (Skuy and Partington 1990). The situation worsened in 1991 when only 39.2 per cent of black candidates passed their matriculation exams (Wren 1992).

TRAINING OF SPECIAL EDUCATORS

It might be considered a luxury to encourage the training of special educators in South Africa when there is such a crisis in regular teacher training. However, more need exists for special education now than ever before.

Intensive, full-time, advanced teacher preparation in special education is in its infancy for black teachers in South Africa. The main reason for this situation is the deliberate attempt by proponents of the apartheid philosophy to neglect black education. The philosophy invented and implemented by Dr Verwoerd, the notorious former Prime Minister and psychologist, was aimed at educating blacks for servitude (Schrire 1991). As previously mentioned, this served to maintain and perpetuate inequalities at all fronts. Consequently, nothing was done to improve the quality of black teachers (Skuy and Partington 1990).

In an effort to improve the quality of black teachers, upon the completion of their high school diploma the trainees are now required to complete a three-year teacher's diploma. A two-year course leading to a diploma in special education is also available. The admission requirement for this course is an approved teacher's qualification (Heyns 1986). Despite these improved requirements, the majority of teachers in black schools across the country are not qualified. Marcum (1982, p. 17) reported that:

> the government's new (1981) policy of progressively introducing compulsory primary education for blacks is expected, if and when fully implemented by the year 2000, will require annual expenditure of roughly four billion and a cadre of 320,000 teachers. This translates into 11,000 new teachers and 10,000 new classrooms per year.

The training of regular teachers about special education is a necessity. It is evident that every black teacher in his or her career will be faced with the task of identifying and addressing learning disabilities. Therefore, under optimal conditions, sound teacher training practices should incorporate the provision of skills in identifying and addressing children with disabilities (Skuy and Partington 1990).

Whereas secondary school teachers are trained at universities, some universities co-operate with technikons or colleges of education in the training of teachers for certain subjects (Heyns 1987–8). All fourteen white universities offer higher specialisation degree and diploma programmes in different areas of special education. These areas include learning disabilities, mental retardation, visual handicaps, and behaviour disorders (Skuy and Partington 1990). On the other hand, segregated black universities offer no teacher-training specialisation in special education. In the past few years more and more of the white universities in South Africa have opened their doors to students from all racial, ethnic, cultural, religious, socio-economic and language groups (Goodey 1987). For those blacks who are not admitted to white institutions, there are sub-departments of the segregated black universities. Part-time studies in the form of in-service training are also available to most African teachers. It is, therefore, important to note that limited opportunities do exist for black teachers who wish to specialise in certain areas of special education.

RECOMMENDATIONS

Special education for blacks is in its infancy in South Africa, but urgency requires it to occupy an integral part of educational reform initiatives that are now emerging. However, there is no possibility now or in the near future of training an adequate number of black special education personnel to meet South Africa's needs of black children with disabilities. Given these problems, the field of special education for blacks must receive immediate attention. One way to achieve this is to review and update the teacher-education programmes for primary, secondary and tertiary levels of education to incorporate some elements of special education programmes for all teacher trainees. In this connection, South African universities and colleges of education, particularly black institutions, should take the initiative in effecting these desirable changes.

Significant changes in education in South Africa can be realised only through the removal of the apartheid system. This system is responsible for the present unequal educational system of the country. Thus it is evident that the arduous task of reconstructing this educational system can succeed only when performed by a government and people committed to equal education for all in South Africa. Nkomo (1991) stated that South Africa has great potential for a prosperous and democratic future if it restructures its education system in a rational manner informed by a democratic ethos.

Limited available resources need to be distributed more equitably throughout the education system. More schools need to be developed to accommodate all children, including those with special needs. Better training of teachers should be another priority. A unified educational system with a single curriculum for all races should be established. Exclusion of persons in education due to their race or disability should be abolished. Development of a well-articulated educational policy that reflects and represents the needs of all South African people is required. This policy can be developed through the implementation of democratic ideals, such as equal representation of all racial groups at all levels of education.

The availability of physical facilities will be meaningless without the services of adequately trained professional personnel. The need for competent, well-trained regular and special educators is evident. Research studies indicate that most black teachers in South Africa need to be retrained. Because children with mild to moderate disabilities are found in all regular schools, teachers should be trained at all levels to meet these children's needs. This task is best accomplished by introducing general and basic courses in special education for all prospective teachers.

CONCLUSION

The rationale for introducing special education in South Africa is to give concrete meaning to the idea of equality in education. This includes equal access to educational opportunities for all children, regardless of their physical, intellectual and emotional disabilities. However, these objectives and recommendations cannot be achieved in the absence of adequately trained teachers in all spheres of special education. This training will help teachers to cope with the problems of children with disabilities in both regular and special schools.

The rising numbers of families with children at risk due to political violence, neglect, torture and abuse is only one reason why special education can play a great role in our changing social conditions. The number of black South African children and youth needing special education services and the growing complexity of their needs indicate that future programmes in special education will be difficult to implement, demand long-term commitments and require a high level of funding.

On the other hand, South Africa's prognosis with regard to redressing educational disparities is good. As a country, South Africa has extensive natural resources. It is evident that education is one of the most important instruments to bring about future stability in South Africa. It is essential for the future stability of South Africa that blacks, with and without disabilities, receive quality education. For this to happen, a considerable improvement in basic education for blacks is a prerequisite. The improvement should occur in content, methods and scope.

REFERENCES

Csapo, M. (1986), 'Separate development: education and special education in South Africa', *International Journal of Special Education*, 1, pp. 49–91.

Donald, D. R. and Hlongwane, M. M. (1989), 'Consultative psychological service delivery in the context of black education in South Africa', *International Journal of Special Education*, 4, pp. 119–140.

Gaunt, J. (1990), 'Now the capitalists search their souls', *Journal of Special Education*, 13–16 July.

Goodey, J. S. (1987), 'Towards multicultural education in higher educational institutions in South Africa', *Journal of Multilingual and Cultural Development*, 8, pp. 354–5.

Green, M. (1991), 'The politics of education: South Africa's lost generation', *The American Enterprise*, 2, pp. 12–15.

Heyns, R. (1986), *South Africa*, CTP Book Printers, Cape Town.

Heyns, R. (1987–8), *South Africa*, Persko Printers, Johannesburg.

Hlatshwayo, T. (1992), 'Kwazamokuhle school for the handicapped', *Southern Africa Today*, June, pp. 16–17.

Horrell, M. (1968), *Bantu Education to 1968*, Cape & Tvl Printers, Cape Town.

KaChoeu, C. (1991), 'The right to education: an elusive quest for the youth in South Africa', *Africa Today*, 38(3), pp. 72–8.

Kriegler, S. (1989), 'The learning disabilities paradigm: is it relevant to the South African context?', *International Journal of Special Education*, 4, pp. 165–71.

Marcum, J. A. (1982), *Education, Race and Social Change in South Africa*, University of California Press, Berkeley.

Nkomo, M. (1991), 'The current crisis in education and the challenge of the future', *SASPOST*, 2(2), pp. 1–5.

Regehr, E. (1979), *Perceptions of Apartheid: Churches and Political Change in South Africa*, Herald Press, Scottdale, PA.

Schrire, R. (1991), *Adapt or Die: The End of White Politics in South Africa*, Ford Foundations, USA.

Seedat, A. (1984), *Crippling a Nation: Health in Apartheid South Africa*, IDAF, London.

Skuy, M. and Partington, H. (1990), 'Special education in South Africa', *International Journal of Disability*, 37 (2), pp. 149–57.

Van Vuuren, D. J., Wiehahn, N. E., Lombard, J. A. and Rhoodie, N. J. (1985), *South Africa: A Plural Society in Transition*, Butterworth Publishers, Durban.

Wren, C. S. (1992), 'For black students in South Africa, dismal scores', *SASPOST*, 4(1), p. 9.

Part III

Emancipatory research

Chapter 18

Accidental emancipatory action? The evolution of a project in which I learned how to work with shifting sands

Susan Brock

From a background in nursing and sociology, Susan Brock discusses her study of the experiences of disabled students in higher education in the context of her developing ideas about research methodology. She considers the characteristics of what has been called 'emancipatory' research and evaluates how far they match her own work. She is committed to an approach which defines its activities in terms set by the participants and which aims to effect positive change in policy and practice. During the course of her research, Susan has come to identify herself as a disabled person.

In my first year as a lecturer, struggling to write up a PhD thesis, I received a letter from the Open University. This letter asked me to contribute to a section of a new Reader which was to be entitled Emancipatory Research. The letter initially threw me into disarray. Lots of questions went through my mind: what emancipation, whose emancipation, what is emancipatory research, and have I actually been engaged in it? I'm not sure that I have, but I hope so.

In this chapter I will outline what I perceive to be emancipatory research and how, if at all, I feel that my research could be described in this way. I will discuss the interplay between the values informing my research process and the 'chance occurrences' which I learned how to treat as 'meaningful events'. I'll then briefly outline the aims and actions of my research and some possible outcomes of the research process.

EMANCIPATORY RESEARCH

In order to start writing this study I had to uncover exactly what was meant by 'emancipatory research'. The most useful article was published by Mike Oliver (1992) and discusses the issues very clearly and precisely. Oliver suggests that traditional research paradigms, such as the positivist and the interpretative, are oppressive and alienating to many of the subjects of the research. Old-style research ignores people's own definitions of disability, assumes that uncovering facts about the world will lead to change, takes the experience of disability away from disabled people and does not make any improvement to the material conditions of people's lives. Further,

> disabled people have come to see research as a violation of their experience, as irrelevant to their needs and as failing to improve their material circumstances and quality of life.
>
> (Oliver 1992)

Oliver makes a convincing case for this and then goes on to outline an approach which, he argues, is neither oppressive nor alienating. At the same time he fully recognises the problems inherent in the idealism of the new research paradigm. He argues that in order to move research into disability forward appropriately we have to do three things. First, we need to change our theory of knowledge and develop theory which is

> adequate to the task of changing the world. [It] must be open ended, nondogmatic, informing, and grounded in the circumstances of everyday life.
>
> (Lather 1987, p. 262; cited in Oliver 1992, p. 107)

Second, we need to change the social relations of research production so that the 'researcher and researched become the changer and changed' (Oliver 1992, p. 107). The new research paradigm will not simply study existing power relations but will seek to challenge and demystify the ideological structures in which power relations are located. In order to do this researchers must learn how to 'put their knowledge and skills at the disposal of their research subjects' (ibid., p. 111). Finally, he suggests that we must develop a research methodology 'building on trust and respect and building in participation and reciprocity' (ibid., p. 107).

FACTORS INFLUENCING THE NATURE OF MY OWN RESEARCH

The first factor which has shaped the content and direction of my own research is the research plan which was submitted by my supervisors in order to obtain funding for my project. The proposal plan of work suggested that:

> This project is designed to explore HE provision for students with physical disabilities in terms of two important dilemmas: the strengths and weaknesses of special versus integrated provision and the reconciliation of personal and vocational needs.
>
> (Taken from the original submission documents)

The project was intended to focus on: various organisations and practices, a comparison of the merits of the 'special initiatives' (three European Social Fund-supported courses), in-depth interviews with students on mainstream courses, the employment opportunities for disabled people regionally, identifying courses that may be able to help meet these requirements, establishing mechanisms for 'continuing liaison, support, needs identification, etc.', and identifying teaching/learning strategies most appropriate to particular disabilities.

I was employed by the university to develop a research plan and undertake this research, and this leads on to the second main factor which influenced my research, my status as an employee of the university. It is well noted in the literature that undertaking research within your employing institution raises a complex range of issues, such as loyalty, integrity and the position of power held by the researcher. These issues are sufficiently complex if you simply intend to 'study what goes on', but, with the assistance and guidance of my supervisors, I intended to attempt to change certain aspects of the institution and the practice of its staff. An onerous task if you are a manager perhaps, but as a 'mere' researcher?

I was to 'explore' provision, but more than this it was decided that I should attempt to focus primarily on 'establishing mechanisms' for liaison and support. In terms of a research project there is a very long practical and conceptual distance between exploring an area and undertaking action which intentionally changes it. As an employee, researcher, and catalyst for potential change it transpired that I would be working in areas which were political minefields. Disability turned out to be an area which was sensitive to the hierarchy, because they felt they only needed to be seen to be 'doing something' to individual staff members, who had been 'working for these poor souls' for years without recognition and to other colleagues, who felt that disabled people should probably not be in the institution anyway if they could not fit in with already operating systems and procedures.

All of these issues affected the nature of my research, but finally it was probably most affected by me, by my experiences, skills and ideas. As an ex-nurse, I graduated in 1989 with a BA Social Science degree. I wanted to do further research but was not sure on what or where I would do it. An advert for this research post was pointed out to me. I applied and was appointed. At the time I had no substantial knowledge of disabled people or their struggles. However, owing to my sociology background I had an idea that disability was, like racial categories, socially constructed, and I also had a sense that disabled people, do not, but should, have a right to higher education. During the course of the research I came to identify myself as a disabled person.

Setting a research agenda

The first thing I had to do was set an agenda for my research. Methodology training on my degree had equipped me with knowledge of a whole host of methods. But no one had said it would be this hard to refine and define an area of study. The agenda was eventually set by my interpretation of a combination of 'good policy and practice' recommendations produced by organisations for disabled people, my own values and ideas, and the ideas and demands of a group of students (see Hurst 1992; Stowell 1987; and Silver and Silver 1991).

The recommendations for good policy and practice are published by the Royal National Institute for the Blind (RNIB), Royal National Institute for the deaf (RNID) and SKILL, the National Bureau for Students with Disabilities, of which the last named is the most prolific. From reading these documents and from observing the institution I concluded that my institution should introduce a range of facilities and procedures that it currently lacked.

My own values led me to feel that disabled people who want to enter higher education should have access to all the facilities and options that other students take for granted. For example, in this sector disabled people's choices of what to study, and where, are often still restricted owing to the absence of wheelchair access or an interpreting service.

At this stage, with these influences, I could have taken the research in many different directions. I could have concerned myself primarily with numbers and tried to establish how many institutions have the different types of facilities. Another way of focusing on numbers would be to focus on the disabled students themselves and how many students with what disability are studying where and with what outcomes. At the time we also did not have any idea of the numbers of students who tried to enter higher education but did not get accepted for one reason or another (Hurst 1992; he has since completed his PhD thesis on this subject).

In higher education institutions are not obliged by their funding body to make any sort of accessible provision. Initiatives that are taken are funded at a local level using monies that the institution has competed for nationally. So, as suggested, the sector traditionally has not made provision.

Focusing on the students, but with a different emphasis, I could also have identified a specific group and closely followed them and studied their trials and successes. I could have worked towards uncovering the minutiae of their experiences. In this way I would have been a fly on their wall, not attempting to change the research field, but at the same time trying to account for the effect of my mere presence. This is the old dilemma, as discussed by Hurst (ibid.), of whether to be the observing participant or the participating observer.

Basically these approaches would neatly have fallen into what Oliver has now called 'the old style of research'. They serve only further to categorise and objectify the disabled students themselves. The research would not have gone any way towards changing the material circumstances of the students, and nor would it have challenged or demystified the relations of power or the ideological structures in which they are located. I would have been counting, describing or reporting. At the very least naïvely, but at worst oppressively and in ways which would only further serve to alienate disabled people from the process and product of my research.

As it turned out, it was impossible to take either of these traditional approaches, first of all because it is not easy to define who exactly is 'a disabled student'. At least it is not easy if you do not make use of World Health Organisation definitions which individualise disability and locate it as an abnormal state.

I have mentioned elsewhere (Brock 1991) how students chose to declare themselves as disabled to the institution at a range of different times. Some students accept the label and/or the identity and are prepared to state this to the university. Other students may not accept the identity or, if they do, may only be prepared to 'share' their subjectively-defined status at particular times and for particular reasons.

With regard to the work that I undertook with these students, many of them only defined themselves as disabled when university facilities and arrangements were not appropriate to their needs or when they needed to make use of facilities and procedures for those designated as disabled.

My own definition of disability is primarily derived from attempting to understand, and be sympathetic to, the complex relationships that individuals with impairments have with the dynamic and often oppressive culture and politics of this institution. I am trying to understand how these relationships serve to create disabled identities.

I was also prevented from taking either of the routes outlined by Oliver (1992) because of three chance occurrences. The first consisted of a statement made in an informal interview by a member of the institution's hierarchy. I asked him what he thought should be the direction and product of the research. He replied that I should find out 'what is happening for disabled people in higher education' and then produce:

a neat, well-argued, set of recommendations which suggest directions that the [higher education] sector could move in.

The second chance occurrence was a discussion that I had with a disabled student I ran into in the university bookshop in the third week of my new job. We went for a cup of coffee and not long into the discussion he asked me a very simple question:

'Why should I spend my time talking to you?'

I must admit I was floored. Why should he, what would he gain from the time he would spend recounting his experience to me? The question that he asked me forced me to consider the relationship between the students and myself as integral to the research plan. When looking through my field papers, I matched up these statements on two sheets of paper. The power-holder knew exactly what he expected of me. The non-power-holder was not even convinced of the worth of my future activities.

The final ground-breaking chance occurrence came about when I asked a group of students to complete a questionnaire. Luckily for me I had included the question:

'What do you think I ought to be researching?'

The answers to this particular question were all very similar, and not at all surprising to people who have actually worked with disabled people. The students wanted me to find out how to stop people parking in their car-parking spaces. They wanted me to ensure that people who parked in front of the only door which they could use to get in and out of the building got wheel-clamped. The students also wanted me to get the doors on the (goods) lift changed so that you didn't have to be 'bionic to open them', and also to check out why there was only one toilet that six of them had to use in the whole of that area of the institution.

For various reasons this was the group's definition of research, and these were the issues that were important to them. Members of this group have been silenced historically and denied a voice of their own. I started to feel that if I wanted to work with such a group then I should engage with the issues that were issues for them, not simply with the issues that appeared safe and comfortable to me.

It also appeared that there might be a story behind why the car-park was arranged in such a way and why staff were penalised when they broke some rules and not when they broke others. The existence of rules and the policing of them tells us much about the rule-makers.

What was needed, therefore, was a research project which would engage with these issues in the arenas in which they were being created. Obviously I couldn't do this nationally or on a grand scale, but I could do it by working within the institution and by getting involved with everyday political struggles and decision-making.

I saw these three chance occurrences as meaningful events. With the help of my supervisors, a shape for the research started to develop. It was decided that I should: try to establish why the above-mentioned power-holder, and possibly others like him, had an interest in maintaining the status quo; seek to understand what the students would like to see placed on an agenda for change; and try to engage in the processes of struggle and change with their guidance. Of course, I was not the only person in the institution working with disabled students. Other staff were involved in working groups and also in obtaining funds for 'special initiatives', but none of them had the luxury of focusing only on issues to do with disabled students.

The shape of the research project was thus born out of conflict and disharmony. It wasn't possible to work both in the ways that the power-holder wanted me to and at the same time achieve something useful for the students.

Despite having gained these insights, however, I still had one problem to solve. I was not sure if a social scientist could legitimately concern herself with car-parking, lifts and toilets. I got around this by taking what I saw as strength from what educationalists call action research, an approach in which an individual sets about making controlled interventions to an already existing situation in order to produce changes in the learning of the students. I obviously expanded, and perhaps perverted, this methodology but it served as an excellent starting point. I adapted the model so that in my variation I did not have to be totally proactive. In fact I did not even need to observe many problems and issues; the students and some staff brought them to me, and so in this way I was responsive. But the model did provide me with a basis on which to study what the students were experiencing as difficult in the institution and the role of the people in the institution who had caused or contributed to those difficulties.

Having studied these I then used my interpersonal skills, my knowledge of what other institutions were doing, the students' ideas and help, and the documents presenting ideas of good policy and practice, in order to try to bring about some sort of institutional change. I undertook many activities on the student side: I helped them to form groups, I assisted them with gaining grants and equipment and I acted as a community service volunteer supervisor and student counsellor. On the institutional side I worked with individual staff, was a very active member of the appropriate committees and conducted some awareness-raising sessions.

CONCLUDING COMMENTS

My research was carried out within a specific social context. Various factors influenced the development and progression of 'the research activity'. By being as sensitive as I could to a whole range of issues which concern the students I tried to ensure that my actions were as little oppressive as possible. Although not explicit, the informing theory was grounded in the pragmatic realities of day-to-day life and I retained an awareness of the overall social setting of the practical and political problems that confront disabled people.

The difficulties involved in adopting such an approach to research are tremendous. Responding to what the participants perceived as an undesirable state, and then reflectively working towards practical solutions that are acceptable to all, is very stressful for the students, the researcher and the other staff in the institution. As an action researcher you have no firm ground on which to stand and you cannot retreat into observation. However, 'research' conducted in their way, by disabled people, or by people who are committed to working with disabled people, is a very effective way of achieving small-scale, but nevertheless important, change.

REFERENCES

Brock, S. (1991), 'More does not mean different, access to Higher Education for students with disabilities', *Journal of Access Studies* 6(2), pp. 165–77.
Hurst, H. (1992), 'Access to Higher Education and people with disabilities: Individual and institutional perspectives', PhD thesis, University of Lancaster, 1990.
Lather, P. (1987), 'Research as praxis', *Harvard Educational Review* 56, pp. 257–73.
Oliver, M. (1992) 'Changing the social relations of research production?', *Disability, Handicap & Society*, 7(2), pp. 101–14.
Silver, H. and Silver, P. (1991), *Facilities for Students with Disabilities in Higher Education* (unpublished report), Oxford Brookes University, Oxford.

FURTHER READING

Stowell, R. (1987), *Catching Up?*, HMSO, London.
Meeting the Personal Care Needs of Physically Disabled Students in College (1988); *Examination Arrangements for Students with a Disability* (1988); *Developing Effective Policy Statements* (1987), National Bureau for Students with Disabilities (SKILL), 336 Brixton Road, London, SW9 7AA.

Chapter 19

Geoffrey and Michelle: a review of the learning needs of two students with profound and multiple learning difficulties

Linda Harris

This study of the perspective on learning of teenagers Geoffrey and Michelle is an edited version of the report of an investigation carried out for the Open University postgraduate course which preceded 'Developing Inclusive Curricula: Equality and Diversity in Education' (E829), for which this volume is a resource. By means of observations, keeping a diary, some video sequences and interviews with parents and professionals, Linda Harris explored the interests and abilities of her two students. Issues raised by her project include: how far students are seen as having 'profound and multiple difficulties' when their behaviour is aggressive or uncooperative; the limits of new materials to stimulate students who choose to remain inactive; and the relevance of the National Curriculum to students who particularly enjoy activities outside the classroom. Linda Harris concludes that she needs to focus on improved non-verbal communication with Geoffrey and Michelle, to give them as much control as possible in school, to organise staff development sessions and to strengthen contact with services based in the local community.

INTRODUCTION

It is very easy for teachers, ever conscious of the demands of government legislation, of the need to meet parental expectations, to overlook the expectations, wishes, needs of their partners in the education process: the pupils. In this study I have chosen to try to discover more about the perspective two of my students have on their education. This is a difficult task because both have learning difficulties which prohibit easy communication. I am interested to find out how I can improve their programme in school so that it is always relevant to their needs, stimulating, and preparing them for the next stage in their lives. I also want to explore the possibly conflicting demands placed on me as their teacher by the expectations of parents, health and social services, and school policy and practice, to see if all these expectations can be met in a programme whose central aim is to meet the educational needs of the students concerned, who are both members of a class for 16- to 19-year-olds with profound and multiple learning difficulties.

The field of special education is a very wide umbrella, encompassing a range of learning difficulties and impairments with a bewildering array of terms and acronyms which can often have very different meanings according to the role and working environment of the user. Therefore, it is important at the outset of this study to define the terms I will be using.

First, what are profound and multiple learning difficulties and how many of the population make up this category? The prevalence of profound and multiple learning difficulties (PMLD) depends upon the definition applied, but Fryers, in Sebba (1988), concluded that it is a little less than 1 in 1,000. Sebba quotes Grossman's definition of PMLD as those with an IQ in the range of below 20 or 25 who may, or may not, have additional physical/sensory impairments. Other definitions do not refer to test scores but concern themselves with functional definitions, describing those with PMLD as having virtually no language, barely ambulant, having difficulty in fine motor tasks and unable to feed, dress or go to the toilet by themselves. However, this very negative description of those with PMLD is not an accurate reflection of the general composition of school-based PMLD provision. Sebba states that classes for pupils with PMLD, often referred to as special care classes,

> frequently include many individuals who are neither profoundly retarded nor have multiple impairments, but who exhibit difficult behaviour which is considered uncontainable in other classes.

For the purposes of this study I shall be using Sebba's wider definition of PMLD pupils as this better reflects the composition of my class, and using the term 'special care class' to identify segregated provision within a special school. When writing about educational developments generally I shall use the term 'pupils', but when writing about Geoffrey and Michelle, the subjects of the study, will refer to them as 'students', in line with their age and position in the school.

In order to review the learning needs of Geoffrey and Michelle it is important to explore briefly the theoretical framework which underpins evolving PMLD practice and to set this in the context of mainstream curriculum development, i.e., the National Curriculum, which has undoubtedly influenced the education of all pupils with learning difficulties.

CASE STUDIES OF GEOFFREY AND MICHELLE

Geoffrey

Geoffrey is 18 years old but looks much younger as he is short and small for his age, making it easy for adults to continue to treat him as a child instead of a young man. His actual height is greater than first appears because he walks with his knees and ankle joints bent into a 'z' position which has the effect of reducing his height by some 15–20 cm. Nevertheless, his height would not exceed 1m.30: he weighs 35 kg. Geoffrey is doubly incontinent. Geoffrey has no speech, produces no babbling sounds, but will laugh to show pleasure and moan to show displeasure. He can communicate 'yes' by touching an adult's hand in response to a question and usually signifies 'no' by turning away and covering his face. Geoffrey's 'no' response is used in almost all situations, but his positive response is confined to choosing food and drinks and to say whether his nappy is wet.

Geoffrey entered school at the age of 3 and has always been in a special care class. His records show that at birth he was considered a 'funny-looking baby' with a cleft palate, which was operated on shortly after birth and again at age 3. He progressed from milk to solid food later than other children but was eating 'lumpy' food until his second operation, when he developed a feeding problem. Again, records show a persistent difficulty, with Geoffrey refusing to eat anything other than liquidised food for several years, often refusing that. Although there were periods when he would feed himself, these were short-lived, as a change of staff or an illness would break the pattern. When he was 16 it was decided to change Geoffrey's feeding habits by giving him control over his eating and drinking. Weight loss was no longer an immediate threat to his well-being and, although his intake of fluid was still very low, he appeared to survive quite happily on it. Therefore, with his parents' agreement, Geoffrey was allowed to refuse all food and drink in school. After several weeks of this new regime Geoffrey was beginning to feed himself again, when he realised that no one was going to sit by him doing it for him. He still continues to drink very little and requires feeding at home where he lives with his parents and older and younger sisters.

Geoffrey learned to walk at the age of 12 and, although he can walk around school and for approximately 400+ yards, he has a mobility problem because of the shape of his legs and his extreme reluctance to walk if he can avoid it. He has physiotherapy in school and wears leg splints as part of his treatment to try to correct the 'z' formation of his legs and feet.

Throughout Geoffrey's records the word 'stubborn' appears very frequently. Despite his limited means of communication, he is very adept at making his feelings understood by a policy of non-cooperation, and making him change his habits, for example, feeding and walking, requires steely resolve. He is capable of simple cognitive tasks such as discrimination by colour and shape but generally resists these activities, preferring to watch his surroundings, or self-stimulating activities, such as twiddling his fingers in front of his eyes, rubbing a piece of plastic or cellophane through his fingers, occasionally hitting his forehead.

It appears, therefore, that Geoffrey's learning difficulties originate in some unidentified failure in the foetus to develop normally, coupled with a second cleft-palate operation which led him to regress in feeding habits and kept him as a 'baby' for a long period. The delayed onset of walking, too, will have affected his physical development but also affected his intellectual development through his inability to explore his environment.

Michelle

Michelle is a 17-year-old girl of West Indian origin. Michelle's records show that she was born in England but was originally sent to live with her grandmother in the West Indies until age 5. However, she had convulsions as a young child and was brought back to England at the age of 3. It was suggested in her admission records that her severe retardation was the result of convulsions or maternal deprivation. At age 14 Michelle moved into residential care as she was becoming too difficult for her mother to handle at home.

Michelle has three words which she uses appropriately: 'please', 'apple' and, more rarely, 'good'. She vocalises quite frequently and will occasionally repeat words she knows, but not appropriately. She is continent and can feed herself but requires pushing to use self-help skills for dressing and undressing. She can follow simple instructions if she chooses to, and can complete simple inset puzzles and various discrimination tasks. However, she is very good at avoiding tasks she does not want to do by passive resistance and, sometimes, by acts of aggression towards other pupils and staff. She appears to enjoy school, likes going out, swimming, and music sessions, where she can exhibit uncontrolled rocking and swaying to the rhythm. She enjoys food and is very adept at taking food from others. She always finds puzzles and other similar-sized items in the classroom which she will sit and complete over and over again, mouthing the pieces frequently as she goes along.

Michelle began school at 3 and has been in and out of special care classes throughout her school career. Her records show her as 'too bright' for special care but her refusal to co-operate with the staff's planned activities for her, and her bouts of uncontrolled and aggressive behaviour, brought her back to special care, and then to a challenging behaviour group. When this was disbanded she moved again to the oldest special care class.

As far as one can tell from the evidence in her records it is likely that Michelle's learning difficulties stem from the convulsions she had as a child of 3. She still takes medication to control epilepsy but has been free from attacks for over a year. Her records also suggest maternal deprivation as a cause and it may be that Michelle's care as a baby was not intellectually stimulating; but intervention at the age of 3 would, in my opinion, have led to greater progress than Michelle has made if this were the sole cause.

THE STUDENTS' PERSPECTIVE – GATHERING THE EVIDENCE

Finding out what Geoffrey and Michelle want from me, their teacher, is a task beset with difficulties. First, their means of communication are limited, and, second, their ability to communicate depends on the awareness of the adults around them to the meaning of their vocalisations and their body language. In these circumstances communication cannot be instant but something which develops as staff learn about each student, learn to attach meaning to sounds, gestures and expressions and respond to them in a consistent manner. When the staff know the students in this way communication becomes more effective.

In order to find out more about the students and their interests it was decided to carry out a series of observations focusing on the students' activities in the classroom to discover what they chose to do by themselves, and if a wider range of activities and materials within the classroom brought about higher activity levels, particularly in Geoffrey who is a very passive student, preferring to sit and watch others rather than make active choices himself.

Observations were carried out three times in two different settings so that results could be averaged to produce a reliable picture of each student's chosen activities throughout a thirty-minute period. In the ordinary classroom setting materials such as books, brightly coloured plastic manipulative material and simple puzzles were available to the students as they usually are throughout the day. In the enhanced classroom setting this material was still available but a water tray, keyboard, drum, variety of papers, crayons, scissors, music, electronic toys and large construction material were brought into the classroom. Items such as water, shiny paper, drum, keyboard and scissors, which were known to be attractive to the students concerned, were deliberately chosen.

At the beginning of the observation period the students were taken to the classroom door and left to choose where they went so that staff had no influence on their position in the room and proximity to materials. Their activity was recorded at minute intervals throughout thirty-minute periods so that the range of their activity could be quantified and, thus, compared between settings.

In addition to the observations described above, a detailed diary was kept of a sample week at school in which the students' responses to the activities on offer were carefully recorded to provide information on how each student showed enjoyment and motivation, and, conversely, lack of interest and dislike. Consistent with everyday practice students were given opportunities to make decisions for themselves regarding drinks, activities, etc. with the aim of making activities more meaningful and establishing consistency of choice, a concept which poor communication skills on the part of the students, and poor interpretation of responses by adults, can make difficult to establish.

Some video footage was also taken to record student responses to the different classroom settings and to record choices made. However, although this provides useful insight into the nature and difficulties of PMLD work for the reader, the absence of a regular member of the staffing team made it impossible to make wider use of the video camera to gather evidence. Supply staff would not necessarily obtain the same responses from the students, through their lack of familiarity with the students and inconsistencies of approach to eliciting responses.

The interactive approach to the education of pupils with learning difficulties requires teachers to look at the whole person in the settings in which they operate to establish a programme which aids them to make sense of their world, to have some element of control of their lives within their settings, and to develop skills which are relevant to their lives. In order to gain a different viewpoint of the two students I interviewed Geoffrey's mother and Michelle's key worker to discover if the students' behaviour at home differed from their behaviour at school, and to gain their views on what each student needed me to provide for them in school. As both students are close to leaving school I also interviewed the deputy manager of the local adult training centre which provides day care to see whether the school programme was adequate preparation for the next stage in their lives and if the transition process could be improved.

ANALYSIS OF THE EVIDENCE

The observation schedules provided information on the range of activity undertaken by each student in a thirty-minute period. The activities were listed, scores averaged and given in percentages, and then classified as either active or inactive (see Tables 19.1 and 19.2). For the purposes of this study the term 'standard behaviour' was used to describe behaviour individual to each student, but which each student habitually carries out, probably as a means of self-stimulation and comfort. In Geoffrey's case this involves holding his hand to his head and flicking his fingers close to his eyes; Michelle likes to handle small pieces of equipment, e.g., puzzle pieces which she drops, picks up, mouths, puts in place, picks up, mouths, drops, and so on. In classifying the activities as active or inactive the following criteria were used: if the student was mobile, using materials available in the classroom purposefully and/or observing activities within his/her environment, this was considered active even if standard behaviour was occurring at the same time, i.e., while observing the environment; if the student was engaged in standard behaviour and taking no notice of surroundings, or totally inactive, this was considered inactive. In this way it was possible to compare levels of activity and inactivity between students and between settings.

Table 19.1 Table of observation data – Geoffrey

Observation	1	2	3	Average (%)
Normal classroom setting				
Active				
Moving	–	–	–	–
Observing	20	3	37	20
Pleasure/displeasure	–	20	3	8
Responding to need	13	7	–	7
Standard/observing	–	–	–	–
			Active	**35**
Inactive				
Standard	47	3	7	19
Standard/staring	–	–	–	–
No activity	20	67	53	46
			Inactive	**65**
Increased activity choice				
Active				
Moving	–	–	3	1
Observing	10	27	10	16
Pleasure/displeasure	–	–	–	–
Responding to need	–	–	–	–
Standard/observing	27	–	33	20
			Active	**37**
Inactive				
Standard	6	10	23	13
Standard/staring	20	–	24	14
No activity	37	63	7	36
			Inactive	**63**

In a normal classroom setting Geoffrey was inactive for 65 per cent of the observation periods. His main activity when active was observing his surroundings and the activities of the other students. Other active pursuits were expressing displeasure; in the case of observation 2, complaining at being moved from his seat to start the observation, and responding to need, i.e. scratching. The enhanced classroom setting where there was increased activity choice had little effect on the range of Geoffrey's activity as his activity level increased by 2 per cent, which is not significant. However, his observation scores did rise from 20 per cent to 36 per cent, which indicates that he found different activities within the classroom interesting to watch.

One interesting feature of his behaviour was that he placed himself very close to a drum, one of his favourite instruments, for an entire observation period without touching it but watching keenly others who did. However,

Table 19.2 Table of observation data – Michelle

Observation	1	2	3	Average (%)
Normal classroom setting				
Active				
Moving	10	–	–	3.5
Observing	–	6	13	6
Non-standard activity	–	–	–	–
Pleasure/displeasure	3	–	6	3
Responding to need	–	–	10	3.5
Standard/observing	–	–	–	–
			Active	**16**
Inactive				
Standard	87	84	67	79
Standard/staring	–	–	–	–
No activity	–	10	4	5
			Inactive	**84**
Increased activity choice				
Active				
Moving	13	10	44	22
Observing	20	7	–	9
Non-standard activity	–	26	10	12
Pleasure/displeasure	4	–	3	2
Responding to need	–	–	–	–
Standard/observing	–	–	–	–
			Active	**45**
Inactive				
Standard	64	54	43	54
Standard/staring	–	–	–	–
No activity	–	3	–	1
			Inactive	**55**

at the end of the observation, when handed the drumstick by an adult, he proceeded to play it. He obviously needs adult intervention/'permission' to use his environment.

Changing the classroom setting had significant impact on Michelle's activity levels as it increased from 16 to 45 per cent with a 25 per cent drop in standard behaviour. Non-standard activity, i.e., using materials for their true purpose, appeared in the enhanced classroom setting and scored 12 per cent. It must be noted, however, that Michelle did use some of the less familiar material in a standard way, showing how ingrained this habitual action is. Scores for movement and observation also increased as she did move around the room to investigate the different materials available to her.

Although unsupported by documented evidence, it was noted during the observation periods that other students in the class produced similar responses. If they were usually inactive through choice, new materials provoked no response; if they usually explored the classroom materials, albeit in their own standard way, they used the wider range of materials.

During the sample week in which the diary was kept it was decided to focus attention on the students' reactions to activities to discover more about their natural, unsolicited responses as a means of communication. At this stage in their education it seems eminently sensible to focus on how they do communicate already, rather than pursue possibly unobtainable goals of increased signing and speech. It is clear from the diary that both Geoffrey and Michelle do have a means of communication which they use to give clear signals of approval and disapproval, with Geoffrey particularly skilled at expressing disapproval. Both students show approval by grinning, smiling and laughing and by an eagerness to participate in the activity. For example, Geoffrey's mobility problems seemed almost to disappear when it was time to board the bus and find a seat, but were evident in the movement session on Tuesday where similar physical activities are practised. Michelle's pleasure and interest are always clearly expressed and her actions and body language make it very clear what she wants to do or to have.

Both students also clearly express disapproval or lack of interest in the class activity. Geoffrey shows his disapproval by turning his body away and/or making whining noises, and displays lack of interest by reverting to standard behaviour. Michelle shows her disapproval usually by passive resistance to the activity, where she refuses to respond to prompts to carry out a task, or by withdrawing herself from the activity and finding her puzzle or sorting ball. It would be interesting to know if Michelle's 'challenging behaviour' label was partly the result of her reacting to pressure to carry out tasks she was not motivated to do but which were part of the required programme for a non-PMLD class. Currently, behaviour problems occur when she is hungry or, very occasionally, when she has to be restrained, e.g., from jumping on the trampoline, but are becoming less frequent.

Highest levels of enjoyment and motivation were expressed during activities outside the classroom, e.g., on the trip to town and at Taplow Adventure Playground. Class-based activity, although not actively resisted, did not provoke the same level of positive response. One-to-one teaching of discrimination tasks using behavioural methods was tolerated by the students but did not really motivate them, although food rewards encourage Michelle to participate. Group activities within the classroom are usually received positively, with both Geoffrey and Michelle ready to take their turn, but, once again, are not as motivating as visits, shopping trips, etc.

The results of the interviews with Geoffrey's mother, Michelle's key worker and the deputy manager of the (ATC) were broadly similar. Both Geoffrey's mother and Michelle's key worker agreed with the study's findings with regard to communication, although Geoffrey did not communicate by touch at home. All three shared similar views on the role of the school in terms of increasing independence and social skills, working in partnership on specific programmes, and stressed the need for school to provide stimulation, interest and different activities. It was evident that the continued development of cognitive tasks and access to the full range of National Curriculum subjects was not mentioned, even though annual review documentation is presented in this way. Stimulation, enjoyment, independence and social skills training were seen as the major priorities for school. When questioned about the usefulness of school reports in the transition process, the deputy manager of the ATC found them of some use but stressed the need for greater detail re current independence/social skills programmes. The school-based physiotherapist (employed by the health authority) who works with Geoffrey was also consulted. She considered it important for Geoffrey to continue to receive physiotherapy and to be kept as mobile as possible through exercise, hydrotherapy and physical manipulation of the joints and limbs to maintain the quality of his life.

MATCHING THE CURRICULUM TO MICHELLE'S AND GEOFFREY'S NEEDS

How does the curriculum meet the needs of Geoffrey and Michelle and the expectations of parents and other agencies? Can Michelle's needs be met in a class designated as PMLD? It is clear from the information gathered that Michelle and Geoffrey both want a curriculum which consists of activities which they enjoy, which they can take an active part in, activities which they understand, and where their limited but spontaneous means of communication are acknowledged, respected and acted upon. Neither is motivated by the cognitive tasks of the traditional developmental curriculum and these tasks have little relevance to their lives as a whole. Indeed, these areas are ignored by parents and other agencies who focus on stimulation and independence and social skills. School expectations, therefore, appear to be out of step with the students' and their carers' priorities in this area. Moreover, school expectations that a broad, balanced curriculum is offered, similar to National Curriculum, is at variance with the legislative requirements placed on schools for this age range. Both Michelle and Geoffrey are over 16 and therefore not required to cover the National Curriculum topics. The government has plans to review the 16 to 19 curriculum, but, as yet, schools are free to deliver a curriculum appropriate to the students, unfettered by legislative prescription.

Geoffrey and Michelle, in order to be as independent as possible, and to prepare them for leaving school, need to maintain and develop their independence skills. Geoffrey also needs to continue his physiotherapy programme to maintain mobility. In a busy day aspects of the daily routine such as self-care can be rushed to make time for class activities. It is vital that these daily, repetitive tasks are given sufficient time and status within the school day for the students to be as independent as possible in feeding, toileting, dressing, etc. Their importance to the students, to their carers and to their next stage in life is clear from the evidence gathered.

Michelle probably does not perceive the need to eliminate her aggressive outbursts as there is sometimes a 'logical reason' for her action, i.e., she wants something and it is being denied. However, as she enjoys a lively programme, going out into the community, etc., her activities in the future could be circumscribed by her adult placement: those who are 'difficult to place' tend to end up in a more restrictive environment.

Provided there is flexibility of curriculum delivery within the school there is no reason why an appropriate curriculum cannot be provided for Geoffrey and Michelle. *The National Curriculum: From Policy to Practice* (DES 1989) states that:

> the use of subjects to define the National Curriculum does not mean that teaching has to be organized and delivered within prescribed subject boundaries.

THE WAY FORWARD

Geoffrey and Michelle have complex learning difficulties which stem from birth and/or early childhood. These barriers to learning cannot be eradicated but they need not be compounded by a curriculum which does not allow them to be active participants in the learning process, to use the skills they have, and to develop skills relevant to their situation and future needs.

In order to improve the match between the curriculum and their needs I propose to review classroom practice with regard to communication. Through the study it has emerged that the students already have an effective communication system which, although it does not include much speech and signing, does work for them. Therefore, I intend to build on this by using this as a means to further their communication skills by focusing on their body language and vocal responses, responding to them and reflecting their responses back to them verbally to increase their understanding of my means of communication. In addition, I shall continue with the policy of decision-making by the students themselves wherever possible to increase their control over, and participation in, activities. As the study has shown the value of close observation and detailed knowledge of each student in understanding their responses, I intend to carry out detailed observations of new students so that I gain a good understanding of them more quickly.

This proposal has implications for staff training as it is vital in furthering the students' understanding of their world that the responses they receive from staff are consistent so that understanding and not confusion is fostered. Therefore, I intend to request that training time be set aside for this activity.

The study has also shown the enjoyment and motivation the students gained from activities off-site. When planning next term's programme I intend to increase our time spent outside school, establishing a programme where social skills are practised as much as possible in real settings. It is to be hoped that staffing and resources will be available to support. Within the classroom I intend to use as many new and different materials and activities to stimulate interest with staff leading the students to explore the possibilities as the observations showed that adult intervention is needed, particularly by Geoffrey.

Independence skills are in danger of relegation to low status because their practice is part of day-by-day routine. Therefore, it is my intention to ensure that sufficient time and importance are attached to routine activities so that there is always time for the students to do as much as possible for themselves. It is only by careful daily practice that skills are slowly acquired. Practice will take place in context but using behavioural techniques such as backward training.

In the interview with the deputy manager of the ATC it became apparent that closer liaison and more detailed records were needed by the ATC as students moved on from school and that schools could work with parents to enable them to cope with the transfer from school to ATC. Therefore, I intend to suggest that it become normal practice to send more detailed records to the ATC, to make a liaison visit and to support parents at this period of transition.

The advent of the National Curriculum and 'entitlement for all' has led to rapid curriculum review and change as special schools have sought to adapt existing practice to new demands. In attempting to implement these changes schools may have veered too far away from their existing curricula in order to embrace the new, threatening existing good practice. Whole-school policy can have the effect of squeezing out the very special provision required by some pupils. Therefore, I intend to continue to resist the 'need' for common documentation etc. to shape the curriculum offered to the students. The needs of the students should shape the curriculum offered, not the need for uniformity and common practice.

REFERENCES AND FURTHER READING

Department of Education and Science (DES) (1984), *The Organisation and Content of the Curriculum in Special Schools*, HMSO, London.

DES (1989), *The National Curriculum: From Policy to Practice*, HMSO, London.

Fagg, S. (1992), 'Perspectives on the National Curriculum', in R. Ashdown, B. Carpenter and K. Bovair (eds) *The Curriculum Challenge*, Falmer Press, London.

Farrel, P. (1992), 'Behavioural teaching: a fact of life?', *British Journal of Special Education* 19(4), pp. 145–8.

Glenn, S. (1987), 'Interactive teaching', in B. Smith (ed.) *Interactive Approaches to the Education of Children with Severe Learning Difficulties*, Westhill College, Birmingham.

Hulley *et al.* (1987), 'Samantha', in T. Booth and S. Swann (eds) *Including Pupils with Disabilities*, Open University Press, Milton Keynes.

Sebba, J. (1988), *The Education of People with Profound and Multiple Handicaps*, Manchester University Press, Manchester.

Sebba, J. (1992), 'The National Curriculum: control or liberation for pupils with learning difficulties?', *The Curriculum Journal* 3(1), pp. 146–60.

Uzgiris, I. and Hunt, J.McV. (1975), *Assessment in Infancy: Ordinal Scales of Psychological Development*, University of Illinois Press, Urbana.

Wilson, E. (1992), 'Contemporary issues in choice making for people with a learning disability', *Mental Handicap* 20 (March), pp. 31–3.

Chapter 20

Personal and political: a feminist perspective on researching physical disability

Jenny Morris

First published as Morris, J. (1992) 'Personal and political: a feminist perspective on researching physical disability', *Disability, Handicap & Society* 7(2), pp. 157–66.

In 1991 the Rowntree Foundation supported a series of seminars on 'Researching physical disability'. A number of the papers presented were published together, in 1992, in a special issue of the journal Disability, Handicap & Society *(now* Disability & Society). *This chapter and chapter 22, by Lesley Jones and Gloria Pullen, were originally prepared for the seminar series. Here, Jenny Morris discusses why disabled people feel alienated by disability research and argues that there is much to learn from feminist theory and methodology, despite its neglect of the experience of disabled women. The challenge for feminist researchers is to integrate this experience into their analysis of social oppression. Adopting a principle of making the personal political will take women and disabled people out of what Jenny Morris describes as a 'research ghetto' into the mainstream, where the study of their lives should be seen as of general relevance to all groups within our present inequitable society.*

INTRODUCTION

This paper is not really about gender and disability, except to point out that research which only includes disabled men is not ungendered research. Thus such research should be called a study of disabled men and not a study of disabled people; similarly research which only includes white disabled people should be called a study of white disabled people.

Nor am I interested in talking about whether disabled women experience a 'double disadvantage' – for reasons which will become clear. Instead, what I want to do is take the original aim of this series of seminars and the agenda laid down by Mike Oliver in his paper and look at what a feminist perspective might have to offer.

In the proposal for the series of seminars on researching disability which were funded by the Joseph Rowntree Foundation, the proposers identified that disability research has, in the main, been part of the problem rather than part of the solution from the point of view of disabled people. Such research, they said, has been severely criticised by disabled people because 'it has been seen as a violation of their experience, irrelevant to their needs and as failing to improve their material circumstances and quality of life'. In his own seminar paper, Mike Oliver identified that disabled people experience disability research as alienation – in the sense of alienation from the product of research, from the research process, from other research subjects and from one's self.

In that paper – and in other writings – he argued for the development of a new paradigm of research – emancipatory research. This must be based on: empowerment and reciprocity; changing the social relations of research production; changing the focus of attention away from disabled individuals and on to disablist society.

As a disabled researcher, seeking to incorporate a feminist and a disability-rights perspective into my research, what can I contribute to these aims?

WHAT CHARACTERISES A FEMINIST PERSPECTIVE AND WHAT MAKES IT RELEVANT TO RESEARCHING PHYSICAL DISABILITY?

My life as a feminist began with my recognition that women are excluded from the public sphere, ghettoised into the private world of the family, our standpoint excluded from cultural representations. When I became disabled I also realised that the public world does not take individual, particular physical needs into account. Just as it assumes that children are reared, workers are serviced somewhere else, i.e., in the private world of the family, so people whose physical characteristics mean that they require help of some kind (whether this need is actually created by the physical environment or not) have no place in the public world.

As a feminist I recognised that men's standpoint is represented as universal and neutral. Simone de Beauvoir wrote: 'the relation of the two sexes is not quite like that of two electrical poles for man represents both the positive and the neutral . . . whereas woman represents only the negative, defined by limiting criteria, without reciprocity'. Women have thus been excluded from a full share in the making of what becomes treated as our culture. When I became disabled I realised that, although disability is part of human experience, it does not appear within the different forms that culture takes – except in terms defined by the non-disabled (just as the cultural representation of women was/is defined by men). A lack of disability is treated as both the positive and the universal experience; while the experience of disability 'represents only the negative, defined by limiting criteria, without reciprocity'.

Patricia Hill Collins's statement (in her book *Black Feminist Thought*) has a doubly powerful meaning for me: 'Groups unequal in power are correspondingly unequal in their ability to make their standpoint known to themselves and others' (Hill Collins 1990, p. 26). Making our standpoint known both to ourselves and to others is a central part of the feminist research agenda, as it must also be of a disability-rights agenda.

WHAT IS MEANT BY THE TERM 'FEMINIST RESEARCH'?

Women have previously experienced research as alienation. 'Objectivity', as Liz Stanley says, 'is a set of intellectual practices for separating people from knowledge of their own subjectivity' (Stanley 1990 p. 11) – or as Adrienne Rich once said, 'Objectivity is a word men use to describe their own subjectivity.'

Building on this recognition of research as alienated knowledge, feminist research is characterised by a method which, as Dorothy Smith says,

> at the outset of inquiry, creates the space for an absent subject, and an absent experience, that is to be filled with the presence and spoken experience of actual women speaking of and in the actualities of their everyday worlds.
>
> (Smith 1988, p. 107)

Does disability research do this for disabled people? Most of it clearly does not, which is one reason why disabled people experience such research as alienation.

This quote from Dorothy Smith also reminds me of one of the reasons why I am uneasy about the use of medical and social models in disability research. Such models are problematic because they do not easily allow the space within the research for the absent subject. The use of models as an analytical tool comes from theory and research which treats us as objects. Is it possible to adapt such an analytical tool for the production of unalienated research?

As Dorothy Smith says in the context of feminist research on women,

> The problem . . . is how to do a sociology that is for women and takes women as its subjects and its knowers when the methods of thinking, which we have learned as sociologists as the methods of producing recognisably sociological texts, reconstruct us as objects.
>
> (Smith 1988, p. 109)

This is the task for disability research also and, again, I am wary of the use of models for they come from a form of thinking which has treated disabled people as objects.

According to Liz Stanley, three things distinguish 'unalienated knowledge' in feminist terms:

- the researcher/theorist is grounded as an actual person in a concrete setting;
- understanding and theorising are located and treated as material activities and not as unanalysable metaphysical 'transcendent' ones different in kind from those of 'mere people'; and
- the 'act of knowing' is examined as the crucial determinant of 'what is known'.

(Stanley 1990, p. 12)

HOW HAVE FEMINIST RESEARCH AND THEORY FAILED TO APPLY THEIR BASIC PRINCIPLES TO DISABILITY?

If we apply the above principles to feminist research concerning disability, however, we see that such research is in fact alienated knowledge as far as disabled people are concerned. This is because the researcher/theorist has not grounded herself as a non-disabled person holding certain cultural assumptions about disability; because the understanding and theorising have not been treated as taking place in the context of an unequal relationship between non-disabled people and disabled people; and because the 'act of knowing', which in this case is predicated on the social meaning of disability, has not been examined as the crucial determinant of 'what is known'.

The feminist research on informal carers is a prime example of the production of alienated research from the point of view of disabled people – as Lois Keith's paper shows (Keith 1990).

However, it is not just the way that feminists have treated disabled people within their research which is problematic, it is also how they have left disabled women out. This is clear if we look at the development of research over the last twenty years.

There were two stages to the development of feminist research. The first was that of 'adding women in' to the previously male-dominated view of the world. This produced some revealing studies in a number of different disciplines, but it was the second stage that was more revolutionary. Feminists found that, rather than just adding women to the subject matter of research, theories and methodologies had to be fundamentally challenged, for existing models and paradigms were inadequate to explain women's (or men's) realities.

In so doing, feminists asserted not only that the personal, subjective experience of women was a legitimate area of research but that how this research was done had to be revolutionised. They went on to develop new paradigms and theories and, finally, a new philosophy which illustrated that feminism is not just about the study of women but about an entirely new way of looking at the world.

The most recent developments in feminist thought have focused on a recognition of the experiences of different groups of women and the relationship between gender and other forms of oppression. Elizabeth Spelman, amongst others, has argued that feminism's assertion of what women have in common has almost always been a description of white middle-class women and that when other groups of women are considered they tend to be 'added on' as subjects of research and theorising. White middle-class women's experiences have been taken as the norm, and other women's experiences have been treated as 'different', as the subject of particular study and analysis. Thus, white middle-class women's reality is the basis of general theory and analysis (in the same way that men's reality was), and the reality of other groups of women is treated as particular, as separate from the general.

Spelman writes, for example:

> Most philosophical accounts of 'man's nature' are not about women at all. But neither are most feminist accounts of 'woman's nature', 'women's experiences' about all women. There are startling parallels between what feminists find disappointing and insulting in Western philosophical thought and what many women have found troubling in much of Western feminism.
>
> (Spelman 1990, p. 6)

Such a recognition has (potentially) as radical an effect on feminist thought as feminism itself has had on world views dominated by men and men's experiences.

Yet there are two groups of women who are missing from Spelman's analysis. In identifying that 'working-class women, lesbian women, Jewish women and women of colour' have been considered as 'inessential' within feminist philosophy, Spelman has – in common with most non-disabled feminists – left out two important groups, namely older women and disabled women. Disability and old age are aspects of identity with which gender is very much entwined but they are identities which have been almost entirely ignored by feminists.

Feminist theory has been broadened, and refined, by the placing of the issues of class and race at the heart of feminism as a philosophy and as explanation. But the issues of disability and old age are either not considered at all, or dismissed in the way that Caroline Ramazanoglu does when she justifies her failure to incorporate disabled and older women into her analysis. She writes: 'while these are crucial areas of oppression for many women, they take different forms in different cultures, and so are difficult to generalise about. They are also forms of difference which could be trans-formed by changes in consciousness' (Ramazanoglu 1989, p. 95). These are really flimsy arguments. Racism also takes different forms in different cultures, yet recent feminist analysis has, quite rightly, argued that black women's experiences and interests must be placed at the heart of feminist research and theory. Her second statement is an extraordinary denial of the socio-economic base of the oppression which older people and disabled people experience – we might as well say that racism can be eradicated by compulsory anti-racism training.

The fact that disability has not been integrated into feminist theory arises from one of the most significant problems with feminism's premise that 'the personal is political'. As Charlotte Bunch acknowledges:

> In looking at diversity among women, we see one of the weaknesses of the feminist concept that the personal is political. It is valid that each woman begins from her personal experiences and it is important to see how these are political. But we must also recognise that our personal experiences are shaped by the culture with all its prejudices. We cannot therefore depend on our perceptions alone as the basis for political analysis and action – much less for coalition. Feminists must stretch beyond, challenging the limits of our own personal experiences by learning from the diversity of women's lives.
>
> (Bunch 1988, p. 290)

Disabled people – men and women – have little opportunity to portray our own experiences within the general culture – or within radical political movements. Our experience is isolated, individualised; the definitions which society places on us centre on judgements of individual capacities and personalities. This lack of a voice, of the representation of our subjective reality, means that it is difficult for non-disabled feminists to incorporate our reality into their research, their theories, unless it is in terms of the way the non-disabled world sees us.

This does not mean that the experience of disability and old age should be 'added on' to existing feminist theory. Integrating these two aspects of identity into feminist thought will be just as revolutionary as feminism's political and theoretical challenge to the way that the experience of the white male was taken as representative of general human experience. Indeed feminism's challenge must remain incomplete while it excludes two such important aspects of human experience and modes of social and economic oppression.

So where does this leave me as a disabled feminist? It means that I want to challenge feminism to incorporate the subjective reality of disabled women, but I also want disability research to incorporate feminist research methods.

TWO CHALLENGES FOR FEMINISM

First, disability is an important issue for women, but the subject of 'disabled women' should not be tacked on as a 'free-standing' research subject bearing no relationship to other research areas in which feminists are engaged.

In my own research, I have recently come across three examples of oppression experienced by disabled individuals where gender issues inter-mesh with disability, although in different ways:

- The rape of a young disabled woman by an ambulance attendant while she was being taken home from a residential college with a broken arm.
- The recording, by a male social worker, in the case notes about a disabled client, that he thought he had discovered her masturbating and the conclusions that he drew from this about her personality.
- A policeman and social worker waiting in a hospital corridor for a disabled woman to give birth at which point they removed her baby from her under a Place of Safety Order on the grounds that her physical disability prevented her from looking after the child.

These incidents are all concerned with violation of one kind or another and they all take place in the context of both unequal power relationships and oppressive ideologies. My challenge to feminists is that they need to ask themselves whether these experiences of oppression are only of interest to disabled women.

The three examples illustrate different ways in which the oppression experienced by women and by disabled people intermesh. However, it is something of a red herring to spend much time analysing the relationship between sexism and disablism. What is more interesting to me is whether the experience of the women described above appears on the main agenda of non-disabled feminist researchers – or is it, at best, tacked on as a supple-mentary issue, on the assumption that disabled women's experience is separate from that of non-disabled women.

Second, I would also argue that it is not very helpful to talk about disabled women experiencing a 'double disadvantage'.

Images of disadvantage are such an important part of the experience of oppression that emancipatory research (research which seeks to further the interests of 'the researched') must consistently challenge them. Therein lies one of the problems with examining the relationship between gender and disability, race and disability in terms of 'double disadvantage'. The research can itself be part of the images of disadvantage.

If disability research is to be emancipatory research then it must be part of disabled people's struggle to take over ownership of the definition of oppression, of the translation of their subjective reality.

As Alice Walker writes, 'In my own work I write not only what I want to read . . . I write all the things I should have been able to read'. I do not think that I, or many other disabled women, want to read non-disabled researchers analysing how awful our lives are because we 'suffer from' two modes of oppression.

WHAT KIND OF DISABILITY RESEARCH DO I WANT TO SEE?

I am interested in identifying the relevance of feminist theory and method-ology for developing disability research which will empower disabled people. There are four main points which I would make in this respect:

1 The role of research in personal liberation. For women like me, as Liz Stanley and Sue Wise write, feminism is a way of living our lives:

> It occurs as and when women, individually and together, hesitantly and rampantly, joyously and with deep sorrow, come to see our lives differ-ently and to reject externally imposed frames of reference for understand-ing these lives, instead beginning the slow process of constructing our own ways of seeing them, understanding them, and living them. For us, the insistence on the deeply political nature of everyday life and on seeing political change as personal change is, quite simply, 'feminism'.
>
> (Stanley and Wise 1983, p. 192)

In a similar fashion, a disability-rights perspective – which identifies that it is the non-disabled world which disables and oppresses me – enables me to understand my experience, and to reject the oppressive ideologies which are applied to me as a disabled woman.

I took to disability research to validate this perspective (in the same way as feminist research has validated a feminist consciousness).

Susan Griffin identified the way in which, during the 1970s, women

> asserted that our lives, as well as men's lives, were worthy of contem-plation; that what we suffered in our lives was not always natural, but was instead the consequences of a political distribution of power. And finally, by these words, we said that the feelings we had of discomfort, dissatis-faction, grief, anger and rage were not madness, but sanity.
>
> (Griffin 1982, p. 6)

I look to disability research to confirm the relevance of these words to disabled people – our anger is not about having 'a chip on your shoulder', our grief is not 'a failure to come to terms with disability'. Our disatisfaction with our lives is not a personality defect but a sane response to the oppres-sion which we experience.

Unfortunately very little disability research does anything other than confirm the oppressive images of disability.

2 *The personal experience of disability*. Researchers such as Vic Finkelstein and Mike Oliver have been arguing for years against the medical model of disability and in so doing they have been making the personal political in the sense that they have insisted that what appears to be an individual experience of disability is in fact socially constructed. However, we also need to hang

on to the other sense of making the personal political and that is owning, taking control of, the representation of the personal experience of disability – including the negative parts of the experience.

Unfortunately, in our attempts to challenge the medical and the 'personal tragedy' models of disability, we have sometimes tended to deny the personal experience of disability. Disability *is* associated with illness, and with old age (two-thirds of disabled people are over the age of 60), and with conditions which are inevitably painful. The Liberation Network of People with Disabilities, an organisation which made an explicit attempt to incorporate the politics of the personal, recognised this in their policy statement. This statement included the point that, unlike other forms of oppression, being disabled is 'often an additional drain on the resources of the individual, i.e. it is not inherently distressing to be black, whilst it may be to suffer from painful arthritis' (*In From the Cold*, June 1981). To experience disability is to experience the frailty of the human body. If we deny this we will find that our personal experience of disability will remain an isolated one; we will experience our differences as something peculiar to us as individuals – and we will commonly feel a sense of personal blame and responsibility.

When illness and physical difficulties – and old age – are so associated with personal inadequacies and are so painful to confront, it is also easy for us, in our attempts to assert control over our lives, to insist that we are young, fit, competent. The truth of the matter is that most disabled people are not young, are not fit, and have great difficulty in developing the competence to control our lives.

The experience of ageing, of being ill, of being in pain, of physical and intellectual limitations, are all part of the experience of living. Fear of all of these things, however, means that there is little cultural representation that creates an understanding of their subjective reality. The disability movement needs to take on the feminist principle that the personal is political and, in giving voice to such subjective experiences, assert the value of our lives. Disability research, if it is emancipatory research (in the way that Mike Oliver defines it), can play a key role in this.

3 *Non-disabled researchers as allies.* All oppressed groups need allies. Non-disabled researchers have two roles as allies:

(a) Non-disabled academics and researchers should ask themselves where are the disabled researchers? students? academics? They should recognise and challenge both direct and indirect discrimination. Unfortunately, most non-disabled people don't even recognise the way that discrimination against disabled people operates within their workplace. Getting disabled people into the positions where we play a full role in carrying out research and disseminating it is as important for disabled people as the same process was and is for women. As Audre

Lourde says, 'It is axiomatic that if we do not define ourselves for ourselves, we will be defined by others – for their use and to our detriment' (quoted by Hill Collins 1990, p. 26).

(b) Non-disabled people, if they make their living from being involved in the field of disability, should ask themselves whether/how they can do research which empowers disabled people.

Non-disabled researchers have to start by questioning their own attitudes to disability. For example, why does Caroline Ramazanoglu dismiss disability and old age in the way that she does? She cannot see either as a source of strength, celebration or liberation in the way that race, class and gender can become through a process of struggle. Non-disabled people need to examine why not.

Feminist research places women's subjective reality (i.e. experience defined in the subject's own terms) at its core. However, when researchers (feminist or not) approach disabled people as a research subject, they have few tools with which to understand our subjective reality because our own definitions of the experience of disability are missing from the general culture.

If non-disabled people are to carry on doing research on disability – as they undoubtedly will – what kind of research should they be doing?

(a) Turning the spotlight on the oppressors. Non-disabled people's behaviour towards disabled people is a social problem – it is a social problem because it is an expression of prejudice. Such expressions of prejudice take place within personal relationships as well as through social, economic and political institutions and, for example, a study of a caring relationship therefore needs to concern itself with prejudice, in the same way that studies of relationships between men and women concern themselves with sexism.

(b) Our personal experience of prejudice must be made political – and space must be created for the absent subject. This point is illustrated by an example of research which needs to be done – namely, research concerning the experience of abuse within institutions. Such research would have three aims:

- naming the experience as abuse;
- giving expression to the anger, pain and hurt resulting from such experiences; and
- focusing on the perpetrators of such abuse, examining how and why it comes about.

The disability movement has started to identify the different forms of abuse that disabled people experience. One example is what has been called 'public stripping'. This is experienced by many disabled people in a hospital setting. For example, a woman with spina bifida described her experience throughout her childhood when she was required by an orthopaedic consultant to be examined once a year. These examinations took place in a large room, with twenty or more doctors and physiotherapists looking on. After the hospital acquired videotaping equipment the examinations were videotaped. She described how, when she was 12, she tried to keep on her bra which she had just started to wear. I quote from the article which described her experience: 'The doctor, in order to explain something about her back, took it off without saying anything to her, but with noticeable irritation. A nurse quickly apologised – not to Anne but to the doctor' (*Disability Rag*, Jan./Feb. 1990). Anne knew that this kind of humuliation was inflicted on her because she was, as one doctor called her, 'significantly deformed and handicapped'.

The prejudice and the unequal power relationships which are an integral part of disabled people's experience of health services has led, in this type of situation, to both abuse and exploitation: abuse because privacy and personal autonomy have been violated, leading to long-lasting psychological consequences for many who have experienced this kind of public stripping; exploitation because, rather than being provided with a medical service (which is why people go to doctors and hospitals), people like Anne are actually providing a service to the medical profession.

4 *Disability research and disability politics are of general relevance to all social groups*. This is not just because disability is found amongst all social groups but also because the experience of disability is part of the wider and fundamental issues of prejudice and economic inequality.

Black people's experience of racism cannot be compartmentalised and studied separately from the underlying social structure; women's experience of sexism cannot be separated from the society in which it takes place; and nor can disabled people's experience of disablism and inequality be divorced from the society in which we all live.

Feminists ask how and why the public world assumes that responsibilities and tasks which take place within the private world will not impinge on the responsibilities and tasks of the workplace. Disability research must ask how and why the public world of work assumes a lack of disability and illness. It is such a focus that takes both women and disabled people out of a research ghetto for these are fundamental questions about the very nature of social and economic organisations. Our society is characterised by fundamental inequalities and by ideologies which set people against each other – the experience of disability is an integral part of this.

REFERENCES

Bunch, C. (1988), 'Making common cause: diversity and coalitions', in C. McEwen and S. O'Sullivan (eds), *Out the Other Side*, Virago, London.

Finkelstein, V. (1980), *Attitudes and Disabled People: Issues for Discussion*, World Rehabilitation Fund, New York.

Griffin, S. (1982), *Made from This Earth*, Women's Press, London.

Hill Collins, P. (1990), *Black Feminist Thought: Knowledge, Consciousness, and the Politics of Empowerment*, Unwin Hyman, London.

Keith, L. (1990), 'Caring partnership', *Community Care* 22 (February), pp. v–vi.

Morris, J. (1991), *Pride against Prejudice: Transforming Attitudes to Disability*, Women's Press, London.

Ramazanoglu, C. (1989), *Feminism and the Contradictions of Oppression*, Routledge, London.

Smith, D. (1988), *The Everyday World as Problematic: A Feminist Sociology*, Open University Press, Milton Keynes.

Spelman, E. (1990), *Inessential Woman*, Women's Press, London.

Stanley, L. (1990), *Feminist Praxis: Research, Theory and Epistemology in Feminist Sociology*, Routledge, London.

Stanley, L. and Wise, S. (1983), 'Back into the personal or: our attempt to construct 'feminist research', in G. Bowles and D. Klein (eds), *Theories of Women's Studies*, Routledge, London.

Chapter 21

Music, sounds, braille and speech – a multi-media computer for blind people

Tom Vincent and Bill Martin

This chapter describes a project which was carried out by a sighted researcher, Tom Vincent, and a composer, Bill Martin, who is blind. The purpose of this collaborative research was to design a score writer for blind composers.

INTRODUCTION

When personal computers first became available in the 1970s, it appeared to be a development that excluded blind people because a visual display was the chosen medium with which to interact with the computer. Subsequently, through the use of synthetic speech, sounds and braille equivalents to the visual display, many blind people now use computers effectively. Indeed, it could be argued for some blind people that the computer has had a more positive impact on their lives than for most sighted people.

The success in using computers to meet the needs of blind people has not come about by accident. The assessment of individual needs, matching the needs to the technology, designing interfaces, the conversion of screen text to speech and/or braille, and developing new skills, have all played a part for the user who is blind.

This chapter draws on the experiences from a research project that set out to design a music score writer for blind composers. The project, as with many others of this type, was a partnership between researcher and user. This jointly authored chapter reflects this partnership, and the different skills that were brought together to achieve a successful outcome. This success is measured in terms both of the prime objective of developing an independent means of score writing, and of integrating the use of the technology into the life of the composer.

BACKGROUND TO THE PROJECT

There are few aspects of our lives where computers do not play a part. This may be directly through their use in the classroom and in the workplace, or through personalised letters that appear as advertising leaflets. New devices are planned for the home that will be called 'entertainment centres' or similar names to disguise the fact that they are computers without the familiar keyboard and monitor. In education, training and employment, many computers are purchased that have a multi-media capability and use high capacity storage devices such as CD-ROM.

What are the implications of these developments for people who are blind? Do they create opportunities or barriers? There are no simple answers to these questions – not least because computers have provided new opportunities for some people and barriers for others. Investigations into the use of computers by blind people has been the subject of research at the Open University since 1979 (Hawkridge and Vincent 1992). A key feature of this work has been a project-based approach within which a blind person with a particular need has participated throughout. A project that sought to overcome the difficulties of a composer in producing printed music scores independently is described here.

ADAPTING COMPUTERS FOR BLIND PEOPLE

For blind learners with good hearing, the greatest advance has been the development of screen readers, which can provide a spoken (synthetic speech) equivalent to the visual screen display for computer software that functions in a text mode. When speech synthesisers were first added to computers in the 1970s, the interface was often simple and crude. Typically, text would be spoken at the time that it was displayed on a computer screen. This was adequate for many applications as text was written to the screen sequentially (like a teletype terminal or printer) rather than to single screen displays where characters can appear anywhere at any time as with most current computer applications. For a sighted person the format of the display is less of a problem as the eye can quickly scan the screen for information.

Development of screen readers in the 1980s significantly improved access for a blind person to computer applications (Edwards 1991). A screen reader usually works in two different modes: review, and live or application. In the review mode, the screen output from an application (word processor, spreadsheet, database) is 'frozen' and the text on the screen can be interrogated with a set of functions through the computer keyboard or a separate keypad. These functions are associated with a speech cursor that can be moved anywhere on the screen, and characters, words or lines of text can be spoken. There are usually additional facilities to assist with 'navigation' around the screen such as the speaking of the x and y co-ordinates of the speech cursor, or directional and positional tones as the cursor is moved. Information about the attributes of a character can be reported, such as the colour or brightness. These review facilities provide detailed access to text or other ASCII characters on a screen but slowly because of the amount of navigation around the screen. In live mode, the screen reader is programmed to match the display of a particular application to various speech windows and event markers. Speech windows define areas of the screen which can be read using a sequence of keystrokes or automatically. These windows are used in conjunction with an event marker which is programmed to monitor changes in pre-defined locations on a screen. For complex screen displays there may be numerous speech windows and event markers that combine to provide a spoken output when appropriate. Skilful programming of screen readers minimises the amount of speech and maximises the amount of information required for the next action. For effective access to computer applications, the live mode is usually more appropriate.

IDENTIFYING THE NEED

Many human activities can be undertaken by a computer. The need to do this may not always be clear. For example, pen and paper is an effective communication medium although technically, it can be replaced by a computer and printer. The identification of needs and the matching of the technology to these needs (assessment) is well developed in some areas of provision for disabled people. This was the starting point for the project with Bill Martin, a blind composer. The problem was well defined, as Bill Martin indicates:

> 'Is this note D, D sharp or E?' I was faced with this question thirty years ago when correcting some publisher's proofs, but my feelings of inadequacy and frustration are as vivid as if it had been yesterday. I attached no blame to my copyist. This was something I would have to live with as long as I chose to dabble in composition. This was a fact of life for all blind musicians, be they composers, students or lecturers. I wonder just how much talent has been lost to the profession over the years because of this seemingly insurmountable problem. It was against this background that I accepted the challenge of becoming involved in this computer-based project which held out the possibility of being able to produce my own scores completely unaided. I had no idea of the physical size or layout of a computer: as head of music in a secondary school, I saw the computer as an expensive toy for my colleagues in the maths department. Little did I realise that I would be glad of their help in solving some of my problems in operating the computer.

MATCHING THE TECHNOLOGY TO THE NEED

The development of word processors that have a braille or speech output has given many blind people an increased independence in writing (Hawkridge and Vincent 1992). In addition, it is significant that the printout from a word processor (whether a letter, essay or report) bears no indication that it was produced using either a screen display or any alternative such as braille or speech. This equalising effect together with increased independence represents a major contribution to the needs of blind people over the last decade.

The need for increased independence in writing is not dissimilar to the needs of blind composers who wish to produce their own printed music scores. Many composers produce their scores in braille which, in turn, has to be transcribed by a sighted person into a conventional printed score. This method of producing scores clearly lacks independence and, in practical terms, can be time consuming. Hence, for example, to produce a score for a lesson or tutorial might currently require preparation several days in advance. By comparison, an independent facility would enable a short score to be produced on demand, such as during a teaching session.

In order to produce a music score writer, there are two options to consider. First, the development of a computer program that can take braille music code and convert it to a printed score. Second, to adopt similar techniques to sighted composers using computers where staves, notes, symbols, etc. are entered from a conventional computer keyboard together with an electronic music keyboard. The first approach was not adopted because of the anticipated problems of (a) interpreting braille music where there is a high degree of contextual meaning, and (b) limitations with editing scores with a braille input.

The second approach requires a further decision as to whether a customised computer program with speech output is developed, or use is made of an existing score writing program for sighted users to which a speech output can be added that gives a blind composer access to the same facilities.

In the early stages of the project, investigations revealed that a suitable score writing program did not exist which could readily be adapted. Several possibilities were excluded because there was a high degree of dependence on using pointers to place notes and symbols on to staves. This technique is difficult to adapt to a speech output. Trials with customised programs met many of the ergonomic requirements but the need to reproduce all the features of music representation in a score was not fulfilled. However, considerable experience was gained in the techniques that would be appropriate for a blind composer.

SONGWRIGHT PROVIDES A NEW OPPORTUNITY

During the early part of 1990, a significant change of strategy occurred as a result of collaboration with a company who distribute the *SongWright* score writing program. The potential of this program both to have a speech interface and to meet the standards required in music representation were high. This potential was increased when the program developer agreed to introduce a modification that would significantly assist with the use of speech.

SongWright is a computer program (used with an IBM-compatible personal computer) that can receive musical notation from both computer and musical keyboards, and play back individual notes or bars using either the internal sound channel on the computer or an external device through a MIDI interface. Inherent in this process is the ability to store a code for a note which has four attributers to describe it. These are: name, value, accidental and link. This feature allows flexible and accurate checking and editing of scores. In addition, the characters in the codes are chosen as far as possible to give an intuitive representation in terms of music. For example, A to G represent pitch in the value attribute, and a number is used for duration in the value attribute (four entered for a quarter-note).

The *SongWright* program score writing program was made accessible for a blind composer using speech output. This involved a detailed study of the score writing process, and then designing a collection of individual speech environments that give access to a wide range of screen displays that appear when using the program.

HAS TECHNOLOGY MET THE NEED?

The answer to this question must rest with the user of the technology. Bill Martin outlines his experience:

> From day one, my adventure into hi-tech equipment has been need-driven. My present workstation has ten applications. The learning of many operating routines can be a formidable problem. From the outset, I have been soundly advised to learn what is necessary for the moment and to add to that knowledge as a new need presented itself: something new to improve the presentation of a document, new print routines to improve the appearance of my music scores, or new routines that allow me to search and read articles on a CD-ROM. This way, the learning of new operating routines is not an abstract chore, but an adventure that pays immediate dividends.
>
> In the spring of 1984, every available inch of shelf space in my music room was filled with box files which contained braille music scores of original compositions and arrangements for my school instrumental groups, braille copies of songs, form lists, records, all those things in fact,

that are needed to run a music department in a secondary school. All these box files were there for my benefit; there was still the problem of storing the print sheet music and the large, varied collection of instruments.

I was advised to approach the Manpower Services Commission (as it then was), for help in obtaining a VersaBraille. I understand that I broke new ground by being the first teacher to be given such equipment.

In the summer of 1987, I saw for the first time a computer and was more than a little frightened of it! I was to be a guineapig working with the Open University to develop a music processor for use by blind composers and blind musicians working with sighted colleagues who needed the facility to print their own scores. Inputting of music would be a complex process and I would first need some word processing skills. It took no more than a weekend to convince me that the typewriter was a thing of the past. Even the electronic typewriter that was interfaced with the VersaBraille, would be a thing of the past. With speech output, I had all the incentive that I could possibly need, to develop the word processing skills that would enable me to write my private correspondence, to do all the writing (including addressing my own envelopes and labels) that goes with the secretaryship of the Visually Impaired Musicians Association (VIMA), magazine articles and reviews, in the complete confidence that I can do all my own editing and that the responsibility for this is mine alone.

The computer is used to produce music scores. However, I use a spreadsheet for recording bank statements and the like. Memory Mate is a domestic database on which I keep my diary, details of CDs and details of VIMA members with their addresses etc. I interface an electronic brailler with the computer which enables me to produce files in braille that can be transferred to the computer. I also have a CD-ROM drive for newspaper archives (*The Times* and *The Sunday Times*). Use of this computer equipment has brought me independence that I never imagined to be possible, not in my wildest dreams. Over the years my workstation has been upgraded and I see the business of coping with new routines as yet another challenge to be conquered. This is an ongoing challenge, I am the beneficiary and I look for opportunities to help other blind musicians to share my good fortune. I hope the day will come when the computer is seen as an essential tool for any blind person who can use it.

It was the independent production of printed music scores that had been identified as the prime need and where the project has led to a solution:

Since *SongWright* and the speech environments were installed on my workstation early in 1990, I have written material for my clarinet and piano students, written arrangements of folk songs to perform with a friend, and written music for flute, clarinet and piano for performance at a public concert (an example is shown in Figure 21.1). The two friends with whom I played this music are fully sighted and when I gave them their parts we played it through as fluently as they would have played from printed parts and they had no complaints.

The speech environments make for ease of inputting, checking and editing and they are proving to be a wonderful asset. Using the computer's sound channel in checking for errors can be a somewhat tedious process, especially in a composition of any length. I have found my electronic keyboard to be invaluable for checking, since, with a midi interface, you can hear the whole composition and not a voice at a time. The program also has the facility to stop and start at any bar you wish. In addition, the program has the facility for direct input from an electronic keyboard and this may be an attractive proposition to some, but as the music then has to be tidied up and thoroughly edited, I prefer not to use it.

To say that this has been a story of unqualified success would be far from the truth. Many blind alleys were explored before a program that could accept speech output was found.

I have thought of scientists as being unlike artists and musicians who can easily become rather depressed when the ideas just won't flow or it is impossible to get something just right: but I have seen at first hand that scientists are creators too, they can also be depressed when things are just not working out. It seemed that the project could flounder over the question of printing text between the staves. For it to work, we must be able to place syllables accurately under the notes and this proved to be a significant challenge in designing a speech environment that could provide feedback on both the text being entered and its exact placement in relation to the stave.

Certain conventions in staff notation are simply not logical in computer terms, it cannot be expected to accept a semibreve rest as a bar's rest in any time other than 4/4 or 2/2. A piece written in 12/8 time had to be hastily re-barred in 6/8 for performance at a recent concert. The program would not accept 12/8 time or a dotted semibreve. There is provision for the user to construct his own symbols such as staccato dots, grace notes and other such symbols which have no defined position on the stave and which can be saved as computer files. I have found no way of doing this without sighted help, but I consider this to be a small price.

In trying to present a balanced account of things as they stand at present, it would be fair to say that none of the above snags is insurmountable and the program allows us to do what we have never been able to do before, to have complete control over the production of our own scores; nothing need be left to chance.

As with all such applications, a degree of computer literacy is essential and backup teaching material is also vital for the user to get to grips with

PRELUDE

For piano   WILLIAM MARTIN

Figure 21.1 Prelude

the program and all it offers as soon as possible. We are asking a great deal of the computer and some complexity of operation must be expected. Whatever the complexities, the ability to produce one's own scores totally without help is all the motivation that a blind musician can want or need. My copyist shares my delight in dispensing with her services, something that was totally unthinkable when we read those proofs. Just what will be the state of play in thirty years' time?

WHAT LESSONS HAVE BEEN LEARNED?

The success of this project has re-inforced the importance of involving the researcher and user throughout a development where technology is applied to an individual need. In this particular case, the researcher had no knowledge of music but had expertise in developing speech interfaces for computers; the user had no knowledge of computers but is a skilled musician. Both have needed to gain an understanding of each other's skills and requirements.

The 'whole-person' approach is a key factor. Introducing a computer into someone's life is a significant decision. For a blind person, the commitment is of a high order as it can involve changes in communication media (such as braille to digitised speech). In this respect, the identification of range of applications that engages the user in frequent use of the technology is a key factor. Another feature is that technology has to be introduced incrementally so that skills can be developed and confidence built in a progressive way. This can involve many months.

Overall, it has shown that the seemingly intractable problem of providing blind composers with a means of independently producing printed music scores can be overcome with an adapted computer. However, the technology alone is unlikely to bring this about without the assessment of individual needs and the provision of training and support.

REFERENCES

Edwards, A. D. N. (1991) *Speech Synthesis: Technology and Disabled People*, Chapman, London.

Hawkridge, D. and Vincent T. (1992) *Learning Difficulties and Computers: Access to the Curriculum*, Jessica Kingsley, London.

Chapter 22

Cultural differences:
Deaf and hearing researchers
working together

Lesley Jones and Gloria Pullen

First published as Jones, L. and Pullen, G. (1992) 'Cultural differences deaf and hearing researchers working together', *Disability, Handicap & Society* 7(2), pp. 189–96.

Taking turns to present their different points of view, Gloria, who is deaf, and Lesley, who is hearing, reflect on their experiences of collaborative research. The problems which arose are not seen as merely linguistic. Although sharing gender, class, race and motherhood, each woman remained outside her research partner's defining culture. It was necessary for them to acknowledge this, in order to be true to themselves and to maintain an equality of control over the research. However, it was also important not to stay locked into a single perspective but to be willing to understand and to compromise. Gloria and Lesley see their long-term, multi-media project as cross cultural, rather than a study in disability.

INTRODUCTION

This article is based on joint research done by the two authors, one Deaf and the other hearing, over several years. It describes some of their experiences and sets them in the context of cross-cultural research. Doing research about the Deaf community involves complex social and cultural processes typical of inter-cultural contact when a hearing researcher is involved.

For the readers of academic journals (largely part of the hearing world), research describes and accounts for behaviour in another culture. Research findings have tended to reflect the dominant hearing culture. The researchers have been drawn into the social processes they are trying to account for. That is to say, they have become involved in the social construction of deafness. This process is by no means new in social science research and has attracted a great deal of comment from ethnographers (for example, Hammersley and Atkinson 1983).

The research relationship is based within broader social relationships, which in important ways create firm distinctions between the researcher and the researched, building upon a belief that the researcher has specialised knowledge and skills and remains largely in charge of research production (Oliver 1991). These social relationships of research production have served to reproduce ideologies of disability and unhelpful conceptions of the Deaf and Deaf culture.

The problems inherent in research relationships cannot be reduced to narrow methodologies or technical issues. Nor can they be described as a set of attitudes on the part of researchers (Baker-Shenk and Kyle 1990). Such problems must be understood to be part of broader socio-cultural patterns and power relations.

The contact between Deaf and hearing culture may be problematic. Deafness has been compared to ethnicity because of inherent cultural conflict (Erting 1978; Higgins and Nash 1983; Johnson and Erting 1984). Deaf people in various social and institutional contexts find themselves set against the potentially debilitating and marginalising assumptions of the hearing culture. Like prevailing racist and sexist ideologies, 'disablist' assumptions form the everyday reality of Deaf people's lives. These cultural circumstances form and structure much of Deaf people's experience in education, at work and in contact with the major institutions of society. Deaf culture offers a 'resource to resist the conflicting assumptions of the hearing world' (Padden and Humphries 1990). The researchers cannot step outside such cultural conflict. Both deaf and hearing researchers must encounter the same patterns of cross-cultural interaction apparent (and problematic) elsewhere.

What is important here is the need to develop awareness of such processes as well as strategies for dealing with their effects.

Doing the research itself involves both Deaf and hearing researchers in a process of cultural exchange resulting from contact between two social groups – otherwise known as acculturation. This article examines the accounts of the socialisation processes of two researchers and attempts to situate this within broader social structural processes. The following accounts may throw some light on the cultural and personal conflicts generated in such work.

These accounts are based upon the research done at the Universities of Bristol (Centre for Deaf Studies), York (Social Policy Research Unit) and Durham (the Centre for Deaf Studies), and at the National Institute for Adult and Continuing Education. We have been involved in mainly qualitative research with Deaf people throughout Europe. Areas of research have been health, education, employment, telecommunications and adult learning. The work has all been done in sign, written and spoken languages. There have been three areas of potential conflict:

- culture;
- language; and
- research challenge.

The first project we worked on together involved interviewing Deaf people in eleven member states of the European Community in their indigenous sign language. The interviews were video-recorded and translated from sign language into spoken language and into English. It is important to stress here that we are discussing research within the Deaf community with those people who use sign language, usually denoted by use of the upper case in Deaf. It is perhaps useful first to set it in the context of changes taking place in the Deaf community. There has been a marked growth in the recognition of Deaf culture and sign language over the last fifteen years. Sign language had been repressed in education since the end of the nineteenth century, but is currently reasserting itself. It has been recognised as an official language by Sweden and there is some progress now towards its recognition within the European Community. Lane (1984) and Groce (1985) have charted the progress of the American Deaf community and the growth of Deaf culture which is part of a world-wide movement Usually people who lose their hearing as adults opt not to become part of the Deaf community (Jones *et al.* 1987) or identify themselves as culturally Deaf.

EACH RESEARCHER GIVES HER OWN VIEW

Gloria

When our project, 'A Social Survey of Deaf People in Europe', started, I was very pleased. Lesley and I had a lot of discussion preparing the project. The only problem was that Lesley was not a fluent signer – but I understood her sign-language mistakes, and her attitude to the Deaf community was good – so I thought it would be all right.

When the travel arrangements were made, we saw the personal differences – I realised Lesley has a problem about arriving hours before the plane or train leaves! I don't! I also realised she speaks some foreign languages – I thought how clever! We discussed Spain on our way there – she'd worked in Spain for six months and was full of it – we agreed she would translate for me.

When we met the President of the Spanish Deaf Association, Lesley was talking to the interpreter in Spanish and I was using International Sign Language with the President. I wish I had a photo of Lesley's face when she saw us communicating – it was her first Deaf experience outside the UK – she realised then that the spoken language was not always important and that Deaf people can communicate in International Sign Language as well as each country having their own sign language.

I realised that the problem was Deaf culture – very important in the Deaf community and Lesley was not fully aware of this. An example was when we first arrived to interview people as part of our research. We would chat first. I'd see Deaf people looking at Lesley and grinning. I knew something was going on so I turned around and was shocked to see Lesley setting up the video equipment and standing there waiting to start! I tried to let her know by my facial expression that this was not the right way to interview people. (You don't rush in and start interviewing. It is important to get to know people first and take time for them to understand what is happening.) Unfortunately, Lesley kept on asking me what she was doing wrong – so I tried to indicate that she should not keep asking or people would notice. Then, in our own sign language, I told her to stop setting up the video and I would explain later at the hotel. The problem was that Lesley couldn't stop and wait until I made it really obvious that we should not go on.

After the interviewing was over that night, we went to our hotel and then I had to explain to Lesley, to make her more aware – but it did mean we got very little sleep.

If we look back, we had a lot of arguments about the problems – luckily we were two strong women – one person did not get too oppressed. So we continued working together and learned from each other's cultures. I often noticed that if there were problems we stayed up very late discussing them. Lesley was trying to keep up with all the late nights and the new culture. I realised she would be smiling, trying to seem cheerful when she was tired – but she would be smiling at the wrong times when people were talking about serious things – she was so tired she didn't understand. Sometimes thinking of her makes me laugh now.

Lesley tried to 'copy' our culture and always wanted to know what was right or wrong, but she will never 'fit' into the culture exactly – she might know the rules, but not the right way of using them. For example – touch – I found it hard to explain exactly how Deaf people use tapping someone on the shoulder. So sometimes when Lesley would tap me on the shoulder I would think it was urgent when it wasn't. It was just her way of tapping someone. It used to make me very frustrated – when someone tapping me normally wouldn't have this effect on me – but it's impossible to explain exactly the cultural norms of Deaf people.

When there was a group of Deaf people and Lesley was the only hearing person, she'd be trying too hard. She used to look put out when people asked if she was hearing as she felt they treated her differently. If they asked, it was important to tell them. They would accept her on different terms. It's important to be honest in the Deaf community. Sometimes after a couple of hours of trying all the time she'd give up and go to bed. She's improved. Now I find it useful if I'm tired and she is not. We can often take over from one another if one of us is tired – it is helpful being able to do that.

Lesley's sign language is not always natural and like a Deaf person's – you can see she is not Deaf and she makes mistakes sometimes – but give her a couple of drinks and she's fine. When she's more relaxed and confident her signing improves. The next day it's back to normal.

As we travelled all over – in the UK as well – I was amazed that Deaf people praised her sign language. Lesley felt pleased with the compliments from Deaf people. The trouble is that some Deaf people were trying to be nice, or they weren't used to seeing people like her – they didn't realise the importance of correct signing. Lesley always used to say 'thank you' then look at me, laughing – so I often teased her about it, saying that her signing was not as good as I hoped it would be, or that it wasn't too bad. We liked to see how Deaf people were amazed at the criticism of her signing – they wouldn't understand why we were laughing.

By the end of the project, and of our time working together, I realised that I had been worried at first about Lesley's skills in sign language and Deaf culture. Hearing people can learn sign language well, not fluent British Sign Language perhaps. The main problem though is that although people like Lesley may learn the 'rules' of Deaf culture, they won't really be behaving as Deaf people do. I feel it is important that people like Lesley learn about Deaf culture and know the rules, but we Deaf people must also accept them as individuals – discuss things, laugh at things together.

It is important to understand that we all have to learn our limits about crossing cultures – it's difficult to change, but perhaps after ten or twenty years in another culture it would be possible to change. However, we don't live in each other's culture – we only work in it. It is vital to understand and be aware of the cultural difference.

As a Deaf person I think it is easier for Deaf people to understand hearing culture as they are exposed to it more, at school for example. Hearing people aren't exposed to Deaf culture in the same way. Perhaps hearing children in schools should spend some time in Deaf culture, just like learning other languages. Perhaps it would be different then.

Lesley

When I first started working with Gloria in the Deaf community I thought I would be all right – I had grown up in a bilingual family so I thought I understood about working in two languages. I thought the language would be the main problem. I was wrong. The culture was the main thing I didn't know. I had a lot to learn.

I realised working with the Deaf community was very different. One of the things I noticed straightaway was time. Time and punctuality seemed to have a very different meaning. Setting up interviews, one after another, at people's houses was hopeless. We would be there for hours at the first house. Leaving a Deaf club meant at least an hour of waiting for goodbyes to be made – especially at first when I wasn't really a part of the goodbyes myself and didn't know how to join in. I was never sure who to kiss and hug and who not to. All Deaf people's stereotypes of hearing people being stiff and formal were confirmed! I would be standing there anxiously worrying about the time and who to kiss goodbye. I have tried to learn to be flexible with both time and goodbyes and not to mind hearing people waiting to close restaurants at three in the morning. Then you definitely feel pulled between two cultures. The timing of research was different too. I was used to arriving at people's houses and starting to interview straightaway after a *short* chat then having a cup of tea and relaxing. The opposite seemed to be true of interviewing Deaf people at home. Time needs to be taken for everyone to get to know one another first and then the interview takes place at the end. It has a purpose, as regional differences in sign language need to be established as well as backgrounds. Most Deaf people attend residential schools so that peer-group networking is very important.

Another aspect of Deaf culture I found difficult was the confrontational aspect. If something went wrong when we were working with hearing people Gloria would explode with rage and want to go in there straightaway and sort them out – everything else thrust aside. We had a few tussles about hearing culture and the way the subject causing offence might be approached in a roundabout way, rather than tackled head on. I actually prefer the direct approach myself, so we worked out a good compromise there, I think, of hearing deviousness and Deaf directness.

We have often noticed hearing professionals looking surprised at our way of working – puzzled at the teasing that goes on, and trying to work out which one of us is 'in charge'. Some hearing people do still try to talk only to the hearing person. We have very good ways of dealing with that now. I always leave the room for a few minutes, then the hearing person is obliged to communicate directly with Gloria.

The other thing I noticed that was different in our cultures was looking at things with interest. On a train recently when we had been working together, a family got on and the mother was having difficulty with feeding her baby. Gloria and I laughed because I was pointedly looking out the window, trying not to stare (but wanting to!) while Gloria watched avidly with interest. When I was trying to look invisible there she was observing, getting the visual information she needed – I could still hear what was going on.

For a long time I felt at a permanent disadvantage working in the Deaf community, abroad especially. I realise now that Deaf people may well feel the same in hearing culture. I always felt I couldn't do anything right, I couldn't sign properly or understand the foreign sign languages or behave in the right way. Amongst Deaf people and interpreters who were from Deaf families I felt like the only one in the netball team who didn't know the rules. I was running around the field trying to keep up – sometimes I wasn't sure which team I was on. There is another problem about not being an interpreter (which is a more clearly-defined role), but interpreting all the same and having another role as researcher. I was amazed recently to find that some interpreters I'd been to a party with were astonished that I was so extrovert, they had always thought I was quiet and repressed and a bit aloof perhaps. It made me realise that I had been behaving very unnaturally in the Deaf community, especially at first when I was nervous and watchful, making sure I did the right thing.

I think it's important to work in the Deaf community on your own terms – as your own person – not as someone trying to be like Deaf people. I'm not Deaf. Gloria's not hearing. We are different.

So how do we manage to reconcile the differences? We have things in common too, which helps. We are both women, so, for example, walking along dark streets at night looking for the Deaf club means that is sometimes the overriding factor. We are both from white, working-class backgrounds. We are both happy eating egg and chips and a pot of tea in a café when we are out interviewing. We both have grown-up children which provides another link.

Apart from cultural differences, we have other differences. Gloria smokes, I don't. We've had to learn to overcome that – and that could have been a real problem. When we're together, Gloria smokes outside on the balconies, hanging out through open windows – we sit in non-smoking seats on trains and planes. We've managed to be flexible about that. In the same way, I think, we've learned to accommodate by accepting each other's faults as well.

I've learned to wait while Gloria does her hair in the morning – even at five in the morning when we're catching a train. I've also learned that Gloria will only eat English food, no matter where we are, and that her tolerance for foreign spoken languages and my difficulty of translating is low. I've accepted that she doesn't like reading letters, or having information written down – that she prefers sign-language information. She accepts the fact that my signing doesn't improve very rapidly. I ask her the same things over and over again and make the same mistakes. I suppose we're learning to trust each other too, to know that doing the wrong thing culturally is not the end of the world. It's how you react that's important. We've also learned to take 'time out'. To say now it's 'Deaf time' or 'hearing time' – so that we can relax or just switch off.

Sometimes when we're with hearing people and Gloria is tired she will indicate to me not to bother interpreting everything that's going on as she's tired. Then I know she will tap my shoulder (gently!) when she wants to come back into the conversation. I feel I can do the same now with Deaf people when I am out of my depth and struggling to follow. Having the confidence to do that has made a lot of difference. It's wearing trying to look bright and alert all the time when you are not.

I think we've always laughed at our differences too. Without a sense of humour I don't think we would have survived. I know my limits though – I'll never understand Deaf jokes. Otherwise the humour has helped a lot.

I've learned a lot – and still have a great deal to learn. I've enjoyed the warmth and friendliness of working in the Deaf community which has made working with hearing people seem rather cool by comparison. I have liked the openness and directness we have come across meeting Deaf people through our work. There seems to be an interest and enthusiasm in Deaf research which is a pleasure to work with. I've been grateful for the chance to work in Deaf research and to learn such a lot.

Gloria

Today we Deaf can work with hearing researchers and be honest. We must be prepared to expect a hearing person not to be like a Deaf person. The most important thing is that the hearing person should accept our culture and be prepared to spend time discussing it as part of the research. I haven't been very patient with Lesley sometimes. I've lost my temper, but when the work is going well and we talk about it afterwards I realise that losing my temper won't help her. I've learned to be more patient because of that. I am sure it is good to work with hearing people with an open mind and to share their culture too. Now I am aware of things about hearing culture that I've learned from Lesley. For example, I know how to interrupt hearing people when they are talking. We cannot stay locked in our own culture all the time. The only way to work on equal terms with one another is to understand each other's cultures.

CONCLUSION

Research in the field of deafness is inevitably cross cultural. This is the case for research with Deaf people who use sign language and identify themselves as part of the Deaf community. The cultural processes and conflicts which are identifiable in interaction between the Deaf and hearing worlds are reflected in the research relationship and the 'moral career' of the researchers. We have not tried to suggest that there will be relatively constant types of reaction to those issues as has been suggested elsewhere, rather that the nature of cultural process will vary over time, context and institutional setting. We offer the insights as illustrations of such processes, which will be subject to variation.

We each act as channels to each other's language, we interpret for each other, so this is a crucial strength or weakness – which may cause problems. There are clear differences of time, touch, visual information and language between the two cultures. There are different ways of establishing a reassuring presence with the people being interviewed. There is a constant need to check out the rightness of the hearing researcher's behaviour. The hearing culture is the dominant one – the funding, dissemination and supervision may well be largely hearing. This leads to an immediate imbalance in any research project. The hearing researcher may well spend a great deal of time as the only hearing person among Deaf people, but such is the everyday experience of Deaf people. The 'decisions' about the research may well be made within hearing groups (e.g., funding bodies) and disseminated amongst hearing forums (conferences, seminars, etc.). We have made a conscious effort to disseminate our research through the medium of sign language in video form and through Deaf networks. There is, however, a noticeable difference between 'Deaf-led' research, where the hearing researcher was working for a Deaf organisation, and working for a hearing organisation. There may well be a short shelf-life for hearing involvement in some Deaf research but we feel the issues are important ones which illustrate a complex process with similarities in other areas of research.

REFERENCES

Baker-Shenk, C. and Kyle, J. G. (1990), 'Research with deaf people. issues and conflicts', *Disability, Handicap & Society* 5, pp. 65–75.

Erting, C. (1978), 'Language policy and deaf ethnicity', *Sign Language Studies* 19, pp. 139–52.

Groce, N. (1985), *Everybody There Spoke Sign Language*, Harvard University Press, Cambridge, MA.

Hammersley, M. and Atkinson, P. (1983), *Ethnography Principles in Practice*, Tavistock, London.

Higgins, P. C. and Nash, J. (1983), *Understanding Deafness Socially*, Charles C. Thomas, Springfield, IL.

Johnson, R. and Erting, C. (1984), 'Linguistic socialization in the context of emergent deaf ethnicity', *Werner-Gren Foundation Working Papers*, in A. Kernan (ed.), *Anthropology*, Werner-Gren Foundation, New York.

Jones, L., Kyle, J. G. and Wood, P. (1987), *Words Apart: Losing Your Hearing as an Adult*, Tavistock, London.

Lane, H. (1984), *When the Mind Hears*, Random House, New York.

Oliver, M. (1991), 'Changing the social relations of research production?', *Disability, Handicap & Society* 7, pp. 101–14.

Padden, C. and Humphries, T. (1988), *Deaf in America: Voices from a Culture*, Harvard University Press, Boston, MA.

Spradley, J. P. (1980), *Participant Observation*, Holt, Rinehart & Winston, New York.

Chapter 23

Inclusive education in Australia: policy development and research

Mark Vaughan

As co-director of the UK Centre for Studies on Inclusive Education (CSIE), Mark Vaughan was invited to speak at a special education conference in New Zealand in January 1993. He took the opportunity to visit Australia, where he wanted to discover, as far as he could, the extent of inclusive educational policy and practice. In particular, he was struck by a commitment to the study of inclusive education unlike anything that is commonplace in the UK. In this chapter, Vaughan analyses political developments and published research in which the main themes are: an endorsement of the right to be educated in non-discriminatory environments, a drive towards high-quality education systems which are flexible, and schools which will encompass a diversity of educational and social opportunities. He argues that the practice of integration in the UK would benefit greatly from a similar variety of detailed research projects and asks why they do not therefore receive similar support.

INTRODUCTION

In 1993 I was invited to open an international gathering in Dunedin, New Zealand, the inaugural Special Education Service Conference, where I spoke about integration and its importance as a human rights issue. Ten years after its inception, the UK Centre for Studies on Integration in Education (CSIE) had become recognised both at home and abroad as one of the first bodies to put integration in education on a human rights platform and to argue for its enhanced status in the rapidly-changing debate and recent legislative reforms in the UK.

Going to New Zealand also enabled me to make brief visits to parts of Australia to collect a range of material on integration. The significance of this material, which goes back more than a decade, seems to me to be that it discusses a breadth of issues, findings and recommendations about some aspects of integrated education which could also be useful, and possibly applicable, to this country.

It is clear from both national surveys and individual state and territory policy directives that Australia is moving towards the practice of integrated education for all but those with the most severe disabilities. A recurring comment from a wide variety of people and institutions is that, with adequate support, many children with disabilities or learning difficulties can be integrated in mainstream classrooms.

After looking through a selection of documents and conducting some interviews, three themes became apparent:

1 Compared with the UK, there is a wider endorsement of the *right* to be educated in environments which are non-discriminatory, and which give the greatest possible 'normal' experience.
2 There seems to be a drive to develop more efficient and *flexible* education systems to deliver the most appropriate education and for that education to be of a high quality.
3 There is a need felt by a range of educators to develop schools which have a *diversity* of educational and social opportunities – that is, they aim to be as effective as possible for all children.

These motivating forces and influences appear to have taken root and are still effective in Australia, in spite of there being no principle of guaranteed integration enshrined in federal legislation. Australians would be the first to admit that they have a long way to go in the development of inclusive school systems. In New South Wales, at any rate, there is no move at all towards inclusive education, but it is interesting to note the difference between states in that country and our own weak integration laws, the 1981 Education Act (in force in England and Wales from 1983 to 1993) and the subsequent 1993 Education Act (Part 3).

This article looks at some of the Australian findings, asks what implications there might be for this country and discusses some possible future action here in the UK.

My personal view about the material is that it reveals a much greater enthusiasm in Australia to discuss progress and developments with integration in the mainstream and to keep findings and the major issues out in the open. When the policy statements of the different state governments in Australia are looked at in comparison with central and local government intentions in the UK, the ambivalence towards integration in the UK is clear.

I am going to look, first, at the policy review carried out in Victoria in 1984 and, second, at the studies of attitudes towards, and the practice of, integration carried out at Macquarie University, Sydney, New South Wales.

POLICY REVIEW IN VICTORIA

In 1984 the State of Victoria education department examined both the overseas debate and local views on the integration of disabled children. It formulated both a new interpretation of a policy for integration and a conceptual framework that was appropriate to the enactment of that policy.

Just two years earlier the education department had drawn up a policy statement that defined integration as 'the maximum useful association between handicapped children and others consistent with the interests of both'. The 1984 review of policy throughout the state condemned it as being 'inconsistent with a rights model' – it had not gone far enough in ensuring access to the mainstream for disabled children.

Progressive though it may have been at the time, it was clear that in Victoria in the early 1980s people were looking for something that would give a disabled student the *right* to ordinary school education with appropriate support services. And while the Victoria report of 1984 stopped short of recommending the abolition of special schools, it argued strongly that all future allocation of resources should be directed 'as a matter of priority' towards maintaining children with special needs in mainstream schools.

The 1984 review document came up with a new definition of integration that contrasts starkly with the general duty to integrate in Section 2 of the UK 1981 Act:

Victoria Review's definition of integration:

(i)   a process of increasing the participation of children with impairments and disabilities in the education programmes and social life of regular schools in which their peers without disabilities participate;

(ii) a process of maintaining the participation of all children in the educational programmes and social life of regular schools.

1981 Education Act's integration duty:

After the wishes of the parents have been taken into account, a child shall be integrated provided:

(i)   the child can actually receive the appropriate education;

(ii) there is no disruption to the education of the non-disabled children;

(iii) there is an efficient use of resources.

The Review adopted five guiding principles which form a strong starting point for any preparation for change in the education of children with disabilities or learning difficulties. They are:

1 **'Every child has a right to be educated in a regular school'**
This declaration was originally given ministerial approval in March 1983 and its implications, according to the Review, are that ordinary schools must provide and have access to a range of educational options and services for all children, whatever the disability or learning difficulty. Interestingly, the Review added that this principle did not imply integration 'if this is not their parents' wish'; thus it can be seen that Victorian

thinking at that time was that there should be a *right* to mainstream education, but not a *requirement* that all children be so placed.

2 **'Non-categorization'**

This principle asks for children's education to be determined by their *additional* educational requirements rather than being categorised as those having a 'specific qualifying disability'. The Review calls for services to be delivered on a 'non-categorisation basis', though this would not mean an end to special expertise such as teachers of the deaf.

3 **'Resources and services should, to the greatest extent possible, be school-based'**

Successful integration, according to the Review will depend on action at the school level, therefore the focus of resources should be school-based.

4 **'Collaborative decision-making processes'**

This calls for equal participation by all those concerned with decisions about a child's progress.

5 **'All children can learn and be taught'**

Previous assumptions of ineducability for some children are abandoned with this principle which challenges the practices of no, or limited, educational provision for certain groups of children.

In addition, the Review said the overall aims of education for children with disabilities or learning difficulties include equalising access so that the child can participate in the same educational programmes as non-disabled children. They also include ensuring equal access to the social life of ordinary schools and reducing the 'handicapped consequences' of a disability if an environment is not altered. Interestingly, the Review said another aim was actually to *maintain* the educational and social integration of all children in the life of ordinary schools. There has been little published research on the effects of the Collins Report (1984). However, there are some indications that its implementation has not proceeded without difficulty.

EDUCATIONAL RESEARCH AT MACQUARIE UNIVERSITY

Attitudes

The attitudes towards integration of those professionals most centrally concerned with its implementation have a powerful influence on the nature and the quality of special educational provision for children with disabilities or learning difficulties.

Research undertaken by staff at the Special Education Centre at Macquarie University, Sydney, New South Wales has provided a range of information in this area. Studies undertaken between 1985 and 1989 covered the attitudes of headteachers (Center *et al.* 1985), teachers (Center and Ward

1987) and psychologists (Center and Ward 1989) demonstrated that professional groups vary considerably in their perceptions of which types of children are most likely to be successfully integrated. A further study (Bochner and Pieterse 1989) looked at the attitudes of pre-school directors; in general, the findings from all of these studies seemed to be that the most enthusiastic group were those responsible for pre-school provision; the most cautious group were the classroom teachers, with heads, resource teachers and psychologists in between.

The 1985 study by Center *et al.* at Macquarie University surveyed school-heads in New South Wales to discover their attitudes to integration and available support services; in particular they were asked about integration of children with moderate learning difficulties. There was overwhelming support for integration as a desirable goal, although the analysis showed the support was conditional on there being appropriate support services.

There were also some differences between schools, with Catholic and country schools showing slightly more positive attitudes towards integration; heads who had been in post for more than seven years were less likely to be positive about integration, as were those who had a special class on-site or who had previous experience with a special class.

The 1989 study on psychologists' attitudes by Center and Ward showed them to have 'a fairly optimistic perspective with regard to mainstreaming when compared with teachers'. The study of 261 psychologists found this optimism 'welcome evidence of professional acceptance of, and consequent support for, the [integration] concept'. However, the Macquarie University report goes on to note that none of the psychologists appeared to be in favour of a 'zero reject' model in which *no* disabled children would be kept out of mainstream education. And the psychologists tended to see their role with regard to integration as 'consultative rather than interventionist' and they attached little importance to knowledge of classroom techniques to facilitate integration. This suggested to the authors that 'the training and deployment of psychologists need considerable modification in systems which are moving towards a fully or partially mainstreamed approach'.

On the premise that positive attitudes are an important, if not crucial, factor in trying to achieve effective integration for children with disabilities or learning difficulties, any information about what the key groups of professionals are thinking and feeling about disabled children can only be a good thing. The absence of such studies in the UK is to be regretted.

The practice of integration

The 1989 study of integration in practice in New South Wales led by Dr Yola Center at Macquarie University was funded by a major grant from the state's Education Department and by other contributions from the NSW Society for Crippled Children, the Spastic Centre of NSW, the Catholic

Office of Education, the Down's Syndrome Programme, the Special Education Centre at Macquarie, the University of Wollongong, the Hunter Institute
of Higher Education and the Mitchell College of Advanced Education.
Researchers from the last three institutions formed part of the research team.

In New South Wales, the researchers studied ninety-one children with a
range of disabilities or learning difficulties who were being educated in
ordinary schools and found that the 'nature of the child's disability does not
appear to affect the success of the placement' provided structured teaching
methods, appropriate support and a positive school ethos are present.

'Few children with the disabilities studied cannot be effectively mainstreamed. *Most of the factors which predict success are modifiable and lie
outside the child*' (author's italics). Sixty-five per cent of pupils were regarded
as successfully mainstreamed, 17 per cent as 'ineffectively placed' and 13 per
cent as anomalous because of data discrepancies; the remainder were 'marginal'. It should be stressed that these data cannot be generalised to all children
with disabilities. They refer only to those children who were mainstreamed at
the time of the study and consequently exclude many children with more
severe disabilities.

Appropriate support and a positive school ethos were stressed by the
researchers as the 'two most important factors' to help bring about effective
integration and, in a school situation, could be summed up as the commitment
by the head and the teachers 'to the principle and practice of integration'. This
team also found that the successful integration of pupils (whatever the
disability or learning difficulty) was facilitated if the parents were committed
to the mainstream placement and were willing to co-operate with the school's
plan for the child.

The team wrote:

> Most difficulties in mainstreaming can be overcome by appropriate organi-
> sational and technical means if positive school attitudes are present. It is
> noted, however, that students with disabilities studied encounter more
> difficulties at the upper primary and high school levels, where degree of
> disability also becomes a critical issue.

What was also of interest was the report's recommendation that a mainstream school 'should be prepared to act as advocate for a disabled child' in
obtaining resources and deploying existing services. On staff training, it
recommended that headteachers receive in-service training on the implementation of effective integration programmes and that classteachers should
have some practical experience of disabled children along with the use of
structured methods of teaching. In addition, the report takes up the issue of
teacher-aides and recommends that there should be training for them.

If placement in a mainstream class is not going to work for some children,
the report said that support classes provide 'an obvious alternative to special

schools'. Dr Center's report concluded that the results of the study 'reflect a high degree of satisfaction with the mainstreamed placements in terms of both academic and social outcomes. Indeed, there is little evidence of outright rejection or major controversy.'

The study demonstrates how useful it would be to have had a similar investigation into practice in our country since the implementation of our own integration law. The early work (1981 and 1982) by Dr Seamus Hegarty and colleagues at the National Foundation for Educational Research (funded by the former Department of Education and Science) remains the most substantial research into integration in England and Wales.

An integration index

As part of the 1987/88 studies, an 'integration index' was completed by the same researchers from the Special Education Centre at Macquarie University. This index, which was carried out in two stages, assessed the educational and social experiences of disabled children in ordinary primary and secondary schools and identified those children who were successfully integrated into regular classes.

The index had three separate aspects to it: 'academic, social and total integration'. The team concluded that the index appeared to be 'effective in discriminating between more and less effective placements' and use of it in the future was expected to give realistic appraisals of children's integration status, something which had not previously been possible.

The index of academic integration consisted of eight parts, measuring:

1 Teacher's rating of academic progress.
2 Parent's rating of academic progress.
3 Child's progress over six months in maths.
4 Child's progress over six months in reading.

These first four were all relative to the class group.
5 Degree of curriculum modification for the child.
6 Appropriateness of class curriculum for the child.
7 Child's time-on-task in basic skills.
8 Amount of child withdrawal from classroom for academic instruction.

The index of social integration for each child contained twelve parts measuring:

1 Teacher's rating of social acceptance.
2 Parent's rating of social acceptance.
3 Peers' rating of social acceptance.
4 Teacher's rating of child's social acceptance by peers.
5 Change in social acceptance over six months.

6 Teacher's rating of child's class behaviour relative to peers.

7 Observer's rating of child's class behaviour relative to peers.

8 Observed playground interaction compared with random same-sex peer from class group.

9 Teacher's rating of playground interaction (from teacher interview).

10 Out of school contact with school friends.

11 Access to other areas of school (assessed by observer) and

12 Participation in general school activities (assessed by observer).

The total integration index was a combination of these first two indices. Using a predetermined cut-off point for evaluating the mainstream placement for a particular child, the researchers found that 63 per cent of the total sample of students in Stage 1 of the study were successfully integrated in terms of academic and social outcomes; children with sensory disabilities were 'unequivocally successful' and those with physical disabilities were almost all well integrated.

At the other end of the spectrum, children with multiple difficulties seemed to be 'overwhelmingly unsuccessful', though the authors pointed out that, tempting though it might be, no assumptions could be made to link *category* of disability and *effectiveness* of disability. For example, while children with behavioural difficulties tended to be not so successfully integrated, 'one highly successful case suggests that this disability may be offset by the presence of other factors related to the child, school and classroom'. They added that most students with emotional difficulties were found to be unsuccessfully integrated, but *none* of them had the combination of appropriate support or structured instructional style found necessary for success.

The Stage 2 study found that 67 per cent of the sample were successfully mainstreamed. Students with physical abilities still appeared to be successful, although they were closer to marginality than in Stage 1.

Children with *intellectual abilities* in primary classes now appeared, as a group, to be slightly below the cut-off point for effective mainstreaming. However, once again, they exhibited more variability than the other groups of children, with about 60 per cent successful and 40 per cent not reaching criterion on either the Integration or the Validation Index, indicating that it was not necessarily the disability which militated against successful integration. The smaller number of cases classified as anomalous (where actual performance is low but acceptance high) compared with other disability groups, suggested that in upper primary classes there is less tolerance for academic and social diversity shown by children with intellectual disabilities.

Another interesting result of this follow-up study concerned the number of successful case studies of children with *multiple disabilities* when compared with the ones described in Stage 1. This suggests that disability *per se* was not the dominant predictor of integration success for this group, as was tentatively suggested in the pilot study, but classroom and school factors were much more closely associated with positive outcomes for children with multiple disabilities, which can only be explored effectively through case-study data (Center *et al.* 1989).

In terms of the new components in the second stage of the study, it would appear that (a) students with *sensory disabilities* in high schools could be regarded as well integrated, although not as unequivocally as the primary students with sensory disabilities observed in Stage 1. Thus, the tentative conclusions of Stage 1 regarding (1) the rank order of successful mainstreaming for different categories of disabilities and (2) increased mainstreaming difficulties in high schools and upper primary classes appeared to have been substantiated by the Stage 2 study.

As far as (b) children with *learning difficulties* who have attended a special school are concerned, the authors felt these results could only be regarded as provisional, pending confirmation with a large sample. However, the data suggested that some difficulties are experienced in reintegration which are predominantly associated with lack of appropriate teaching strategies and resource support, particularly at the primary level.

In their conclusions the authors said that both Stage 1 and Stage 2 of the study showed that the new indices permitted 'a more objective grounding of otherwise relatively subjective judgements' of the educational experiences of disabled children in mainstream settings.

A significant finding, according to the team, was that 'children from all disability groups observed can be successfully mainstreamed into regular infants and primary classes, providing appropriate teaching methods are used and adequate support is available'. If this turned out to be generally true with all disabled children, they added that it would seem reasonable for parents to seek an integrated place for their child.

CONCLUSIONS

John Elkins wrote in 1985 that Australian society was 'now more sensitive to the injustice implicit in past educational practices' with regard to disabled children, though he thought it might take a generation of non-disabled children being educated alongside their disabled peer-group 'before the idea of segregation is obliterated'. He felt that much damage had been done in the past because of inappropriate views of the potential of disabled students:

> Future special education will benefit greatly if the needs of disabled children are considered, not only by psychological and medical researchers, but by historians, sociologists and anthropologists, philosophers and lawyers. Even more important may be the influence of succeeding generations of citizens if in today's schools past discriminatory attitudes and practices toward disabled children can be eliminated. Just as the curriculum has had to be reformed to remove sexism and

racism, every opportunity must be taken to free students from the tyranny of ignorance and fear of their disabled peers.

(Elkins 1985)

Indeed, Gillian Fulcher (1989) felt the progressive Victoria Review document of 1984 had not lead to all the fruitful changes that might have been anticipated when it was first published. In her view, increasing bureaucratiaation and politicisation of issues surrounding disability were partly behind the 1984 Review's 'failure' to be fully implemented. Fulcher argued that the 'rights theme' of the Victoria Review had a weak institutional basis and that the continued failure by disabled people to achieve an integral place in society was due to the 'weakness of rights issues in current Australian social and political life' (Fulcher 1989, pp. 231–2).

In the UK we need a variety of research projects to look at integration in practice at all age levels – from pre-school, through infant and junior schools and on up to secondary level and further education. It is important to find out much more about the attitudes of key personnel in the education services towards integration. And the development of an index to help evaluate integrated education – and what schools are trying to achieve via integration – would be a major advance not only for researchers in this country, but also for classroom practitioners.

Why is it that no university in this country has ever been inspired to establish something like the Special Education Centre at Macquarie University in Sydney, New South Wales?

REFERENCES AND FURTHER READING

Bochner, S. and Pieterse, M. (1989), 'Pre-school directors' attitudes towards the integration of children with disabilities into regular pre-schools in New South Wales', *International Journal of Disability, Development and Education* 36.

Center, Y. and Ward, J. (1987), 'Teachers' attitudes towards the integration of disabled children into regular schools', *Exceptional Child* 34.

Center, Y. and Ward, J. (1989), *Attitudes of School Psychologists Towards the Integration of Children with Disabilities*, reprints from Dr Yola Center, Macquarie University Special Education Centre, Sydney, NSW, Australia.

Center, Y., Ward, J. and Ferguson, C. (1991), *Towards an Index to Evaluate the Integration of Children with Disabilities into Regular Classes*, Macquarie University Special Education Centre, Sydney, NSW, Australia.

Center, Y., Ward, J., Ferguson, C., Conway, B. and Linfoot, K. (1989), *The Integration of Children with Disabilities into Regular Schools – A Naturalistic Study, Stage 2 Report*, Macquarie University Special Education Centre, Sydney, NSW, Australia.

Center, Y., Ward, J., Parmenter, T. and Nash, R. (1985), 'Principals' attitudes towards the integration of disabled children into regular schools', *Exceptional Child* 32.

Collins Report (1984), 'Conceptual framework and guiding principles for a policy of integration', in *Integration in Victorian Education: Report of the Ministerial Review of Educational Services for the Disabled*, Melbourne.

Elkins, J. (1985), 'Disability and disadvantage: special education in Australia – past, present and future', in *Melbourne Studies in Education*, Melbourne University Press, Melbourne.

Fulcher, G. (1989), *Disabling Policies? A Comparative Approach to Education Policy and Disability*, London, Falmer Press.

Gow, L. and Ward, J. (1991), 'Progress towards integration: impressions from a national review and recent Australian research', *Australian Disability Review* 4, p. 91.

Hegarty, S., Pocklington, K. and Lucas, D. (1981), *Educating Pupils with Special Needs in the Ordinary School*, Windsor, NFER-Nelson.

Hegarty, S., Pocklington, K. and Lucas, D. (1982), *Integration in Action*, Windsor, NFER-Nelson.

Jenkinson, J. (1987), *School and Disability: Research and Practice in Integration*, Hawthorn, ACER.

Thomas, D. (1985), 'The determinants of teachers' attitudes to integrating the intellectually handicapped', *British Journal of Educational Psychology* 55.

Victoria Department of Education (1984), *Victoria Review* (Collin's Report), Victoria.

Westwood, P. (1982), *Integration of Handicapped Children in South Australia*, Magill.

Westwood, P. (1985), *Students with Special Educational Needs in Secondary Schools in South Australia*.

ACKNOWLEDGEMENT

The author wishes to thank Dr Yola Center for her valuable comments and suggestions which have been incorporated in this final version.

Chapter 24

Exclusion and reintegration: policy and practice for junior pupils

Rose Mahony

As with Chapter 19, this study of policy and practice for pupils excluded from mainstream primary schools in a shire county is an edited version of the report of an investigation carried out for the Open University postgraduate course which preceded 'Developing Inclusive Curricula: Equality and Diversity in Education' (E829) and for which this volume is a resource. From her first-hand knowledge of current provision in her area, her analysis of policy documents and children's statements of special educational need, interviews and visits, Mahony aimed to be in a position to develop practice in a new, voluntary-sector unit so that children referred there could be reintegrated into the mainstream within two years. This looked as if it was going to be extremely difficult.

INTRODUCTION

What is happening in the local county primary schools? Although figures are not available there has clearly been a recent dramatic increase in the number of infant and junior children permanently excluded from mainstream education.

The four child-guidance centres and the two school-based units for children classed as being emotionally and behaviourally disturbed are over-subscribed and there is a waiting list for the one county special school which caters for such children.

When my own independent school agreed to go into partnership with the county to provide a junior facility for excluded pupils, we received an initial batch of fifteen referrals aged from 6 to 11. Many of them had been out of school for months and in three cases parents had become so desperate they had enlisted the help of the local MP to find suitable education for their children. At a time when educational philosophy is advocating inclusion and equality of opportunity for all children it seems strange that so many should be put out of the system.

Peter Housden, Director of Education for Nottinghamshire LEA gave a paper in 1992 entitled 'Bucking the market: LEAs and special educational needs'. He referred to:

> those children our educational system so often placed 'at risk' of failure, blighting both the lives of these vulnerable children and the society that allows it to happen.

(Housden 1993)

Since the death of Jamie Bulger earlier in the year the media have high-lighted individual cases of young children who seem to be running out of control into a life of violence and crime.

A sense of 'moral panic' has been identified as society attempts to explain and find solutions to the problem. Government plans to reintroduce 'Borstal'-type institutions where 'bad' children would be 'out of sight and out of mind', whilst they may be vote-catching, have been universally condemned by child-care charities. However, no one seems to have an alternative solution. Policies are produced which attempt to make short-term improvements in the situation but which are unable to tackle the root causes of the problem. Poor housing, social disadvantage, poverty and racism are not going to be countered by committee meetings and local policy documents. Perhaps one area of hope lies in education where children caught in a cycle of deprivation can be helped. At that level the balance can be weighted in their favour to give them at least an opportunity to succeed.

AIMS OF THE PROJECT

In the light of the situation described above I want to examine three issues of policy and practice:

1 What are the reasons for the increase in the number of junior exclusions in the county?
2 How does the county special needs policy work as applied to the group of young people who are described as being emotionally and behaviourally disturbed?
3 How should the newly-developed independent/county junior unit set about devising a policy for the reintegration of young people described as being emotionally and behaviourally disturbed?

This is an enormous subject and is the focus of a great deal of national research but my hope is that this project will provide valuable information which will help to direct and improve the development of policy and good practice in the newly established junior unit at my own school.

BACKGROUND TO THE UNIT

The Beech Down junior unit is based in its own premises, separate from the residential school. It takes children who have been permanently excluded from mainstream junior schools and who have a statement of special educational need. It is a day school taking pupils from four local areas.

The unit can take up to ten pupils aged from 5 to 11 and it is staffed by a teacher in charge, two non-teaching assistants and a part-time social worker. The aim of the unit is to return pupils to mainstream within two years. This gives a focus to the work and makes it essential that all those concerned with the young people referred should be working towards their successful reintegration. Linda Jordan, writing about 'integration policy in Newham, 1986–90', says:

> As has often been said, integration is a process, not a state.
>
> (Jordan 1992, p. 384)

The unit's policy is to begin this process from the day the child enters and to continue it in partnership with parents and professionals until support is no longer necessary.

The unit is managed independently and governed by the organisation's child-care policies. However, these have been produced with residential pupils in mind and are therefore not always relevant. There is a need for the unit to develop its own policy which reflects its close links with county and local mainstream junior schools.

METHODS OF INVESTIGATION

In order to examine the reasons behind the number of exclusions in the county I have analysed the papers and statements of educational need of all the recent referrals to the unit. I have also interviewed an educational psychologist, a headteacher of a referring school and the head of special educational needs for the county.

I have visited the county education department and gained copies of the policy statement on special needs and the most recent annual report on the state of special education in the county. In order to examine how the county's policies relate to the children in our unit I have read other policy documents from other local authorities as a comparison.

To fulfil the third aim of the project I visited a similar unit which has worked with considerable success over a number of years, both to sustain young people with behaviour problems in mainstream schools and to return them to schools after a period of exclusion.

Throughout the investigation I have attempted to discover what provisions are available for the support of special needs in the county and how the services work in practice. In order to describe the situation I have looked at an attempt the unit made to reintegrate a 9-year-old boy back into main-stream. The lessons learned from that experience contribute significantly to my thoughts on the development of future policy and practice.

WHAT ARE THE REASONS FOR THE INCREASE IN THE NUMBER OF JUNIOR EXCLUSIONS?

All the professionals interviewed agreed that there has been an alarming rise in the number of excluded junior pupils in the county.

The annual education report for 1992/93 says at point 101: '149 pupils benefited from attendance at primary adjustment centres compared with 73 in 1991–92'.

This doubling of the figure in a year suggests the nature of the problem but not the cause.

My analysis of the papers for the pupils referred to the Beech Down unit showed that in every case the county guidelines had been followed. Each pupil had been temporarily excluded on a number of occasions and then had been indefinitely excluded for a violent incident against either another pupil or a teacher. All of the pupils were assessed as being of average intelligence or above and in no case was any disapplication of the National Curriculum necessary. However, all were considered to be under-achieving and suffering from low self-esteem.

In every case the school had employed the use of the local psychological service to provide guidance on ways of effectively handling the pupils. The same strategies occur again and again: part-time support from a non-trained assistant, withdrawal of the child into a support group, calling in parents to support the child in school, or sending the child home at certain specified times. The usual workplace of these youngsters prior to the final exclusion has been the headteacher's office where they have been isolated from their peers both for their own and the other pupils' safety.

In my discussion with a local primary school headteacher she expressed the opinion that there had been a noticeable change in the infants coming into her school over recent years. Children were coming in at 5 without the basic social skills necessary for school:

> If they're not fed, if they've not had a good night's sleep, if they don't feel good about themselves, you can forget learning, they're not going to learn, they're going to disrupt, they're going to mope, they're going to be unhappy, they don't stand a chance.

The head of special educational needs for the county confirmed that the county has a number of 5- and 6-year-olds who have been permanently excluded and for which the county has no provision.

Another factor highlighted by all the professionals was the demands made by the National Curriculum together with the publishing of league tables of test results for schools.

The performance of individual children was not the cause for concern, but the effect that their disruption had on their peer group. In discussion with a local educational psychologist he made the following distinction between different types of special needs pupils:

> The ones that are less likely to be O.K. are the ones with behavioural difficulties – because of the reputation of the school – two kids with massive behaviour difficulties can create havoc to a school's reputation. Two kids with learning difficulties are marvellous to have in a school because they don't count towards any league tables – they're excluded from that, they bring in the revenue and they keep the numbers up.

He referred to headteachers having low tolerance levels towards pupils with emotional difficulties and described the exclusion of these pupils as 'damage limitation'. Stressed teachers trying to cope with the demands of the National Curriculum in open-plan classrooms simply could not cope with the disaffected child.

The introduction of LMS (Local Management of Schools) has also had an effect as headteachers have attempted to attract children from well-motivated and affluent homes. The 'problem' children have been 'weeded out' and following exclusion have been transferred to other local schools with spaces. Gradually sink schools have developed.

The educational psychologist again:

> If a school is empty . . . the sink school becomes even more sink because they'll have the spaces, and the rejectees from most schools will end up there. In fact I've been fending that off on behalf of one of the local secondary schools. The other schools are actually chucking kids out into this school and I'm getting lumbered with numbers of kids to deal with who are all problems and so there is a disproportionate number of kids in that school with problems. Therefore the parents take them away and put them to other schools and what's happening is – it's ending up almost like a special school.

He quoted figures for a local primary school which in 1976 had 250 juniors and 150 infants. Now it has 49 primary pupils and 35 of those have problems.

The message for schools would seem to be clear. Remove the difficult pupils if you want to be successful.

Under LMS schools have to be concerned about their public image. So money is more likely to be directed into computers, music or testing schemes than into provision for most special educational needs. To keep class sizes down an extra class teacher may be employed, rather than a special needs teacher.

As the government has taken increasing amounts of power and funding away from the LEAs and given it to individual schools so the LEAs have become increasingly enfeebled and headteachers have taken the power into their own hands to remove difficult pupils.

HOW DOES THE COUNTY SPECIAL NEEDS POLICY WORK AS APPLIED TO THE GROUP OF YOUNG PEOPLE WHO ARE DESCRIBED AS BEING EMOTIONALLY AND BEHAVIOURALLY DISTURBED?

In the government White Paper *Choice and Diversity: A New Framework for Schools* (DES 1992) a distinction is drawn between pupils with special needs and those who simply 'behave badly'. LEAs are instructed to make alternative provision for those young people which will remove them from mainstream schools. In the county, it is to be hoped that this is not the real reason behind the county's interest in Beech Down. Are children who are described as emotionally and behaviourally disturbed now to be written off as simply 'badly behaved'? Do they no longer qualify for special support in their education?

A local authority document called *Meeting Special Education Needs – A Statement of Policy* was produced in 1991 by those working in the special needs department at County Hall in consultation with the quality-assurance department and special needs co-ordinators in local schools. The statement is divided into three sections:

1 The underlying principles.
2 The policy.
3 Implementation of the policy.

It meets the criteria laid down by Tony Booth in his definition of policy:

I define policy as a co-ordinated attempt to control the direction of practice. It involves the elaboration of a set of principles and a plan on which actions might be based and also a definite intention and commitment to implement such a scheme.

(Booth 1987, p. 204)

The statement emphasises the entitlement of children with special needs to receive a 'broad and balanced curriculum'. It stresses the high quality of educational experience which should be made available to the children and demands that achievements should be celebrated.

The policy is set within the county's equal opportunity policy and as such it is understood that no discrimination should exist on the grounds of gender, race or handicap.

The wording of the section relating to parents is interesting for whilst the policy is clear that the support of parents is 'integral' to the education of a child with special needs, it is also stated that 'Parents should be given opportunities to be active partners in decisions relating to their child's education.' What is an opportunity? Does it mean an opportunity to attend a high-powered meeting of professionals or comment on a complicated type of written statement? Certainly, the bewildered parent who turned up at Beech Down junior unit for an interview two weeks ago did not feel like an active partner. He was quite happy with his child's progress in mainstream and was unaware that the school was about to exclude his son. He knew that there were problems but was confident that they could be worked through.

The government has made an effort to increase parents' rights by issuing the Parents' Charter guide, 'Children with Special Needs'.

This gives written information about assessment and statementing procedures for parents. Now legislation is to be introduced to extend parents' rights over the choice of school for their child:

> The government proposes to give parents of children with statements of special educational needs a similar legislative right to state a preference for their child's school as other parents.

> (DES 1993)

A new Special Educational Needs Tribunal is to be established to hear appeals.

When I asked how this might affect the placement of children in the county the head of special needs in the county remarked that to date no appeals made to the Secretary of State had been successful. However, he acknowledged that parents' opinions would have to be more carefully considered within the proposed new framework.

Section B of the policy statement makes clear the authority's commitment to early intervention and identification of educational need. The benefit to be gained by those with physical and mental handicaps is clear as the requirement to provide resources and support is outlined. Regular reviews are required to monitor the appropriateness of the provision. However, once again children seen to have emotional and behaviour difficulties (EBD) do not seem to fit comfortably into the policy. The head teacher that I interviewed said that the professionals did not like to statement infants in spite of the need that has been clearly identified. This is in contradiction to the intent mentioned above, in the policy statement.

Section C of the county document covers the implementation of the policy. The requirements made of teachers and governors are all in line with good educational practice. It is an impressive statement which should benefit all children who require extra help with their education. Schools are encouraged to keep all children within their community and it is made clear that the authority will only remove children from mainstream with great reluctance. School performance in this area will be monitored by the quality-assurance team and the plan for special education is to be regularly reviewed.

Although this is a good policy document, there are indications that the term 'special needs' is being used particularly for those with identifiable 'handicaps'. For example, it refers to the authority's commitment to provide training for teachers 'wishing to gain advanced qualification in special educational needs including physical, sensory and learning difficulties'. The omission of any mention of behaviour management, anti-racist practice or counselling skills suggests that the focus is not on the 'badly behaved'. In the light of the increase in exclusions for behaviour problems this would seem to be an oversight.

Whilst there is a clear commitment to inclusion in the county's policy, this does not extend to EBD pupils. Provision for this group is having to be extended as head teachers use their right to exclude pupils permanently. It would seem that the policy statement is too broad to be meaningful. The gap between the policy-makers and the practitioners is too wide.

HOW SHOULD THE NEWLY-DEVELOPED JUNIOR UNIT SET ABOUT DEVISING A POLICY FOR REINTEGRATION OF YOUNG PEOPLE DESCRIBED AS BEING EMOTIONALLY AND BEHAVIOURALLY DISTURBED?

Two major points have emerged from the first two sections of this project. The first is that schools do not want to keep children who are very difficult to manage, the second is that county policy does little to encourage schools to keep these children. The educational psychologist whom I interviewed told me that a teacher in a local school was so delighted when he told her that a particularly difficult pupil in her class was to be sent to the junior unit that she almost kissed him. It cannot be denied that 'aggressive and disruptive pupils make life almost impossible for those who have to work with them in the normal school structure. Their refusal to conform works against everything that schools are trying to achieve.'

However, it cannot be acceptable that pupils excluded between the ages of 5 and 11 should not be allowed back into mainstream.

David Ruebain, writing as a school governor, makes three recommendations for an integration scheme which seems to provide a sound basis for action:

1 Develop clear policy directives both in general and in particular and ensure that the discussions around them are generated at the outset.
2 Appoint an individual or team to oversee the development, ensuring they have clear channels to all sectors of the authority with the power to influence, assist and react to even the most localised problem.
3 Back up the programme with resources to fund in-service training, seminars, building, transport and all other necessary features.

(Ruebain 1987, p. 200)

Using this as a basis for the unit's policy the following points can be made:

1 For the unit successfully to reintegrate its pupils it will need to ensure that local schools are committed to accepting pupils back and are prepared to work to that end by maintaining regular contact with the child, its family and the unit staff. There must be a clear understanding of this statement of policy and joint co-operation to produce the means by which reintegration will be achieved. For every child a written plan needs to be produced which is the result of collaboration between professionals, those acting in the parental role *and the child*.

   Schools should not be allowed to operate an 'out of sight, out of mind' scheme but should maintain contact and particularly ensure that parents remain involved in the life of the school.

2 To oversee the development the school intends to form a 'board of studies'. This will be composed of individuals who have a particular interest in reintegrating pupils back into mainstream schools. Already, a local junior school headteacher, the head of a local withdrawal unit and an educational psychologist have accepted invitations to join the board. Parents and teachers should also be involved. The chair is to be taken by the county's head of special needs which should ensure that David Ruebain's 'clear channels' to those with the power are established.

   This board will monitor progress, analyse practice and develop future policy. It should safeguard the rights of the individual as well as the needs of the wider community.

3 The independent school has a commitment to make this project work and to supplement the money provided by the county to ensure that the scheme does not fail for lack of resources. In addition to this, there is a willingness to share expertise and knowledge to encourage and support the reintegration programme.

Warnock (1978) suggested that 'firm links should be established between Special and Ordinary Schools in the same vicinity' and the unit will work to encourage exchanges of staff and resources.

The county has a clear set of guidelines for teachers in mainstream schools who are in charge of pupils with statements of special educational provision. They provide detailed instructions on practice and procedure with regards to setting goals, reviewing progress, planning ahead, adapting materials, providing extra resources, and keeping records. They stress the need to encourage a positive attitude in pupils towards their difficulties. These will be the basis of the units' daily work as the staff seek to raise their pupils' self-esteem, moderate their unacceptable behaviour and help them back into school.

The journal *Support for Learning* published an article in August 1993 called 'Exclusions: the challenge to schools' by Philip Garner. In his article he looks at a number of issues which need to be considered in the exclusion–integration debate. He says that mainstream schools should have some 'ownership' of the problems relating to excluded pupils and that schools should be rewarded for holding on to difficult pupils. He also makes an interesting statement:

> attending to the needs of a student who is prone to be excluded from school on account of his or her disruptive behaviour is as likely to benefit the whole school community as it is to assist the excluded student in question.
>
> (Garner 1993, p. 102)

How many schools examine their own failure when a pupil is excluded, instead of focusing on that of the pupil?

Trying to normalise excluded children's educational experience in a segregated unit is the most difficult part of the work, and convincing them that they can succeed where they have already failed is a daunting task. It requires change on both sides and some willingness from the professionals to compromise.

When I visited a local withdrawal unit and spoke to the teacher in charge, she expressed the view that once pupils have been out of school for six months, they will never make it back. I would agree that if nothing changes they are unlikely to reintegrate successfully, but if the time out is spent productively by both the pupil and the school then things could be different.

This is all very well in theory, but in reality schools are not given to change and parents and pupils do not alter their attitudes and habits a great deal. The unit's first attempt to reintegrate a pupil was a failure. A brief look at his case history will highlight some important points.

The boy, whom I will call Simon, was permanently excluded from his mainstream junior school at the age of 8. He went to a local withdrawal unit for four mornings a week until he moved to the Beech Down junior unit as its first pupil. He was a bright and lively pupil but was given to sudden and violent mood swings. Many of these could be related to lack of supervision at home since he was often dirty, hungry and tired when he arrived at school. It was noticeable that his behaviour improved dramatically after he had been given something to eat.

After some months in the unit it was decided to begin a reintegration programme, but his previous school did not want him back and felt that other parents and pupils (and teachers?) would be too hostile to allow him to succeed. Another local school was sought, but his reputation went before him. Only the local Catholic school was prepared to try.

Following meetings and discussions between the unit staff and the staff of the school, a planned series of accompanied visits was organised. Simon's parents visited and agreed to the placement. At first everything went well, but as soon as the unit support began to be withdrawn Simon's behaviour deteriorated and he started to run away and hit out at other children. At the same time his behaviour at home became very difficult and his parents were unable to contain him. He is now awaiting a placement at an out-of-county residential school.

What can we learn from this experience? Can it be reflected in the policy of the unit to ensure that other pupils are prevented from similar failures?

Certainly, the fact that pupils will not now be accepted unless their local schools will have them back is an important point. Ideally, children should be educated at their community school where they can develop a sense of belonging and of responsibility to their home area.

Perhaps the most important lesson to be learned is that children must be committed to a plan if it is to work. This is where I believe that Simon's reintegration went wrong. He may not have been very old but he had already had very negative experiences of school which had damaged his confidence. He needed to be sure that this would not happen again. He should have been more involved in the reintegration scheme so that he felt he 'owned' the action that involved him. He was bright enough to realise that he did not belong in a middle-class Catholic school six miles from his home – we were not!

CONCLUSION

In this project I have considered the plight of the difficult pupils, the ones labelled as EBD. As their numbers increase so schools' tolerance for them decreases.

In spite of local authority policies which encourage inclusion and the support of special needs pupils in mainstream schools, the headteachers have the power to exclude and few parents are able to stand up to them. By the time the pupils arrive at Beech Down junior unit both they and their families are angry and demoralised. Their confidence in the education system has collapsed and chances of success are slight.

It is to be hoped that the suggestions made for the unit policy will go some way towards redressing the balance in favour of the child. Certainly, the partnership of the independent and the local authority promises to bring a new and more caring aspect into the work of reintegration. Commenting on her enquiry into special educational needs, Mary Warnock said: 'People have said we fudged the issue of integration, but we fudged it as a matter of policy' (1978).

It would seem that the issue is still not clear, particularly where children with behaviour problems are concerned. The government seems inclined to dismiss them as merely badly behaved and allow them to be removed from the system; those who know these children must work to ensure that they are not overlooked. We shall forget them at great cost to the health of society.

REFERENCES

Booth, T. (1987), *Preventing Difficulties in Learning*, Blackwell, Oxford.
Booth, T. and Potts, P. (eds) (1983), *Integrating Special Education*, Blackwell, Oxford.
DES (1978), *Special Educational Needs* (The Warnock Report), HMSO, London.
DES (1992), *Choice and Diversity: A New Framework for Schools*, HMSO, London.
DES (1993), *'Special Educational Needs: Access to the System. A Consultation Paper'*.
Garner, P. (1993), 'Exclusions: The challenge to schools', *Support for Learning*.
Housden, P. (1993), 'Bucking the market: LEAs and Special Educational Needs', National Association for Special Educational Needs (NASEN), Nottingham.
Jordan, L. (1992), *Policies for Diversity in Education*, Routledge, London.
Ruebain, D. (1987), 'The development of an integration scheme: a governor's view', in T. Booth and W. Swann (eds) *Including Pupils with Disabilities*, Milton Keynes, Open University Press, pp. 195–200.
Warnock, M. (1978) in V. Makins (ed.) 'Handicapped given the hope of a new deal', *Times Educational Supplements*, 26 May 1978.

Chapter 25

Special educational needs: from disciplinary to pedagogic research

Graham Vulliamy and Rosemary Webb

First published as Vulliamy, G. and Webb, R. (1993) 'Special educational needs: from disciplinary to pedagogic research', *Disability, Handicap & Society* 8(2), pp. 187–202.

This chapter discusses trends in research over the past twenty years. The controlled experiments of psychologists which attempted to measure and predict, for example, the learning capacities of children with a particular disability, were superseded by more qualitative approaches, for example, the evaluation of policy and practice by means of interviewing and observation and by the work of sociologists, who asked awkward questions about vested interests and the function of socially-constructed categories, such as 'educationally sub-normal'. Further, disabled people are now engaged in 'emancipatory' research, representing their own experience, challenging the status quo and actively intervening to improve the quality of their lives. However, these new approaches still retain a disciplinary allegiance. Graham Vulliamy and Rosemary Webb argue that a 'pedagogic' approach is more appropriate: one in which practitioners, working collaboratively, generate questions, put forward solutions and evaluate the outcomes from a variety of perspectives. They have worked with teachers on what they call an 'outstation' MA course at York University and this chapter is a version of the introduction to their edited collection of students' project-work: Teacher Research and Special Educational Needs *(1992), David Fulton, London.*

INTRODUCTION

Research on special educational needs in Britain has widened in scope markedly over the last two decades. What is surprising, however, is that such developments have been, with very few exceptions, restricted to what Bassey (1981, 1983) refers to as 'disciplinary' research. This is despite the fact that one of the main problems identified by special needs researchers – that of the apparent gap between research and practice – is precisely the source of the rationale behind Bassey's arguments for 'pedagogic research' conducted by practitioners. In other educational spheres collections of pedagogic research carried out by teacher-researchers have explicitly addressed the conventional theory–practice conundrum and, it has been argued, made significant contributions to teachers' professional development and to changes in classroom practice and school policy (see, for example, Hustler *et al.* 1986; Lomax 1989, 1990, 1991a; Webb 1990b).

In this article, we will examine both why teacher research has been relatively neglected in special education and what the essence of its contribution might be.[1] We believe that teacher research, based as much of it is on case studies of the processes of teaching and learning, is particularly suited to the area of special needs, where teachers are often concerned to understand pupils with unique learning difficulties. We argue here that the reluctance of special needs researchers to embrace pedagogic research and the qualitative research strategies which underpin it is a consequence of the fact that special educational needs research in this country has tended to be dominated by those trained in the discipline of psychology. This discipline has characteristically used positivist research strategies, such as experiments and surveys, which attempt to produce law-like generalisations based upon the statistical analysis of large samples.

THE BROADENING OF TRADITIONAL APPROACHES TO SPECIAL NEEDS RESEARCH

A historical overview of special needs research over the last two decades indicates that many of the marked changes in emphasis during the 1980s were prompted by the implications of the Warnock Report, published in 1978, and the subsequent 1981 Education Act. Wedell (1985a) notes that 'this Act gave "official" recognition to the concept of "special educational need", and to the concern of special education with meeting children's needs rather than with categorizing them' (p. 1). Thus the focus of research needed to shift from descriptive studies of children's conditions and disabilities to studies of the ways in which various educational needs might best be met. This, in turn, directed research attention towards ways of improving the learning experiences of children, and evaluating and disseminating improvements, whether in special or in ordinary schools. Such a change of emphasis is readily apparent in a comparison of reviews of special needs research conducted prior to the 1981 Act (Cave and Madison 1978; Wedell and Roberts 1981) – where the more traditional research, including investigations of children grouped by category of diagnostic classification, predominates – with an agenda for future research drawn up by a 1982 special needs research symposium. The latter concluded that priority should be given to six areas:

1 the evaluation of intervention approaches;
2 the methodology for evaluating intervention;
3 within the area of descriptive research, emphasis on the study of functional impairment, rather than the characteristics of diagnostic categories of children with special needs;
4 the process of innovation;
5 the methods of disseminating research information;
6 the preparation of critical summaries of existing relevant research, particularly in areas which extend across disciplines.

(Wedell 1985b, p. 23)

Such a research agenda inevitably required a shift from the more traditional emphasis of psychology upon studies of specific children, either as individuals or groups, to a broader range of approaches. This range included both new substantive themes, such as implementation and change, and new methodological ones, such as qualitative evaluation styles, which for some time had characterised educational research on curriculum evaluation and innovation in general. This, in turn, brought the special needs research community more directly into contact with alternative research strategies arising from critiques of the methodological positivism underlying more traditional approaches. As early as 1968, the psychologists Bracht and Glass had raised some fundamental problems about such approaches when they developed the concept of 'ecological validity' in their discussion of the external validity of experiments. Ecological validity refers to the extent to which behaviour observed in one context can be generalised to another. Put simply, the problem with more traditional research methods in education, whether experiments or questionnaire surveys, is that they are unlikely to give an accurate portrayal of the realities of teaching and learning in a natural or conventional setting. The strictures of experimental design are such that only rarely does the experimental setting approximate to the normal conditions of schooling to which generalisations need to be made. Questionnaire surveys cannot penetrate the gap between 'words and deeds' (Deutscher 1966) and, especially in the evaluation of innovations, are prone to the reproduction of the rhetoric contained in the aims and documentation of the innovation. It is considerations such as these which have led to compelling arguments that traditional positivist research strategies in education and the social sciences have been over-preoccupied with reliability (the consistency of a measuring instrument) at the expense of validity (Deutscher 1973). Somewhat ironically, perhaps, Bracht and Glass's (1968) early discussion of 'ecological validity' was picked up much later by qualitative researchers in education who see the maximisation of ecological validity as one of the main rationales for their approach (see, for example, Atkinson 1979; Hammersley 1979; Evans 1983).

The influence of such critiques of positivism, together with the new research agenda, can be clearly seen in a 1984 special needs research symposium on the methodology of evaluation studies in special education. Thus, for example, Corrie and Zaklukiewicz (1985) comment in their paper that much previous work:

> has tended to be limited by the somewhat narrow conception of research as being above all, quantitative and statistical in character. Quantitative procedures, particularly survey techniques, have featured prominently throughout the entire history of research in this area . . . as have psychometric approaches to individual functioning and development.
>
> (p. 123)

Following an overview of the major criticisms being made of previous research in special education (Schindele 1985), the symposium was devoted to two approaches to evaluation which, in very different ways, marked new departures. The first of these, the use of single-subject and small-N research designs, whilst still operating within a positivist and quantitative research strategy, nevertheless attempts to overcome some of the previous weaknesses of more traditional evaluation strategies by focusing upon an in-depth evaluation of practice. Kiernan (1985) provides an overview of the defining features of single-subject research designs. They involve the investigation of the behaviour of a single individual (or a small group in small-N designs), where the intention is to test specific hypotheses concerning critical variables. However, where in more traditional experiments the use of control groups is intended to enable the replication of effects across individuals, any replication in single-subject designs is across time, context or other variables, and the analysis concerns only the behaviour of the single individual. An example of such a study is Barrera *et al.*'s (1980) investigation into the effectiveness of three different models of language training – using signs, words and a combination of the two – for a 4½-year-old 'mute' autistic boy. This involved giving the child twenty minutes of direct language training with each of the three models in a random order each day and using a trained observer, supplemented by video recordings to ensure reliability, to monitor the child's responses. The results showed that the total communication model was substantially superior to both the oral and the sign-alone training models.

Evans (1985) suggests that single-subject experimental designs have a particular relevance for special needs research for a number of reasons. First, the nature of some children's special needs may be particularly individualistic in character, with few other children displaying exactly the same range of needs. Second, the designs enable teachers to monitor and record the progress of an individual child over time against pre-set objectives. Third, whilst sophisticated statistical techniques have been developed for the interpretation of causal effects in single-subject designs (McReynolds and Kearns 1982; Halil 1985), it is still possible for teachers to 'eyeball' the numerical data and reach conclusions which can immediately be put into practice.

The second major evaluation approach considered at the 1984 research symposium was the use of qualitative research. There are several important distinguishing features of such research. It provides descriptions and accounts of the processes of social interaction in 'natural' settings, usually based upon a combination of observation and interviewing of participants in order to understand their perspectives. Culture, meanings and processes are emphasised, rather than variables, outcomes and products. Instead of testing preconceived hypotheses, qualitative research aims to generate hypotheses and theories from the data that emerge, in an attempt to avoid the imposition of a previous, and possibly inappropriate, frame of reference on the subjects of the research. This implies a far greater degree of flexibility concerning research design, data collection and analysis, with aspects of each of these sometimes occurring simultaneously throughout the duration of a research project, than tends to be the case with quantitative research. (For more detailed summaries of the defining characteristics of qualitative research, see, for example, Corrie and Zaklukiewicz 1984, pp. 125–7; Burgess 1985, pp. 7–10; Bryman 1988, pp. 61–9; Vulliamy 1990a, pp. 7–14.)

Hegarty (1985) argues that qualitative research is particularly suited to a number of topics in special education. These include investigations into pupils' and teachers' perspectives and experiences of special education programmes; clarifying the implications of various policy options; evaluating innovations; and providing detailed accounts of various forms of special education provision. However, to date, there have been relatively few published qualitative research studies on the theme of special educational needs, despite the prominent impact of qualitative research on educational research more generally. Moreover, it is noticeable that, of the few such published studies that do exist, a high proportion have been initiated or conducted by researchers from outside the special needs research community, as, for example, with Jamieson et al.'s (1977) study of the integration of visually-impaired children into ordinary schools and Bell and Colbeck's (1989) action enquiry project into the integration of a number of special needs units into a large primary school.

Given the strong legacy of positivist research in the special needs community, but the recent recognition also of the need for alternative approaches, it should not be surprising that calls are made for a judicious blending of quantitative and qualitative approaches (e.g., Corrie and Zaklukiewicz 1985, p. 124). As Vulliamy (1990b) notes, in other areas of education and social science research, the integration of quantitative and qualitative research techniques has taken a number of forms, with varying rationales, possibilities and problems. Mittler (1985) suggests that, within special needs research, one of the most fruitful areas for such a combination of approaches is in the evaluation of policy changes and innovations. Thus, for example, Hegarty et al.'s (1981) study of the education of pupils with special needs in ordinary schools used a combination of a nationwide questionnaire survey of LEAs and detailed case studies of schools, including interviews with individual teachers, parents and pupils. Mittler (1985) concludes that 'this approach provides rich possibilities for concentrating on process variables without neglecting product outcomes' and that the detailed case studies of the practice of integration in schools 'are likely to be more influential and useful to policy makers than are any number of multivariate regression analyses' (p. 174).

We have suggested that one of the main concerns of special needs researchers during the 1980s has been to broaden their research styles in response to the growing critique of more traditional positivist research. A second central preoccupation has been to address the problem of the perceived gap between theory and practice, which was identified in each of two major reviews of special needs research (Cave and Madison 1978; Wedell and Roberts 1981). While the broadening of research approaches discussed above is seen as one potential means of increasing the relevance of research to practice (Corrie and Zaklukiewicz 1985), other ideas have centred around trying to bring researchers and teachers into a closer partnership with each other. Thus, for example, Wedell (1985b) suggests that more opportunities should be available to practitioners for periods of secondment when they could be engaged on research projects, and Kiernan (1982) considers a partnership which 'asks teachers to provide feedback on ongoing research or to act as consumers evaluating the products of research' (p. 26). Here there is no attempt to redefine the traditional subordinate roles of teachers in relation to researchers and the approach is similar to the earliest forms of teacher–researcher collaboration advocated by Boone (1904) and by Buckingham (1926), where teachers were used by clinical psychologists as field-workers.

However, an alternative strategy intended to break down such hierarchies has been suggested by Mittler (1974), who argues for a communality of approach between teachers and researchers in special needs, whereby 'teaching is better when it is informed by a research attitude' and 'conversely, research can only benefit from retaining the humanity and open-mindedness of the teacher' (p. 80). Wood (1981) also discusses the benefits of the close collaboration between researcher and teacher in an investigation into teaching strategies with hearing-impaired children. He argues that unless researchers and teachers work together in classrooms 'it seems inevitable that we shall continue to spawn unworkable, unrealistic or invalid theories and that the teachers' intuitions about what works and what does not will go unheard and untested' (p. 432). A recent example of the increased collaboration between teachers and researchers in special needs research can be found in the work of the National Curriculum Development Team (Severe Learning Difficulties) based at the Cambridge Institute of Education. The team sought to provide INSET on key issues associated with the implementation of the National Curriculum in special schools and were commissioned by the National Curriculum Council (NCC) to produce a publication in the curriculum guidance series (NCC 1992a), together with an INSET pack to support the implementation of the advice in the guidance (NCC 1992b). Seconded teachers from seven LEAs in the eastern region collected evidence through spending a series of two-week periods in schools working with staff on National Curriculum-related development. The resulting materials, which the team produced to address the issues identified, were revised and extended as a result of widespread piloting in schools and the collection of staff feedback (see, for example, Rose 1991, on strategies for promoting groupwork in schools for pupils with severe learning difficulties).

This review of new directions in special needs research has so far restricted itself to developments from within what might be termed the mainstream special needs research community. However, the 1980s also witnessed a dramatic increase in research and theorising on special educaion from writers who do not share many of the basic assumptions of the traditional psychological and medical models of special needs. Such critiques came from sociologists, and also from those with disabilities themselves who sought to provide a more radical perspective on the provision of education for those with special educational needs.

THE SOCIOLOGICAL CONTRIBUTION

Whilst the publication of the Warnock Report helped generate a new research agenda for the special needs community, it also contributed to sociologists taking a more direct interest in special education than had previously tended to be the case in Britain. Thus, in an early critique of the Warnock Report, Lewis and Vulliamy (1979, 1980) argue that for both methodological and theoretical reasons the report's definition of 'special educational needs' is misguided and that the report compounds its definitional problem by an implicit theory which neglects the importance of social factors in the creation of learning difficulties. Rather than accepting psychological categories as given, sociologists consider the social processes leading to the construction of such categories and the social and political implications of their use, both at the micro and the macro level. This has involved examining the ways in which legislation and the vested interests of various professional groups may contribute to the legitimation of inequalities in the education of specific groups of pupils. A detailed example is Tomlinson's (1981) study of the decision-making processes involved in the categorisation of 'educational subnormality'. She draws an important distinction between normative categories, such as 'blind' or 'deaf' where there is widespread agreement as to the nature of the label used, and non-normative ones, such as 'educationally subnormal' or 'disruptive'. For the latter, she argues that:

There are no adequate measuring instruments or agreed criteria in the social world to decide upon these particular categories, whether descriptive or statutory. There can be, and is, legitimate argument between professionals, parents, other interested groups and the general public, over what constitutes these categories. The answer to the question 'what is' an ESN-M child or a maladjusted child will depend more upon the values, beliefs and interests of those making the judgments than on any qualities intrinsic to the child.

(Tomlinson 1982, pp. 65–6)

Using a combination of historical research and a case study of the provision for forty ESN-M children in one local education authority in the mid-1970s, she found that those given such provision were mainly the unwanted and troublesome pupils. These were largely from lower socio-economic backgrounds, with a severe over-representation of black children. As she herself points out, such research is conducted from an entirely different value position from mainstream psychological research on this theme:

It turned back-to-front the literature on ESN-M children which attempts to trace causal explanations for educational subnormality in low social class or cultural disadvantage. . . . It pointed out that categorising children as ESN-M may be more of a solution to a problem of social order than an aid to education.

(Tomlinson 1982, p. 12)

The writings of disabled sociologists go further in advancing a radical political and social theory of disability. Barton and Oliver (1992) provide a useful summary of this work and its underlying theoretical orientation:

They are critical of 'personal-tragedy' models of disability. For them, the difficulties of participating in society are not due to personal limitations, but arise from the prejudices, discriminatory policies and practices and social restrictions of an unadaptive society. Disability is a fundamentally political, social issue, which is a form of oppression.

(Barton and Oliver 1992, p. 70)

The successful establishment of a new academic journal, *Disability, Handicap & Society*, in 1986 is testimony to the influence of these newer sociological approaches. The latter are critical of the privileged status previously given to psychological explanations in discussions of special educational needs and disability in general. By individualising problems, attention is wrongly diverted from the inherently political nature of the social and educational processes which help produce such 'problems'.

A recent special issue of this journal (Vol. 7, no. 2, 1992) is based on a series of seminars on 'Researching Disability' held in London in 1991. Both traditional positivist research strategies and qualitative or interpretative approaches are criticised for failing to involve disabled people, to represent the reality of their experience and, most importantly, to contribute to changes of direct benefit to them. It is argued that both paradigms are equally alienating as far as disabled people are concerned because the social relations of research production

> are built upon a firm distinction between the researcher and the researched; upon the belief that it is the researchers who have specialist knowledge and skills; and that it is they who should decide what topics should be researched and be in control of the whole process of research production:
>
> (Oliver 1992, p. 102)

Researchers, who lack awareness of how disability is socially produced and so fail to challenge notions of disability as medical or social problems located within individuals, frame their research questions and conduct their research in ways which those with disabilities find oppressive. Consequently, the contributors to the special issue call for a change in the social relations of research production. Zarb (1992, p. 125) suggests that the first steps would be to ensure greater participation in the research process through consultation between researchers and disabled people at all stages in the design and conduct of the research, subjecting research to the critical scrutiny of research participants and making researchers accountable to the disabled people their work represents. The special issue also discusses the possibility of developing an emancipatory research paradigm which could faithfully represent experiences of disability, challenge the status quo and institutionalised disablism, redefine the 'problem' by shifting the focus to the disabling attitudes and practices of able-bodied society and make fundamental and significant contributions to improving the quality of the lives of those with disabilities.

There are clear parallels between the criticisms levelled at disability research and those made of educational research by classteachers regarding its irrelevance to those researched, the distorted representation of their experience and its failure to bring about change. The previous section documented how ways forward such as those suggested by Zarb have been adopted to bring special education researchers and researched into closer and more fruitful relationships. However, as is discussed in the next section, it is necessary to look outside the traditions of psychology and sociology to find the development of an emancipatory approach to research, where the research agenda, data collection, and analysis and dissemination of findings are controlled by those at the centre of the research.

APPROACHES TO TEACHER RESEARCH

The above review of new directions in special needs research throughout the 1980s indicates that a variety of fresh theoretical and methodological orientations has been pursued. What is striking, however, is that such new directions are still firmly placed within the traditional educational disciplines of psychology and sociology. The development of various styles of teacher research, which have come to the fore in mainstream educational research (see, e.g., Elliott 1991; Webb 1990b; Lomax 1989; Hustler *et al.* 1986), are conspicuous by their absence, with the exception of Ainscow's (1989) book and a few other isolated examples, such as Burton's (1989) project on combating sexism in a special school and Stephenson's (1990) research on the integration of four young children with special educational needs in a nursery department.

While the origins of various brands of teacher research go back to the turn of the century where, as suggested, earlier teachers remained in a totally subordinate role to researchers, contemporary approaches in Britain are best viewed as being derived from the pioneering work of Lawrence Stenhouse in the 1960s and 1970s (for a review of teacher research from its origins to the present day, see Webb 1990a). He argued that both curriculum development and teachers' professional development would be enhanced by teachers systematically studying the processes of teaching and learning (Stenhouse 1975). He questioned the traditional model of the relationship between educational research and educational change, whereby teachers were expected to adopt those curricula and pedagogic styles that had been 'proved' by academic researchers to be successful. Instead, he argued that teachers should take the fruits of researchers and curriculum developers as working hypotheses to be systematically tested in order that they might be evaluated, rejected or refined. An early example of this was the use of teacher researchers in the development of the Schools Council Humanities Curriculum Project between 1967 and 1972 (see Elliott 1991, ch.2). Since that period, and especially within the last decade, the influence of teacher research has grown considerably, giving rise to some distinct 'schools', each with its own set of intellectual and theoretical influences – for example, the case-study tradition developed at the Centre for Applied Research in Education at the University of East Anglia (Walker 1985) and the 'living educational theory' approach associated with Whitehead's group at the University of Bath (Whitehead 1989; McNiff 1992).

It might be helpful here to differentiate three very broad approaches to teacher research which, between them, account for the vast majority of current teacher-research enquiries. The first broad approach is case study. As a research strategy, case study has a long history in both anthropology and sociology where it is associated with ethnography and the intensive study, using participant observation, of a particular group or institution. Where schools have been the objects of study, this has led to the development of theories of schooling located either within an anthropological framework (e.g., Spindler 1982) or a sociological one (e.g., Hammersley and Woods 1976). However, Stenhouse specifically distinguished the use of case study in teacher research from its anthropological and sociological counterparts. He argued that, since ethnographers are strangers to the situations they study, this was an inappropriate strategy for teachers and educational researchers who tend to be very familiar with classrooms. Instead of using participant observation, he envisaged that the analysis of schools and class-rooms would be based upon an accumulation of documents ('the case record') which would include those created through interviews and direct observation (Stenhouse 1978). Compared to the more traditional ethno-graphic participant observation studies, this involves much shorter periods of field-work with a greater reliance on data derived from the transcripts of tape-recorded interviews. While interviews usually play a central part in teacher-research case studies, a variety of other research techniques may also be adopted, including observation, teacher and pupil diaries, questionnaires and the analysis of teachers' and pupils' written materials.

A second broad approach to teacher research is represented by evaluation studies. Stenhouse (1975) argued that it should be teachers themselves who should play the major role in evaluating the potential of innovations in their own classrooms or schools. However, he was very critical of the traditional 'evaluation by objectives' model, arguing that undue attention to learner outcomes and objectives restricted the scope of evaluation. Thus traditional approaches tend to neglect key aspects, such as the actual processes of innovation and a sensitivity to the context in which innovation is attempted. In this, he shared with a growing body of evaluators, both in the United States and in Britain, a desire to promote alternative qualitative approaches to educational evaluation based upon the disciplined use of case study (for a review of such approaches, see Norris 1990).

Many of the key characteristics of case-study evaluations are exemplified in Parlett and Hamilton's (1977) depiction of 'illuminative evaluation'. Parlett and Hamilton set their alternative approach to evaluation, which is strongly influenced by sociological and anthropological traditions, in the context of a critique of the traditional experimental design which has been dominant in psychology and special needs research. They characterise the traditional pre-test/treatment/post-test/design for curriculum evaluation as operating within an agricultural-botany paradigm. They argue that this has five major weaknesses:

1 It is impossible to control all relevant parameters in an educational context.
2 It assumes that innovations do not change over time, and can even prevent policy-makers adapting to changed circumstances for fear of contaminating the research design of the evaluation.
3 It concentrates only on that which can be measured and only on the intended consequences of an innovation.
4 The use of large samples for adequate statistical control leads to the neglect of atypical cases, which may be of great interest.

5 Such evaluations often fail to address the concerns both of the participants in the innovation and its sponsors.

In a striking analogy, they liken the traditional evaluator 'to a critic who
reviews a production on the basis of the script and applause-meter readings,
having missed the performance' (p. 22).

Parlett and Hamilton describe their alternative approach as follows:

> Illuminative evaluation takes account of the wider contexts in which
> educational programmes function. Its primary concern is with descrip-
> tion and interpretation rather than measurement and prediction. . . . The
> aims of illuminative evaluation are to study the innovatory programme:
> how it operates; how it is influenced by the various school situations in
> which it is applied; what those directly concerned regard as its advantages
> and disadvantages; and how students' intellectual tasks and academic
> experiences are most affected. It aims to discover and document what it is
> like to be participating in the scheme, whether as teacher or pupil; and, in
> addition, to discern and discuss the innovations' most significant features,
> recurring concomitants and critical processes. In short, it seeks to address
> and to illuminate a complex array of questions.
>
> (Parlett and Hamilton 1977, p. 10)

The third broad approach to teacher research is action research. While this
term can be used in a variety of different ways, within the context of teacher
research it has come to be identified specifically with teachers' enquiries
which consist of a cycle or spiral involving identifying a problem, devising
and implementing a proposed solution and researching the effects of this
(see, e.g., McTaggart and Kemmis 1981; McNiff 1988). Elliott connects this
process specifically with the heightened teacher awareness required for
improvement to practice:

> This total process—review, diagnosis, planning, implementation, monitor-
> ing effect – is called *action research*, and it provides the necessary link
> between *self-evaluation* and professional development.
>
> (Elliott 1981, p. ii)

A study of the impact on teachers of carrying out research in the context of
the part-time, research-based outstation MA run by the University of York
reveals the kinds of contributions that teacher research can make to teachers'
personal and professional development (Vulliamy and Webb 1991, 1992a).
They included an increase in self-confidence, the skills of using evidence as a
basis for decision-making, a deeper understanding of the teaching–learning
process from the pupils' perspective following the collection of pupils' data,
and the ability to make a greater contribution to curriculum development
within their areas of responsibility.

Action research is always a form of self-reflective enquiry. It is an
approach which requires teacher-researchers to use evidence to identify

issues and gain understanding of problems with which they are directly concerned. As with case study, a wide variety of data-collection techniques tends to be used. While action research can be undertaken by individuals, it is frequently a collaborative enterprise (Westgate *et al.*, 1990). This emphasis on collaborative enquiry can make it particularly appealing to groups of teachers, who share common pedagogic, curricular or policy concerns. This is because it facilitates the investigation of a problem from a variety of perspectives and across different subject areas and hierarchical levels. Also, if a number of teachers are involved it strengthens the likely impact and take-up of change.

While in some action-research traditions the emphasis is upon improving practice through insights derived from critical reflection following the systematic collection of evidence, in others it is upon improving practice through changing the values and perspectives of teachers. Thus, for example, Whitehead (1989) advocates the use of video to highlight for teachers the 'living contradictions' of their values in action; Griffiths and Tann (1991) consider a range of techniques, such as the use of images and metaphor, to help uncover teachers' 'personal theories'; and Lomax (1991b) discusses the importance of communities of 'critical friends' in providing validation of explorations of the relationships between teachers' values and educational change.

What distinguishes all three broad approaches to teacher research from more conventional educational research, whether positivist or qualitative, is that research questions are derived directly from the practical experience and concerns of the teacher, rather than being derived from traditional educational disciplines or areas, such as sociology, psychology or curriculum studies. Bassey (1981, 1983), in drawing a distinction between 'disciplinary' and 'pedagogic' research, argues that much traditional educational research, carried out by specialists and couched in their language, has been rejected by practising teachers as of little use in assisting them to analyse classroom situations and in devising solutions to practical problems. By contrast, 'pedagogic' research has as its main aim the improvement of practice (rather than the contribution to theoretical knowledge within a discipline) and employs research techniques, ways of presenting findings and publication outlets that are eclectic, pragmatic and readily accessible to teachers. A major characteristic of 'pedagogic' research revealed by a study of the impact of the outstation MA programme (Vulliamy and Webb 1991, 1992a) was the ways in which it gave teachers access to pupils' perspectives and experiences. This led teachers to revise their assessments of pupils, to recognise the contribution that pupils could make to curriculum evaluation and development and to consult them in the planning of subsequent research and innovation. This finding has important implications for teacher research into special educational needs where it is vital that the concerns of the pupils experiencing those needs are adequately described and represented.

CONCLUSION

The recent development of qualitative research in special educational needs, often from a radically-different perspective from the more traditional psychological edifice for such research, has deepened our theoretical understanding of the role of special educational needs in the British educational system. However, we have argued here that it has done little to overcome the divorce between theory and practice which special needs researchers have themselves identified as a key problem. For historical reasons, which we have charted here, special needs research has been slow to accommodate the style of 'pedagogic' research suggested by Bassey (1981, 1983) and by other advocates of practitioner research. The potential benefits of such research for the area of special educational needs can be seen in the accounts of teachers themselves in both the Ainscow (1989) and Vulliamy and Webb (1992b) edited collections. They testify to the processes of enhanced professional development and to the modifications of classroom practice and school policies arising from the systematic collection and analysis of evidence within their own educational contexts.

It is sometimes argued that a major limitation of such teacher-research enquiries is that, whilst they might lead to improved practice for isolated teachers, the findings are not generalisable to other contexts and cannot therefore be used to advance theoretical understanding. In countering this, we believe that Bassey's (1981, 1990) distinction between 'generalisability' and 'relatability' is an important one. He argues that the products of much traditional educational research, whilst supposedly generalisable because they have been derived from large samples, are perceived by most teachers as unrelatable to the realities of their specific classrooms. By contrast, given the in-depth portrayal of a particular case, be it the use of a specific curriculum package or a certain classroom management style, then teachers can readily relate aspects of such a portrayal to their own experiences. Through the publication of teacher-research enquiries, the aim is to generate theories which are of direct relevance to other teachers, by offering them alternative ways of understanding and acting in their own situations. It is our contention that research on the theme of special educational needs would have much to gain from such approaches.

Correspondence: Dr Graham Vulliamy, Department of Educational Studies, University of York, Heslington, York YO1 5DD, United Kingdom.

NOTE

1 Much of this article is extracted from our edited book *Teacher Research and Special Educational Needs* (Vulliamy and Webb 1992b). The book contains accounts of case-study research and evaluation carried out by teachers in ordinary and in special schools.

REFERENCES

Ainscow, M. (ed.) (1989), *Special Education in Change*, David Fulton, London.

Atkinson, P. (1979), *Research Design in Ethnography, Course DE304, Block 3B, Part 5*, Open University Press, Milton Keynes.

Barrera, R. D., Lobato-Barrrera, D. and Sulzer-Azaroff, B. (1980), 'A simultaneous treatment comparison of three expressive language training programs with a mute autistic child', *Journal of Autism and Developmental Disorders*, 10, pp. 21–37.

Barton, L. and Oliver, M. (1992), 'Special needs: personal trouble or public issue?', in M. Arnot and L. Barton (eds), *Voicing Concerns: Sociological Perspectives on Contemporary Education Reforms*, Triangle Books, Wallingford, pp. 66–87.

Bassey, M. (1981), 'Pedagogic research: on the relative merits of search for generalisation and study of single events', *Oxford Revew of Education*, 7, pp. 73–94.

Bassey, M. (1983), 'Pedagogic research into singularities: case studies, probes and curriculum innovations', *Oxford Review of Education*, 9, pp. 109–21.

Bassey, M. (1990), 'On the nature of research in education' (Part 2), *Research Intelligence*, 37, pp. 39–44.

Bell, G. and Colbeck, B. (eds) (1989), *Experiencing Integration*, Falmer Press, London.

Boone, N. (1904), *Science of Education*, Scribner, New York.

Bracht, G. H. and Glass, G. V. (1968), 'The external validity of experiments', *American Educational Research Journal*, 5, pp. 437–74.

Bryman, A. (1988), *Quantity and Quality in Social Research*, Unwin Hyman, London.

Buckingham, B. R. (1926), *Research for Teachers*, Silver, Burdett, New York.

Burgess, R. G. (1985), *Strategies of Educational Research: Qualitative Methods*, Falmer Press, Lewes.

Burton, K. (1989), 'Bringing about gender equality of opportunity in a special school', in P. Lomax, (ed.), *The Management of Change*, Multilingual Matters, Clevedon, Avon.

Cave, C. and Madison, P. (1978), *A Survey of Recent Research in Special Education*, NFER, Windsor.

Corrie, M. and Zaklukiewicz, S. (1984), 'Leaving special education: issues for research', *Scottish Educational Review*, 16, pp. 10–18.

Corrie, M. and Zaklukiewicz, S. (1985), 'Qualitative research and case-study approaches: an introduction', in S. Hegarty and P. Evans (eds), *Research and Evaluation Methods in Special Education*, NFER–Nelson, Windsor.

Deutscher, I. (1966), 'Words and deeds: social science and social policy', *Social Problems*, 13, pp. 133–254.

Deutscher, I. (1973), *What We Say/What We Do: Sentiments and Acts*, Scott, Foresman, Glenview, Ill.

Elliott, J. (1981) 'Action-research: a framework for self-evaluation in schools', Teacher–Pupil Interaction and the Quality of Learning Project, Working Paper, No. 1, Schools Council, Cambridge.

Elliott, J. (1991), *Action Research for Educational Change*, Open University Press, Milton Keynes.

Evans, J. (1983), 'Criteria of validity in social research: exploring the relationship between ethnographic and quantitative approaches', in M. Hammersley (ed.), *The Ethnography of Schooling*, Nafferton Books, Driffield, pp. 173–201.

Evans, P. (1985), 'Single case and small-N research designs: introduction', in S. Hegarty and P. Evans (eds), *Research and Evaluation Methods in Special Education*, NFER–Nelson, Windsor, pp. 27–31.

Griffiths, M. and Tann, S. (1991), 'Ripples in the reflection', in P. Lomax (ed.), *Managing Better Schools and Colleges: An Action Research Way*, Multilingual Matters, Clevedon, Avon, pp. 82–101.

Halil, A. (1985), 'Statistical methods in single-case studies', in S. Hegarty and P. Evans (eds), *Research and Evaluation Methods in Special Education*, NFER–Nelson, Windsor, pp. 80–105.

Hammersley, M. (1979), *Analysing Ethnographic Data, Course DE304, Block 6, Part 1*, Open University Press, Milton Keynes.

Hammersley, M. and Woods, P. (eds) (1976), *The Process of Schooling*, Routledge & Kegan Paul, London.

Hegarty, S. (1985), 'Qualitative research: introduction', in S. Hegarty and P. Evans (eds), *Research and Evaluation Methods in Special Education*, NFER–Nelson, Windsor, pp. 109–13.

Hegarty, S., Pocklington, K. and Lucas, D. (1981), *Educating Pupils with Special Needs in the Ordinary School*, NFER–Nelson, Windsor.

Hustler, D., Cassidy, T. and Cuff, T. (eds) (1986), *Action Research in Classrooms and Schools*, George Allen & Unwin, London.

Jamieson, M., Parlett, M. and Pocklington, K. (1977), *Towards Integration: A Study of Blind and Partially-sighted Children in Ordinary Schools*, NFER, Windsor.

Kiernan, C. (1982), 'Teachers and researchers in special education', *Special Education: Forward Trends*, 9, pp. 25–6.

Kiernan, C. (1985), 'Single-subject designs', in S. Hegarty and P. Evans (eds), *Research and Evaluation Methods in Special Education*, NFER–Nelson, Windsor, pp. 32–50.

Lewis, I. and Vulliamy, G. (1979), 'Where Warnock went wrong', *The Times Educational Supplement*, 30 November.

Lewis, I. and Vulliamy, G. (1980), 'Warnock or Warlock? The sorcery of definitions: the limitations of the report on special education', *Educational Review*, 32, pp. 3–10.

Lomax, P. (ed.) (1989), *The Management of Change*, Multilingual Matters, Clevedon, Avon.

Lomax, P. (ed.) (1990), *Managing Staff Development in Schools: An Action Research Approach*, Multilingual Matters, Clevedon, Avon.

Lomax, P. (ed.) (1991a), *Managing Better Schools and Colleges: An Action Research Way*, Multilingual Matters, Clevedon, Avon.

Lomax, P. (1991b), 'Peer review and action research', in P. Lomax (ed.), *Managing Better Schools and Colleges: An Action Research Way*, Multilingual Matters; Clevedon, Avon, pp. 102–13.

McNiff, J. (1988), *Action Research: Principles and Practice*, Macmillan Education, London.

McNiff, J. (1992), *Creating a Good Social Order through Action Research*, Hyde Publications, Dorset.

McReynolds, L. and Kearns, K.P. (1982), *Single Subject Designs for Intervention Research in Communicative Disorders*, MTP Press, Lancaster.

McTaggart, R. and Kemmis, S. (1981), *The Action Research Planner*, Deakin University, Geelong, Victoria.

Mittler, P. (1974), 'Research and the teacher', *Special Education: Forward Trends. Proceedings of the Annual Conference, National Council for Special Education, Birmingham*, NCSE, London.

Mittler, P. (1985), 'Approaches to evaluation in special education: concluding reflections', in S. Hegarty and P. Evans (eds), *Research and Evaluation Methods in Special Education*, NFER–Nelson, Windsor.

National Curriculum Council (1992a), *The National Curriculum and Pupils with Severe Learning Difficulties*, National Curriculum Council, York.

National Curriculum Council (1992b), *The National Curriculum and Pupils with Severe Learning Difficulties: INSET resources*, National Curriculum Council, York.

Norris, N. (1990), *Understanding Educational Evaluation*, Kogan Page, London.

Oliver, M. (1992), 'Changing the social relations of research production', *Disability, Handicap & Society*, 7, pp. 101–14.

Parlett, M. and Hamilton, D. (1977), 'Evaluation as illumination', in D. Hamilton *et al.* (eds), *Beyond the Numbers Game*, Macmillan Education, London, pp. 6–22.

Rose, R. (1991), 'A jigsaw approach to group work', *British Journal of Special Education*, 18, pp. 54–8.

Schindele, R.A. (1985), 'Research methodology in special education: a framework approach to special problems and solutions', in S. Hegarty and P. Evans (eds), *Research and Evaluation Methods in Special Education*, NFER–Nelson, Windsor.

Spindler, G. (ed.) (1982), *Doing the Ethnography of Schooling*, Holt, Rinehart & Winston, New York.

Stenhouse, L. (1975), *An Introduction to Curriculum Research and Development*, Heinemann, London.

Stenhouse, L. (1978), 'Case study and case records: towards a contemporary history of education', *British Educational Research Journal*, 4, pp. 21–39.

Stephenson, S. (1990), 'Promoting interaction among children with special educational needs in an integrated nursery', *British Journal of Special Education*, 17, pp. 61–5.

Tomlinson, S. (1981), *Educational Subnormality*, Routledge & Kegan Paul, London.

Tomlinson, S. (1982), *A Sociology of Special Education*, Routledge & Kegan Paul, London.

Vulliamy, G. (1990a), 'The potential of qualitative educational research strategies in developing countries', in G. Vulliamy, K. Lewin and D. Stephens, *Doing Educational Research in Developing Countries*, Falmer Press, London, pp. 7–25.

Vulliamy, G. (1990b), 'Research processes: postscript', in G. Vulliamy, K. Lewin and D. Stephens, *Doing Educational Research in Developing Countries*, Falmer Press, London, pp. 159–67.

Vulliamy, G. and Webb, R. (1991), 'Teacher research and educational change: an empirical study', *British Educational Research Journal*, 17, pp. 219–36.

Vulliamy, G. and Webb, R. (1992a), 'Teacher research: process or product?', *Educational Review*, 44, pp. 41–58.

Vulliamy, G. and Webb, R. (eds) (1992b), *Teacher Research and Special Educational Needs*, David Fulton, London.

Walker, R. (1985), *Doing Research: A Handbook for Teachers*, Methuen, London.

Warnock (Chairman) (1978), *Special Educational Needs*, HMSO, London.

Webb, R. (1990a), 'The origins and aspirations of practitioner research', in R. Webb (ed.), *Practitioner Research in the Primary School*, Falmer Press, London, pp. 12–33.

Webb, R. (ed.) (1990b), *Practitioner Research in the Primary School*, Falmer Press, London.

Wedell, K. (1985a), 'Foreword', in S. Hegarty and P. Evans (eds), *Research and Evaluation Methods in Special Education*, NFER–Nelson, Windsor, pp. 1–2.

Wedell, K. (1985b), 'Future directions for research on children's special educational needs', *British Journal of Special Education*, 12, pp. 22–6.

Wedell, K. and Roberts, J. (1981), 'Survey of current research in the UK on children with special educational needs', Social Science Research Council, unpublished report.

Westgate, D., Batey, J. and Brownlee, J. (1990), 'Collaborative action research: professional development in a cold climate', *British Journal of In-Service Education*, 16, pp. 167–72.

Whitehead, J. (1989), 'Creating a living educational theory from questions of the kind "How do I improve my practice?" ', *Cambridge Journal of Education*, 19, pp. 41–52.

Wood, D. (1981), 'Theory and research in classrooms: lessons from deaf education', in: W. Swann (ed.), *The Practice of Special Education*, Basil Blackwell, Oxford, pp. 417–33.

Zarb, G. (1992), 'On the road to Damascus: first steps towards changing the relations of disability research production', *Disability, Handicap & Society*, 7, pp. 125–38.

Name index

Subject index

Legislation and organisations from countries other than Great Britain are followed by the name of the country in brackets.